America, Christian or Secular?

Readings in American Christian History and Civil Religion

Jerry S. Herbert, Editor

America, Christian or Secular?

America, Christian or Secular?

Readings in American Christian History and Civil Religion

Jerry S. Herbert, Editor

MULTNOMAH PRESS
PORTLAND, OREGON 97266

Cover design: Tom Williams

AMERICA, CHRISTIAN OR SECULAR?
© 1984 by Christian College Coalition, Inc.
Published by Multnomah Press
Portland, Oregon 97266

Printed in the United States of America

The Christian College Coalition is an association of over seventy Christ-centered, fully accredited, liberal arts colleges and universities.

Library of Congress Cataloging in Publication Data

Main entry under title:

America—Christian or secular?

   Bibliography: p. 297
   Includes index.
   1. Christianity—United States—Addresses, essays, lectures.
2. United States—Religion—Addresses, essays, lectures.   3. Civil Religion—United States—Addresses, essays, lectures.
I. Herbert, Jerry S.
BR515.A45   1984   261.7   84-11478
ISBN 0-88070-067-X (pbk.)

84 85 86 87 88 89 90 – 10 9 8 7 6 5 4 3 2 1

Contents

69362

Preface

Referring to America's founding generation, Wheaton College historian Mark Noll argues that since "it did not occur to Bible-readers that Western civilization and scriptural values could move in different directions, it was very difficult even for leaders devoted to Scripture to conceive of the possibility that the Bible might have an independent role in constructing culture."[1] Blind to this distinctive biblical role, Noll believes, the founders uncritically accepted a cultural framework constructed of parts from the pagan classical world, the Reformation, the Enlightenment, and the pragmatic requirements of early American life. In short, Noll argues, America simply was not founded only on the Bible. Indeed, "the use of the Bible in the formation of political thought [was] a rare and unexpected thing."[2]

Evangelical author Francis Schaeffer, on the other hand, speaks repeatedly of the lost "Christian Reformation base" of the United States.[3] Unlike Noll, he supports the idea that America had essentially Christian origins. But he agrees with Noll on one point: The Bible has an independent role to play in the formation of a culture. "How much that is needed today," Schaeffer affirms, "to train students not only to be vaguely 'devoted to Scripture' but to struggle in the concrete needs of today in having the Bible provide 'an independent role in constructing culture.' " It is precisely this belief in the culture-forming role of the Bible that leads Schaeffer to object to Noll's position on America's founding. "Flattening out the Bible's influence in the past in the United States [as Noll would do] is no help to this—it makes everything a flat continuum rather than showing the radical change that has come in the West in general and in the United States."[4]

The disagreement illustrated here between Schaeffer and Noll is, in a nutshell, what this volume is all about. The key question? What was the basis of America's founding, and what does it mean for the way Christians ought to act now in American public life? In other words, what was America and what ought it to be: Christian or secular?

It is noteworthy that the disagreement voiced among evangelicals over "Christian America" is not whether Christians *ought* to influence the life of their country, but *how* they ought to, and on what basis. This is, perhaps, another sign of Evangelicalism's re-emergent self-identification as a reforming influence in American culture. I welcome this re-emergence. Quite frankly, the motivation for compiling this book sprang from the same concern both Schaeffer and Noll expressed: to train students who are "devoted to Scripture" in what it means to have the Bible provide "an independent role in constructing culture."

The present volume is an outgrowth of my work with the Christian College Coalition's American Studies Program, an intensive work-study program for outstanding undergraduates from the Coalition's member institutions. The program is designed to challenge students to explore how a biblical perspective can and should affect contemporary public issues. We seek to train students to take seriously the authority of scriptural norms for public policy and, indeed, for the reformation of culture. The issues we study frequently relate to questions about the role of religion in American life, about Christianity's influence on the development of America's public and legal institutions, and about the way America goes about her politics. All of these questions are part of the current controversy over whether we ever had a Christian America. The present collection of readings is designed to provide a balanced overview of some of the major arguments raised by the controversy.

I am grateful to my colleagues on the A.S.P. staff who were of such encouragement during the preparation of this volume and who graciously assumed some extra responsibilities during the summer to allow me time to work on the project. Kim Holt deserves a special word of thanks for having done so much typing and organizing in my behalf. Thanks also goes to John Hays for his cheerful and efficient help with photocopying and design, and to Rich Gathro for his unfailing prayer support and those special words of encouragement. Dr. John Bernbaum contributed valuable insight and comments while the manuscript was being prepared, and Jeannie Herbert made numerous editorial suggestions that greatly improved the final draft. Of course, they cannot be held accountable for the final product, but their help was deeply appreciated. Finally, I must thank Jeannie, Scott, and Mark for their patience with their husband's and father's short fuse and long absences during the final days of the project.

Jerry S. Herbert

Preface, Notes

1. Mark A. Noll, "The Bible in Revolutionary America," in *The Bible in American Law, Politics, and Rhetoric,* ed. James T. Johnson (Philadelphia: Fortress and Scholars Press, 1983), p. 24.

2. Noll, "Bible in Revolutionary America," p. 24.

3. See, for example, Francis A. Schaeffer, *How Should We Then Live?* (Old Tappan, N.J.: Fleming H. Revell, 1976), pp. 110, 249.

4. Francis A. Schaeffer to Mark A. Noll, 20 November 1982, p. 11 (photocopy). See Introduction, note 21.

Acknowledgments

Grateful acknowledgment is made to the following for permission to reprint previously published material:

Association for Public Justice Education Fund: "American Civil Religion" by Rockne M. McCarthy, and "Public Justice and True Tolerance" by James W. Skillen from *Confessing Christ and Doing Politics,* edited by James W. Skillen. Copyright © 1982 by Association for Public Justice Education Fund, Inc., Box 56348, Washington, D.C. 20011. Used by permission; all rights reserved.

Commentary: "In Defense of Religious America" by Terry Eastland. Reprinted from *Commentary,* June 1981, by permission. All rights reserved.

David C. Cook Publishing Co.: "The Christian Idea," "From a Christian America to . . . ?" and "Plan for Action" by John W. Whitehead. Used by permission. *The Second American Revolution* © 1982 John Whitehead. Illustrations © Wayne Stayskal. Published by David C. Cook Publishing Co., Elgin, Ill. 60120.

Discovery Foundation: "Faith of the Founding Fathers" by David Gill taken from *A Nation Under God?* edited by C. E. Gallivan and published by Word Books, Publisher, Waco, Tex. Copyright © 1976 by Discovery Foundation, Inc., Palo Alto, Calif. Reprinted by permission of Discovery Foundation, Inc.

William B. Eerdmans Publishing Co.: "Civil Religion and the Foundations of the Republic" and "The Republican Vision of Thomas Jefferson" in *Disestablishment a Second Time: Genuine Pluralism for American Schools* by Rockne M. McCarthy, James W. Skillen, and William A. Harper. Copyright © 1982 by Christian College Consortium. Used by permission of William B. Eerdmans

Publishing Co., 255 Jefferson Ave., SE, Grand Rapids, Mich. 49503.

The Seabury Press: "America's Myth of Origin" in *The Broken Covenant: American Civil Religion in Time of Trial* by Robert N. Bellah. Copyright © 1975 by The Seabury Press, Inc. Used by permission.

Transaction: "Religion and the Legitimation of the American Republic" by Robert N. Bellah. Published by permission of Transaction, Inc., from *Society,* vol. 15, no. 4. Copyright © 1978 by Transaction, Inc.

John Wiley and Sons: "Pluralism and Law in the Formation of American Civil Religion" by Phillip E. Hammond adapted from "Religious Pluralism and Durkheim's Integration Thesis" in *Changing Perspectives in the Scientific Study of Religion,* edited by A. W. Eister. Copyright © 1974 by John Wiley and Sons; reprinted with their permission. This adaptation appears in Bellah and Hammond, *Varieties in Civil Religion,* published by Harper and Row.

Contributors

Robert N. Bellah is Ford Professor of Sociology and Comparative Studies at the University of California, Berkeley. Since his ground-breaking article "Civil Religion in America" appeared in 1967, he has been a recognized authority on civil religion. A member of the Society for the Study of Religion, Dr. Bellah is a contributor to numerous professional journals and is the author of several books, including (with William McLoughlin) *Religion in America*, Houghton, 1968; *The Broken Covenant: American Civil Religion in Time of Trial*, Seabury, 1975; and (with Phillip Hammond) *Varieties in Civil Religion*, Harper & Row, 1980. He received his Ph.D. degree from Harvard University.

Terry Eastland serves as Special Assistant to the Attorney General of the United States in Washington, D.C. Mr. Eastland previously worked as a journalist, serving as the editor of both the *Greensboro* (N.C.) *Record* and the *Virginian-Pilot* (Norfolk, Va.). He is a contributor to *The American Spectator, Commentary, National Review, Policy Review, The Wall Street Journal,* and other publications, and he co-authored (with William Bennett) *Counting by Race*, Basic Books, 1979. A native of Dallas, Texas, he is a graduate of Vanderbilt University and holds a B.A. degree in philosophy from Oxford University.

David W. Gill is Dean and Associate Professor of Christian Ethics at The New College for Advanced Christian Studies in Berkeley, California. He is the founding dean of New College, and was formerly co-editor of *Radix Magazine*. Dr. Gill is the author of *The Word of God in the Ethics of Jacques Ellul*, Scarecrow Press, 1983 (based on his doctoral dissertation), as well as many articles and reviews on Christian social ethics. A graduate of the University of California, Berkeley, and San Francisco State University, he received his Ph.D. from the University of Southern California.

Phillip E. Hammond is a sociology professor at the University of Arizona, Tucson. The son of a minister, he has long been interested in the sociology of religion and is a member of the Society for Scientific Study of Religion. Dr. Hammond has written numerous articles which have appeared in sociology, education, and public opinion journals. He is the author of *The Campus Clergyman,* Basic Books, 1966; and co-authored (with N. J. Demerath III) *Religion in Social Context,* Random House, 1970; and (with Kenneth Dolbeare) *The School Prayer Decisions,* University of Chicago Press, 1971. His Ph.D. is from Columbia University.

Jerry S. Herbert is Associate Director of the Christian College Coalition's American Studies Program in Washington, D.C. Prior to his arrival in Washington, he served as Executive Director for the Carolina Study Center in North Carolina, a Christ-centered educational institution founded to help believers integrate their faith with their academic and professional work. He also taught political science at Duke University (from which he received his Ph.D.), and he is the author of several articles dealing with a Christian approach to public service and political action.

Rockne M. McCarthy is Professor of History and Coordinator of the College Studies Institute at Dordt College in Iowa. With expertise in both civil religion and American history, Dr. McCarthy is a contributor to *Fides et Historia, Pro Rege, The Banner,* and other journals. As a Fellow at the Center for Christian Scholarship at Calvin College, Michigan, he co-authored *Society, State, & Schools,* Eerdmans, 1981. He also authored (with James Skillen and William Harper) *Disestablishment a Second Time: Genuine Pluralism for American Schools,* Eerdmans, 1982. A graduate of Covenant Theological Seminary (St. Louis), he earned his Ph.D. from St. Louis University.

James W. Skillen is Executive Director of the Association for Public Justice in Washington, D.C. Dr. Skillen frequently speaks on college campuses across the country. He also has addressed major conferences, including the annual Pittsburg Jubilee Conference, the 1979 International Seminar on Christian Politics held in the

Netherlands, and the 1982 International Conference of the Association for Christian Philosophy. He is the author of numerous articles and books dealing with Christian political thought and witness, including *International Politics and the Demand for Global Justice,* Dordt College Press, 1981; and (as editor and contributor), *Confessing Christ and Doing Politics,* APJ Education Fund, 1982.

John W. Whitehead is a practicing attorney in Manassas, Virginia, specializing in constitutional law. He is the founder of The Rutherford Institute, a non-profit legal and educational organization designed to educate the general public on the Judeo-Christian heritage of America's legal and political system. A popular lecturer, Mr. Whitehead is a frequent speaker in churches and on college campuses. He is the author of several books, including *The Second American Revolution,* David C. Cook, 1982; and *The Stealing of America,* Crossway, 1983. He received a juris doctor degree from the University of Arkansas School of Law.

Introduction

The Founding Fathers of the United States (in varying degrees) understood very well the relationship between one's world view and government. . . . They knew they were building on the Supreme Being who was the Creator, the final reality. . . . What we find then as we look back is that the men who founded the United States of America really understood that upon which they were building their concepts of law and the concepts of government. And until the takeover of our government and law by this other entity, the materialistic, humanistic, chance world view, these things remained the base of government and law.[1]

With these words noted evangelical author Francis Schaeffer restates his frequently voiced belief that the United States, which once had a "Christian Reformation base," has now lost it. In so doing he articulates what George Marsden called "one of the opinions most persistently and widely held in the American evangelical community"; namely, "that America had essentially Christian origins from which lamentably it turned in the twentieth century."[2] This opinion is the focus of the present volume.

How Christian was America's founding? How has Christianity shaped American society? Are we or have we ever been a Christian nation? Evangelicals, and many fundamentalists as well, seek answers to such questions not simply out of a curiosity about history. Rather, these kinds of questions are frequently asked out of a desire to shape and legitimize certain patterns of Christian political activity. So it is necessary to ask a further question as well. How should America's heritage shape Christian political activity today? To address these kinds of questions this volume brings together readings from two types of writing: American Christian history and civil religion.

Christian history seeks to uncover and affirm America's Christian (if not distinctively evangelical) past so as to legitimize efforts to return to the faith of the founders and to the sacred intent of the Constitution. Explorations into civil religion seek to explain the religiosity and moral tendencies of American public life so as to influence efforts at reshaping an American public philosophy. Clearly this book cannot provide an exhaustive treatment of all the significant topics touched on by writings in American Christian history and civil religion. However, an attempt has been made to select a group of readings that permits a balanced look at some of the more important arguments advanced by evangelicals in the current controversy over a Christian America. From the pen of Christian writers come the historical and philosophical arguments for and against the idea that America was founded on Christian principles. From evangelical and non-evangelical scholars come articles on the origins and development of America's civil religion. These latter readings provide a broader sociological context for evaluating the Christian America idea, a context frequently slighted in discussions of this kind.

Christian America Defended

Although belief in a Christian America has been part of America's self-understanding in the past, the current popular controversy over America's Christian history and over efforts to politically and legally reaffirm the Christian heritage of the United States began in earnest during the nation's bicentennial celebration.[3] At the time it seemed as if there were an explosion of books calling on Christians to remember America's Christian heritage and to begin working to restore Christian principles to public life. The publication of such books does not seem to have abated much since.[4] These materials vary widely in their approaches, methodologies, and conclusions. However, there are two major dimensions of the Christian America argument that these kinds of writings tend to emphasize.

First, there is an emphasis on the statements and rhetoric of America's founding generation. For example, frequently quoted is Benjamin Franklin's plea for prayer before the Constitutional Convention when he reminded the delegates that "we have been assured . . . in the Sacred Writings, that, 'Except the Lord build the house, they labor in vain that build it!' I firmly believe this."[5] Another favorite quote is James Madison's declaration that "we have staked the whole of all our political institutions upon the capacity of mankind for self-government, upon the capacity of each and all of us to govern ourselves, to control ourselves, to sustain ourselves according to the Ten Commandments of God."[6] And there is John Quincy Adams's statement that "the highest glory of the American Revolution was this: it connected in one indissoluble bond, the principles of civil government with the principles of Christianity."[7] Similar statements abound as writers drive home the point that our founders knew the scriptures, believed in God, and generally affirmed Christian beliefs.

Second, there is an emphasis on tying Christianity to American law. Heavy emphasis is put on the traditional legal sanction granted Christianity in America. We are told how the United States Supreme Court in 1892 declared America to be "a religious people . . . a Christian nation." We are reminded that in 1931 the Court reiterated its affirmation that Americans were a "Christian people," and that again in 1952 it affirmed once more that "we are a religious people and our institutions presuppose a Supreme Being."[8] Further it is held that the American legal system (particularly as it is expressed in the Constitution) rests upon English common law which rests in turn upon biblical law.[9]

Although there are some differences of opinion in conclusions (e.g., how strictly "Christian" revolutionary America actually was),[10] Francis Schaeffer best summarizes, perhaps, the overall thrust of these writings when he declares that the United States originally enjoyed a "Christian consensus" which gave America both "form and freedom in society and government."[11] He and others point out that the United States unfortunately no longer has this Christian consensus, and non-Christian groups with unchristian ideas are misusing the Christian-based system established by the Constitution. In an often quoted passage, Rosalie Slater explains it this way:

> To understand the American Christian Constitution as the Christian form of government, it is necessary to consider its two spheres—the spirit and the letter—the

internal and the external. Both spheres must be active in order that the Constitution function to preserve the basic republican spirit of individual liberty. Today we still have the letter of the Constitution. That is, we still go through most of the legal processes of the structure of the Constitution in enacting legislation, and in the executive and judicial branches. But the spirit which was intended and understood by our Founding Fathers is missing—the Faith of our Fathers—and as our nation has fallen away from its foundations—the essence of that faith—our Constitution has become a hollow shell.[12]

These writings argue that in rhetoric and law the American republic was founded upon Christian beliefs and principles. If the republic is to endure, we are told, Christians must work to reassert America's traditional Christian foundation in law and public life. However, there is considerable disagreement among Christians over whether Christianity really is the foundation of America's political and legal traditions.

Christian America Denied

Critics argue that there is little hint, even among Christian scholars, that the American republic was established on an especially Christian base, or that the historical period of America's founding was uniquely Christian in some way.[13] The scholarship of evangelical historians Nathan Hatch of the University of Notre Dame, George Marsden of Calvin College, and Mark Noll of Wheaton College is representative of the work that has recently criticized the Christian America idea.[14] We should note two common themes which emerge from their writings.

First, we are told that there was a mixture of Christian and non-Christian influences shaping early American culture. Consequently, a distinctively Christian (biblical) public philosophy never developed. Marsden reasons that if one wishes to claim that America had a "Christian Reformation base" (Schaeffer's term), then one must rely heavily on an appeal to our Puritan heritage. But Marsden claims that the Puritans failed to establish "truly Christian dominant cultural principles." Thus he concludes that "the entire case for a now-lost Christian America rests on rather nebulous foundations."[15] Noll points out that even though most historians acknowledge that Christianity had significant influence on colonial America's political thought, there is widespread agreement that it did not *by itself* supply the substance of that thought.[16] In other words, though Puritanism influenced the general shape of American culture, the public philosophy of early America cannot be said to have been distinctively biblical.[17]

Second, it is argued that revolutionary America's public philosophy emerged from a synthesis of the Christian and Enlightenment world views. Marsden shows how Thomas Jefferson (perhaps the most "Enlightened" of the founders) and John Witherspoon (perhaps the most Calvinist) agreed that humans possessed a natural and innate ability to grasp the truth about the world and about morality, without needing divine grace or revelation.[18] America's government was founded on eighteenth century political theory which at its roots, we are told, had a distinctly anti-Puritan (anti-Calvinist) view of human nature.

> Virtually all the prevailing political thought of the day in America was based on the assumption that the light of natural reason was strong enough to reveal the eternal principles of God's law to any unprejudiced right-thinking person. Depravity, it seemed, may have touched the wills of humans, but it was no longer considered to have blinded their intellects.[19]

This is why, Marsden explains, the deist Thomas Jefferson and the near-atheist Thomas Paine shared with evangelical Calvinist patriots a single political orthodoxy. Evangelicals of the day "had lost any strong sense that reason for the Christian and the non-Christian will often point in different directions. [Thus] . . . at the time of the American Revolution there was no distinctly 'Christian' line of political thought as opposed to secular political thought."[20]

In short, the critics argue that the absence of a distinctly Christian political way of thinking makes the claim of a Christian America suspect. Indeed, the very fact that atheists, deists, and Calvinists found common ground in the prevailing climate of political thought demonstrates the mixture of Christian and non-Christian influences in early American culture.

The Christian America Debate

We can see that the proponents and critics of a Christian America emphasize different things. The critics look at America's public philosophy and are hard pressed to find anything distinctly Christian. The proponents look at the rhetoric of the founders and the courts, see the connections between America's early legal tradition and English common law, and find much that is Christian. For example, Francis Schaeffer finds it "strange and unwarranted" to conclude, as Mark Noll does in a recent article, that evidence of America's Christian base remains "inconclusive" and "at best problematic."[21] Although Schaeffer recognizes that other influences were present at America's founding, he argues that "this does not negate the existence of the biblical mentality involved."[22] Schaeffer finds the founders to be a "biblically knowledgeable group of men naturally having this knowledge shape their conclusions."[23] He holds that it is crucial to see how the founders' work "to base the Constitution in the Creator who gave inalienable rights stands in stark contrast to the French Revolution which did not."[24] But Noll wonders whether this is enough.

Noll claims his study of the founders does not show even the most evangelical ones holding to such biblical convictions as belief that (1) all human groups, even the new American states, are crippled by sin and need to feel the effects of redemption, or that (2) it is God's gracious providence which undergirds political life, not simply nature or human nature that is the basis for politics. Instead, Noll claims the founders believed "a political theory which affirmed that politics is rooted, in Witherspoon's words, in 'conscience enlightened by reason.' "[25] Noll argues that "Witherspoon and his colleagues left their explicit Christian faith at home in thinking about politics," and in so doing "they thoroughly confused nature and grace."[26] For they thought their approach to politics was essentially "Christian" even though it was virtually identical with the rationalist view which saw political life rooted in nature without any immediate link to God's revelation or grace.

Schaeffer agrees that "the founders of the United States did not have this clarity of thought in regard to the unity of nature and grace under Scripture," but he emphasizes that there was a "convergence" of the thinking of men such as Jefferson and

Witherspoon "at the point of a Creator who was not just an abstraction but Nature's God."[27] This was crucial, he argues. Furthermore, he points out:

> Our society, culture, government, law and consensus . . . have in the last years gone through a tremendous revolution. Whatever the very real deficiencies of the past years, there was a Christian influence in it, which was sufficient enough to be called a Christian ethos or consensus. . . . We must not baptize the whole of the past. . . . But, a thousand times but, to play down the radical change that has come in these years because of either the less than perfection of the founders or the serious inconsistencies in the intervening years, is destructive.[28]

Schaeffer appeals for a balance: one that acknowledges the less than perfect Christian influence in the original founding of the republic, but one that also emphasizes the tremendous loss in the past several years of "a Christian memory" in America.[29] He stresses that deriding past biblical influence in the United States only helps rob Christians "of a drive for applying biblical principles in our day [in] politic[s] and culture." To miss the Bible's influence in early America, Schaeffer complains, "helps the lack of energy and the accompanying accommodation which has made today's 'evangelicals' nearly so worthless in today's public life."[30]

George Marsden believes, on the other hand, that it is not failure to emphasize America's Christian history that erodes effective Christian witness in public life, but failure to understand it. Since early American culture expressed a mixture of Christian and non-Christian influences, he argues that continuing to refer to the mixture as "biblical" or "Christian" or "Judeo-Christian" or "Reformation based" does nothing but "attribute the authority of God's Word to what is in reality a compromise between Biblical and extra-Biblical influences." And, he claims, "it is such confusions, i.e., designating large sections of the American heritage as more-or-less Christian, that have helped lower the guard of Christians in distinguishing what is truly Biblical from what is merely part of their cultural heritage."[31]

The writings of Schaeffer, Noll, and Marsden conveniently

outline the broad characteristics of the Christian America debate among evangelicals. Although it seemed unnecessary to include their full debate in the present collection of readings,[32] the general contour of their argument outlined above nicely sets before us the major themes and issues addressed more fully in the following chapters. Proponents of a Christian America argue that the theism of the founders, and America's early legal tradition, fundamentally expressed a Christian consensus or ethos that stands in sharp contrast to today's secularism. The critics argue that the willingness of early American Christians to adopt the political thought forms of the Enlightenment expressed the fundamentally unbiblical ambiguity in the cultural consensus.

Defenders of the Christian America idea fear that minimizing the Christian character of America's original consensus undermines contemporary Christian efforts to reform American public life in a biblical way. Critics fear that labeling early American culture as Christian when it was actually a mixture of things only increases the chance that Christians today will not grasp how America's early cultural principles (particularly as expressed in the new republic's public philosophy) paved the way to secularism's dominance in modern America. They argue it only makes it more difficult for Christians to discern how to reform American public life in a biblical way.

Despite these significant differences, however, there is agreement on both sides that America's cultural consensus has undergone significant change since the nation's founding. Whether resulting from a sharp break with the past or from a gradual unfolding of what was already present in the past, it is agreed that other-than-Christian influences now predominate. Whatever the color of America's earlier consensus, now its cast is definitely non-Christian (if not anti-Christian). This shift has been noted by other observers as well.

Civil Religion

Scholars recognize that America's traditional consensus is crumbling and they wonder about the vitality (or even viability) of a society which experiences the crumbling of its prevailing cultural ethos. The recent interest in civil religion reflects this concern.[33] As John Wilson points out:

> The intent of the [civil religion] proposal was no less than the revitalization of the culture, specifically through its religious medium, so that in a time of global trials as the twenty-first century approached, the nation might renew, perfect, and sustain its broadly liberal commitments.[34]

Although he admits that civil religion can be "exasperatingly elusive," Wilson calls it a "cultural consensus" and describes it as "a synthesis including broadly religious symbols and values (which had derived from Protestant forms of Christianity) and patterns of behavior in the public realm."[35] As a working concept, civil religion provides a framework for interpreting the role of religion in American culture. It can be a powerful aid in clarifying the origins, content, and development of America's cultural consensus, for it recognizes the important religious dimension of American society. As Wilson explains:

> Americans have characteristically understood from the outset of national life that within their culture, some form of public religion—republican Protestantism, pure Christianity, or The American Way of Life—has served as a basic religious medium in the culture and as such has been enormously significant in the society.[36]

A major reason for including a discussion of civil religion in this collection of readings relates to our interest in understanding whether America's early cultural consensus was really Christian. A crucial question in the civil religion debate is whether American cultural principles gave rise to a public consensus (civil religion) that was a kind of "republican Protestantism" or a generalized "American Way of Life" or a type of "pure Christianity." So by including civil religion readings in this collection, some further light can be shed, from a sociological viewpoint, on the origins and content of the early American cultural consensus.

There is, however, a further reason why discussion of American civil religion is helpful: the connection between perception and action. Both sides of the Christian America debate recognize the connection between how Christians perceive the founding of America and how they will act in American public life today. On the one side are Christians who perceive America's traditional consensus as being basically Christian. They would hope, of course, that America's public consensus (civil religion) might be as purely Christian as possible. But however mixed it might remain, they urge Christians to revitalize American society by working politically and legally to renew, perfect, and sustain the "Christian base" that was part of America's traditional civil religion.

On the other side are Christians who perceive America's traditional civil religion to be a synthesis of Christian and non-Christian influences. They believe that there is a fundamental difference between biblical norms and values and the received norms and values of Western culture, particularly as they were given expression by the Enlightenment.[37] They believe mixing such norms and values, as is done in American civil religion, subverts truly Christian (biblical) public action. They urge Christians to acknowledge the fundamental difference between biblical norms and the pervasive public philosophy of America's founding, and to work toward truly biblically based public and political service. The readings on civil religion help explain and clarify this dimension of the Christian America debate.

Our Discussion

This volume engages seven authors in a "discussion" of four major questions pertinent to the Christian America controversy. Each of the four parts of the book focuses on one of the questions, and each part is introduced by a short essay. These introductory essays highlight significant issues raised by each writer and bring these issues into direct contact with the arguments of the other writers, thus helping to combine all of the authors' articles into a single, common discussion.

Part One addresses the question, "Is America Christian?" It introduces the reasons for believing in a Christian America and illustrates the place and influence of religion on America's founding. It also introduces the concept of civil religion and uncovers how civil religion found expression in the cultural consensus of colonial America.

Part Two explores the religious beliefs of America's founders as it seeks to answer the question, "Were the founders Christian?" Again the concept of civil religion is found useful, this time in examining the relationship of the founders' religious beliefs to their understanding of public philosophy.

Part Three asks, "Is American civil religion Christian?" It looks at some of the key dimensions of civil religion and evaluates the extent to which its content and its impact on American public life were Christian. Here the discussion moves from an emphasis on belief systems (or on the ideological component of civil religion) to an emphasis on the institutional (structural) impact on civil religion.

Part Four involves two calls to action. The question is "Is there a response that is Christian?" Each call to action reflects a different viewpoint based upon the divergent assumptions and conclusions expressed earlier in the volume's "discussion." They are presented for the reader's reflection and personal response.

This volume is designed for college students taking courses in American society, history, and politics, but it should also prove helpful to those of the general reading public who are interested in the contemporary debate over our nation's Christian heritage, and in how Christians ought to participate biblically in American public life today. It is hoped that this short collection of readings shall be instrumental in identifying some of the major themes of the Christian America controversy. In so doing, perhaps some light may be shed on areas of agreement, thereby uncovering a possible basis for effective and responsible Christian service to our nation's public life.

Introduction, Notes

1. Francis A. Schaeffer, *A Christian Manifesto,* rev. ed. (Westchester, Ill.: Crossway Books, 1982), pp. 31, 33, 39.
2. George Marsden, "America's 'Christian' Origin: Puritan New England as a Case Study," in *John Calvin: His Influence in the Western World,* ed. W. Stanford Reid (Grand Rapids: Zondervan Publishing House, 1982), p. 241.

3. The idea has persisted in American life that the United States is fundamentally a Christian republic, and that the role of the Church is to build toward the time when the civilization of the country would be fully Christian and when Christians and Christian principles would triumph in history. For an introduction to the study of this American idea, see Robert T. Handy, *A Christian America: Protestant Hopes and Historical Realities* (New York: Oxford University Press, 1971); and Ernest Lee Tuveson, *Redeemer Nation: The Idea of America's Millennial Role* (Chicago: University of Chicago Press, 1968).

4. Some of the first included James C. Hefley, *America: One Nation under God* (Wheaton, Ill.: Victor Books, 1975); Rus Walton, *One Nation under God* (Washington, D.C.: Third Century Publishers, 1975), first published that year by Plymouth Rock Foundation, Marlborough, N.H., and his *In the Spirit of '76: The Citizen's Guide to Politics* (Washington, D.C.: Third Century Publishers, 1975). Later came others such as Verna M. Hall, ed., *The Christian History of the American Revolution: Consider and Ponder* (San Francisco: Foundation for American Christian Education, 1976); Tim LaHaye, *The Bible's Influence on American History* (San Diego, Calif.: Master Books, 1976); John Warwick Montgomery, *The Shaping of America* (Minneapolis, Minn.: Bethany Fellowship, 1976); and perhaps most notably Francis A. Schaeffer, *How Should We Then Live? The Rise and Decline of Western Thought and Culture* (Old Tappan, N.J.: Fleming H. Revell, 1976). Schaeffer covered more than simply America's founding, but affirmed the country's early Christian base which is now lost and in need of being restored.

These were followed by books such as Peter J. Marshall, Jr., and David B. Manuel, Jr., *The Light and the Glory* (Old Tappan, N.J.: Fleming H. Revell, 1977); Harold O. J. Brown, *The Reconstruction of the Republic* (Rochelle, N.Y.: Arlington House, 1977), republished in 1981 by Mott Media, Milford, Mich.; Rus Walton, *Fundamentals for American Christians* (Marlborough, N.H.: Plymouth Rock Foundation, 1978), later published as *Foundations for American Christians* (Nyack, N.J.: Plymouth Rock Foundation/Parsons Publishing, 1979); Verna M. Hall, ed. *The Christian History of the Constitution of the United States of America: Christian Self-Government with Union* (San Francisco: Foundation for American Christian Education, 1979); and Rosalie J. Slater, *Teaching and Learning America's Christian History* (San Francisco: Foundation for American Christian Education, 1980).

More recent books include Marshall Foster and Mary-Elaine Swanson, *The American Covenant: The Untold Story* (Thousand Oaks, Calif.: The Foundation for Christian Self-Government, 1981); Gary DeMar, *God and Government: A Biblical and Historical Study* (Atlanta, Ga.: American Vision Press, 1982); and perhaps most notably Jerry Falwell, *Listen, America* (New York: Bantam Books, 1981); Francis A. Schaeffer, *A Christian Manifesto* (Westchester, Ill.: Crossway Books, 1981); and John W. Whitehead, *The Second American Revolution* (Elgin, Ill.: David C. Cook Publishing Co., 1982).

The works of what Thomas E. VanDahm called the Christian Far Right ought also to be mentioned. (See his "The Christian Far Right and the Economic Role of the State," *Christian Scholar's Review* 12 [January 1983]:17-36). Beginning before the bicentennial, these works helped provide additional theoretical support for the Christian America theses. Important writings include Rousas John Rushdoony, *This Independent Republic* (Fairfax, Va.: Thoburn Press, 1964); and his *The Nature of the American System* (Nutley, N.J.: Craig Press, 1965); and Gary North, ed., "Symposium on Christianity and the American Revolution," *The Journal of Christian Reconstruction* 3 (Summer 1976): entire issue.

5. For example, see Hefley, *America*, pp. 9, 20; and Foster and Swanson, *American Covenant*, p. 11.

6. For example, see DeMar, *God and Government*, pp. 137-38; and Walton, *One Nation*, p. 33.

7. For example, see Foster and Swanson, *American Covenant*, p. 13; and Hall, *Christian History of the Constitution*, p. 372.

8. See John W. Whitehead, *The Separation Illusion* (Milford, Mich.: Mott Media, 1977), p. 18; DeMar, *God and Government*, p. 123; Foster and Swanson, *American Covenant*, p. 13; and Hefley, *America*, p. 11.

9. This argument is very widespread. For examples of some of the ways it is presented, see DeMar, *God and Government*, p. 134; Schaeffer, *Christian Manifesto*, pp. 38-51; Whitehead, *Second American Revolution*, pp. 28-32, 193-200; Walton, *One Nation*, pp. 16-24, 52-55; and Hefley, *America*, pp. 38-43.

10. For differences on how "Christian" early America was, compare Schaeffer, *How Should We Then Live?*, p. 110; and his *Christian Manifesto*, pp. 31-33; with Walton, *One Nation*, p. 16; Foster and Swanson, *American Covenant*, pp. 3, 14; and Hall, *Christian History of the Constitution*, p. iii.

11. Schaeffer, *How Should We Then Live?*, p. 110. Also see Foster and Swanson, *American Covenant*, p. 13. (Compare Foster and Swanson, p. 14; with Hefley, *America*, p. 42.)

12. Slater, *Teaching and Learning*, p. 240. This passage is also quoted in DeMar, *God and Government*, p. 135; and Foster and Swanson, *American Government*, pp. 90-91.

13. Some representative scholarship in this area from professing Christians includes Charles W. Akers, *The Divine Politician: Samuel Cooper and the American Revolution in Boston* (Boston: Northeastern University Press, 1982): Edwin Scott Gaustad, comp., *Religious Issues in American History* (New York: Harper & Row, Publishers, 1968); and his *Documentary History of Religion in America*, vol. 1 (Grand Rapids: William B. Eerdmans Publishing Co., 1982); C. C. Goen, *Revivalism and Separatism in New England, 1740-1800* (Hamden, Conn.: Archon Books, 1969); Nathan O. Hatch, *The Sacred Cause of Liberty: Republican Thought and the Millennium in Revolutionary New England* (New Haven, Conn.: Yale University Press, 1977); Richard F. Lovelace, *The American Pietism of Cotton Mather: Origins of American Evangelicalism* (Grand Rapids: Christian University Press, 1979); George M. Marsden, *Fundamentalism and American Culture: The Shaping of Twentieth Century Evangelicalism, 1820-1925* (New York: Oxford University Press, 1980); Mark A. Noll, *Christians in the American Revolution* (Grand Rapids: Christian University Press, 1977); and John D. Woodbridge, Nathan O. Hatch, and Mark A. Noll, *The Gospel in America: Themes in the Study of American Evangelicalism* (Grand Rapids: Zondervan Publishing House, 1979).

14. See, for example, Nathan O. Hatch and Mark A. Noll, eds., *The Bible in America: Essays in Cultural History* (New York: Oxford University Press, 1983); George M. Marsden, "America's 'Christian' Origins: Puritan New England as a Case Study," in *John Calvin: His Influence in the Western World*, ed. W. Stanford Reid (Grand Rapids: Zondervan Publishing House, 1982); and Mark A. Noll, "The Bible in Revolutionary America," in *The Bible in American Law, Politics, and Rhetoric*, ed. James T. Johnson (Philadelphia: Fortress and Scholars Press, 1983).

15. Marsden, "America's 'Christian' Origins," p. 241.

16. "Recent scholarship concerning the Revolutionary period has shown conclusively that Christian doctrines were *not* the immediate source of the political foundations of the American Revolution." Noll, "From the Great Awakening to the War for Independence: Christian Values in the American Revolution," *Christian Scholar's Review* 12 (February 1983): 99. See also his *Christians in the American Revolution* (Grand Rapids: Christian University Press, 1977), wherein he argues that "recent scholarship on the widely shared political ideology of the Revolution" suggests that it was not the Christian world view that was at its root, but rather "the distinctly political values of the Whig world view" (p. 150).

17. Marsden, "America's 'Christian' Origins," p. 242.

18. Marsden, "America's 'Christian' Origins," p. 250-51.

19. Marsden, "America's 'Christian' Origins," p. 250-51.

20. Marsden, "America's 'Christian' Origins," p. 253.

21. Francis A. Schaeffer to Professor Mark A. Noll, 20 November 1982, pp. 6-7 (photocopy). This letter is in response to Noll's article "The Bible in Revolutionary America," and is part of a series of exchanges between Schaeffer and Noll and George Marsden from November 1982 to March 1983. Citing from contemporary personal correspondence is usually not done, but in this case all parties agreed the subject discussed was of such consequence that the correspondence could be shared with others. I am grateful to David John Seel, Jr., for the privilege of reviewing copies of these letters. Material from the correspondence was previously made public in articles by G. Aiken Taylor ("Francis Schaeffer: America's Historical Underpinnings," *Presbyterian Journal* [2 March 1983]:7-8, 13) and Ronald A. Wells ("Whatever Happened to Francis Schaeffer?" *Reformed Journal* [May 1983]:11-13).

22. Schaeffer to Noll, 20 November 1982, p. 5.

23. Schaeffer to Noll, 20 November 1982, p. 6.

24. Schaeffer to Noll, 20 November 1982, p. 5. See also Francis A. Schaeffer to Professor Mark A. Noll, 20 December 1982, wherein Schaeffer contrasts the founders' faith in the Creator with the French Revolution's faith in autonomous human reason as the absolute and final authority (p. 4).

25. Mark A. Noll to Dr. Francis Schaeffer, 8 December 1982. Noll complains that Witherspoon even criticized Jonathan Edwards "for thinking that 'moral philosophy' (including politics) needed some special insights from God's grace or His revelation" (p. 2).

26. Noll to Schaeffer, 8 December 1982. The founders' general efforts, Noll writes Schaeffer, "opened up the same path way for nature to eat up grace that (as I learned from you) is a recurring evil in Western civilization" (p. 2). See also George M. Marsden to Francis Schaeffer, 13 January 1983. Marsden points out that even John Witherspoon, "the 'best' of the founders," held to a nature/grace dualism. He reminds Schaeffer that it is he, Schaeffer, who correctly sees such a dualism "as leading to a view of autonomous nature eventually getting out of hand in Western culture." And Marsden claims that "for most of the other founding fathers an autonomous view of nature (and a growing confidence in human nature apart from God's grace) was already pretty much out of hand" (pp. 2-3). What Marsden cannot understand is why Schaeffer does not apply the same standards to America's founders as he does to today's "weak" evangelicals and Protestant "modernists." He sees Schaeffer arguing that "the fact that [the founders] knew the Bible (so did the modernists), believed in a Creator (so did Voltaire), is sufficient. Why not face the weaknesses of

their Christianity (if any) or the degree of their compromise with the secular thought-forms of their era?" (p. 3).

27. Schaeffer to Noll, 20 December 1982, p. 3.

28. Schaeffer to Noll, 20 December 1982, p. 5.

29. Francis A. Schaeffer to Professor George Marsden, 14 March 1983, p. 1.

30. Schaeffer to Noll, 20 December 1982, p. 9.

31. George M. Marsden to Dr. Francis Schaeffer, 13 January 1983, p. 3.

32. A good introduction to their debate may be found already by comparing Schaeffer, *A Christian Manifesto,* with Mark A. Noll, Nathan O. Hatch, and George M. Marsden, *The Search for Christian America* (Westchester, Ill.: Crossway Books, 1983).

33. The current discussion of civil religion began with the publication of Robert N. Bellah, "Civil Religion in America," *Daedalus* 96 (Winter 1967):1-21; reprinted with commentary and rejoinder in Donald R. Cutler, ed., *The Religious Situation* (Boston: Beacon Press, 1968), pp. 331-393. A convenient introduction to the American civil religion debate is provided by Russell E. Richey and Donald G. Jones, eds., *American Civil Religion* (New York: Harper & Row, Publishers, 1974).

For further reading see Robert N. Bellah, *The Broken Covenant: American Civil Religion in Time of Trial* (New York: The Seabury Press, 1975); Cherry Conrad, *God's New Israel: Religious Interpretations of American Destiny* (Englewood Cliffs, N.J.: Prentice-Hall, 1971); Sidney E. Mead, *The Nation with the Soul of a Church* (New York: Harper & Row, 1975); and his *The Old Religion in the Brave New World: Reflections on the Relation Between Christendom and the Republic* (Berkeley, Calif.: University of California Press, 1977); Elwyn A. Smith, *The Religion of the Republic* (Philadelphia: Fortress Press, 1970); Cushing Stout, *The New Heavens and New Earth: Political Religion in America* (New York: Harper & Row, 1974); and John F. Wilson, *Public Religions in American Culture* (Philadelphia: Temple University Press, 1979).

Books by evangelical authors touching on civil religion include Perry C. Cothan, *Politics, Americanism, and Christianity* (Grand Rapids: Baker Book House, 1976); Robert D. Linder and Richard V. Pierard, *Twilight of the Saints: Biblical Christianity and Civil Religion in America* (Downers Grove, Ill.: InterVarsity Press, 1978); James W. Skillen, ed., *Confessing Christ and Doing Politics* (Washington, D.C.: Association for Public Justice Education Fund, 1982); William Stringfellow, *An Ethic for Christians and Other Aliens in a Strange Land* (Waco, Tex.: Word Books, 1973); Jim Wallis, *Call to Conversion: Recovering the Gospel for These Times* (New York: Harper & Row, 1981); and Robert Zwier, *Born-Again Politics* (Downers Grove, Ill.: InterVarsity Press, 1982).

34. By "broadly liberal commitments," Wilson refers to the classical Liberal values which have traditionally been part of American public life (e.g., liberty, individual rights, due process, etc.) which are adhered to by both liberals and conservatives today. Wilson, *Public Religion,* p. 19.

35. Wilson, *Public Religion,* p. 18. Also see why Wilson prefers *public religion* to the term *civil religion* (p. viii).

36. Wilson, *Public Religion,* p. 19. For a critique of "The American Way of Life" as a sort of "secularized Puritanism" which represents both the basic spiritual reality of American life as well as the common content expressed by the nation's three chief faiths, Wilson refers us to Will Herberg's important *Protestant, Catholic, Jew: An*

Essay in American Religious Sociology (Garden City, N.Y.: Doubleday, 1955; republished, Chicago: University of Chicago Press, 1983).

37. In doing so they follow the example of the nineteenth century Calvinist theologian and Dutch prime minister Abraham Kuyper. Contemporary statements of this approach have recently come from the work of the Calvin Center for Christian Scholarship, Calvin College, and the Association for Public Justice, a national Christian citizens' movement. See Rockne M. McCarthy, Donald Oppewal, Walfred Petersen, and Gordon Spykman, *Society, State, & Schools: A Case for Structural and Confessional Pluralism* (Grand Rapids: William B. Eerdmans Publishing Co., 1981); and Rockne M. McCarthy, James W. Skillen, and William A. Harper, *Disestablishment a Second Time: Genuine Pluralism for American Schools* (Grand Rapids: Christian University Press, 1982).

Part I

Is America Christian?

America is founded on Christian principles. This assertion, perhaps more than any other, has excited controversy among Christian people concerned about the place of religion in American history. Is America, or has it ever been, a Christian nation? Evangelicals and others argue over the extent of Christian influence in the founding and later socio-political development of the American republic. Questions about America's Christian heritage shape the debates over countless issues dealing with religion in American life. In a sense, then, all of the readings in the present volume could be grouped under the question of whether America was or is Christian. The readings selected for Part 1, however, introduce some of the more central arguments in the dispute over the Christian character of the founding of America, arguments which resurface throughout the book.

Christian Influences

In the first chapter, John Whitehead explains that the Christian world view recognizes absolute standards "by which all moral judgments of life are to be measured." He then puts forward one of the more common arguments advanced by those who emphasize the Christian character of America's beginnings. He argues that the fundamental principles of the Christian world view "were passed on in substance and without significant alteration to the American colonies" from Samuel Rutherford's *Lex Rex,* through John Locke and John Witherspoon, to America's founders. He shows how James Madison in particular was influenced by the evangelical Witherspoon, how the Declaration of Independence expressed the Judeo-Christian base upon which the Republic was founded, and how incompatible with the views of the founders are the current "relativistic" and "nontheistic" ways of looking at government. Following in a similar vein in the next chapter, Terry Eastland declares that "as a matter of historical fact, the founding fathers believed that the public interest was served by the promotion of religion."

At this point it is interesting to note both the similarities and differences between Whitehead's and Eastland's arguments. Although not contradicting Whitehead, Eastland is willing to be a little more explicit when he declares that Protestant Christianity was, for most of our history, the "established religion" of the republic. Like Whitehead, he discusses the kinds of beliefs that were part of this Protestant world view and how they shaped the founders' views of government and public life. Here we discover themes similar to those in Whitehead's discussion: the sovereignty of God, human depravity, the need to develop human character through exercising certain spiritual and social virtues (sobriety, honesty, prudence, self-denial, temperance, etc.). Once again, however, Eastland goes further than Whitehead by explaining how this "common moral and religious tradition" he calls Protestant Christianity was, "as a general metaphysic, . . . understood in ways Catholics and Jews and deists could accept." This observation raises an interesting point for us.

Notice how a tradition can be considered "Christian" even though it is accepted in common not only by Christians, but by Jews and deists as well. What Whitehead calls the absolute moral standards of the Christian world view planted in the colonies ought to be compared carefully with what Eastland describes as the common moral Christian tradition established in the early republic.

Much of the heat generated by the debate over whether America was founded as a Christian nation arises from differences of opinion on the significance of ambiguity in America's heritage. Was the nation founded on a generalized religiosity, or on a relatively consistent biblical Christianity? Did the cultural consensus rest on shared moral precepts, or on distinctively Christian convictions? Is it even helpful to ask such questions given the sharp contrast between the obvious theism of the founders and today's secularism? Robert Bellah touches on these questions in the final chapter of this section.

A Combination of Influences

The concept of civil religion can be a difficult one to grasp, but it can also be quite useful in shedding important light on the complex origins and nature of America's founding. In a far-ranging and helpful discussion, Bellah argues that the difficulties surrounding the place of religion in American public life today are rooted in "fundamental unclarities" about the nature of the American republic that go back to its formative period. The American regime is a mixture of classical Roman republicanism and Enlightenment liberalism, Bellah explains, and they are antithetical to each other.

The inner spirit of classical republicanism (with its belief that good politics expresses a people's common way of life) is at war with the liberal constitutional regime (with its belief that good comes from actions of individual citizens motivated by self-interest). Charles Louis de Montesquieu's belief in the republican (classical) virtues of public spiritedness is just the opposite of John Locke's liberal belief that individuals should be free to pursue exclusive self-interest. But America embraces both Montesquieu and Locke. The American democratic experiment, Bellah points out, encompasses two fundamentally contradictory regimes: republican virtue and liberal individualism. He then argues that religion has been used in America to evade the resultant incompatibilities in our political life.

Republicanism, according to Bellah, needs a civil religion. Republicanism sees the state as having an ethical, educational, and even spiritual role to play in society. This is because it will survive only so long as it reproduces republican customs (public virtue) among its citizens. Is America then a Christian republic where biblical religion serves as a civil religion, helping to produce Christian virtue among its citizens? Bellah responds with both yes and no. Christianity has had significant impact on American civil religion, but has not itself been that religion.

Bellah cites the Declaration of Independence as an expression of Christianity's influence in shaping the republican side of the American regime. In arguments similar to Eastland's and Whitehead's, he describes the God of the Declaration as a distinctly "biblical God" who is not just a First Principle, but who stands above the nation, judging and justifying its national existence. Biblical religion, Bellah argues, has given America much of its public moral and religious symbolism, but this symbolism has remained relatively abstract.

America's civil religion, according to Bellah, is rather formalized, consisting, for example, of stock references to the Deity, but containing very little "theology" about the Deity to interpret. It is also marginal, Bellah explains, because it has no constitutional or legal support. It is to be found more in the common moral and religious traditions of the people than in constitutional sanction. It is marginal because America adopted a liberal constitutional regime wherein the religious symbolism of civil religion is viewed as illegitimate. It is only because liberalism in America is in "uneasy tandem" with republicanism that it did not entirely repudiate the religious symbolism of the Declaration of Independence. However, any further elaboration of religious symbolism beyond that of a formal and marginal civil religion had to be kept purely private.

Bellah's point is that America's civil religion is biblical in its religious symbolism, but this symbolism is sparse and highly formalized. Since the liberal side of the American regime resulted in a formal and marginal civil religion, Bellah believes the religious community (often through evangelical "awakenings") has provided the sense of national community and purpose and preserved the public virtues of republicanism. Biblical religion, practiced privately within the contours of a liberal society, provided the public moral and spiritual context for national community, tempering self-interest with public virtue and concern for the common good.

In a nation that was founded on the desire to retain the rhetoric and spirit of republicanism within the structure of a liberal constitutional state, the private practice of biblical religion was indispensable in evading the inherent incompatibilities. But today, in a point made by both Whitehead and Eastland, Bellah observes that religion is no longer as vital or as respected in society as it once was. Indeed, the relevance and credibility of religion is under attack. Consequently, Bellah concludes, the evasion of incompatabilities is no longer possible, and the legitimacy of the American republic itself, once provided by religion, is being undermined.

1. The Christian Idea

John W. Whitehead

We live in a world that is structured by ideas. Our presuppositions and ideas create our world view, the grid through which we view the world. More important, our presuppositions are the basis upon which we act. As a man "thinketh in his heart, so he is" (Proverbs 23:7).

We are more than mere products of our environment. Men and women project their inward thoughts out into the external world where, in fact, their thoughts affect their environment. Ideas thus have consequences, which can be productive or destructive—depending upon their basis or foundation.

Ideas are seldom neutral. For example, we are hearing such ideas as "separation of church and state," "individual autonomy," "right to abortion," "death with dignity," or even "the death of God" expressed with increasing frequency. Each of these phrases portrays something that could initially be characterized as objective or neutral—the expression of an abstract "idea." Their supposed neutrality is belied by their very real and often physical impact in the external world. Words are important since they reveal the faith of the speaker, and all men have faith, consciously or unconsciously, in some basic world view.

What Is the Christian World View?

The Reformation taught that the Bible has something to say about every area of life. Man should base his world view, the Reformers taught, upon the principles of the Bible. The Bible is the grid through which man should view the world.

The Christian world view teaches a unified view of truth. Its principles deal in absolutes that do not vary according to circumstances but should, in fact, govern the actions of man as he responds to constantly changing conditions.

Although biblical principles represent absolute norms, they have never been applied perfectly because people, being fallen, have never carried them out perfectly. However, when biblical principles have been administered with some consistency, they have brought about positive results. In fact, as one views the diminishing number of countries that have any vestige of political freedom, the line between free countries and unfree ones can be seen to correspond to that between those countries that were strongly influenced by the Reformation and those that were not. We may include those Roman Catholic countries such as France that were influenced by Reformation thinking.

An even clearer line can be drawn between the countries that have never had any Christian base (whether Roman Catholic or Reformation in character). Poland has raised the aura of freedom through the Solidarity Union in its resistance to Communist Russia. This was made possible because of the strong influence of Roman Catholicism in Poland. So much of the Eastern Orthodox world is now under communism that Orthodoxy constitutes an exception.

The Christian world view teaches that man is created in the image of God. The implications of man made in God's image can be summarized by saying that man, like God, has personhood, a measure of self-transcendence, intelligence, morality, love, and creativity.[1] In essence, to say that man bears God's image affords man a dignity above and beyond all other creatures.

The fact that man and woman were made in the image of God is intimately connected to the concepts of authority and of power to govern and man's relationship to the revealed law of God. In Genesis 1:26 we read, "God said, Let us make man in our image, after our likeness: and let them have dominion . . . over all the earth, and over every creeping thing." In 1:28 the grant of dominion is reiterated with the added emphasis that man is to "replenish the earth, and subdue it." In the light of the Christian world view, we see that man's dominion is a delegated authority under God. Adam's naming of every creature in Genesis 2:19 was his first authoritative act.

The commands in Genesis 1 (vv. 26 and 28) are commonly called the "cultural mandate"—the mandate from God as revealed to Adam, yet unfallen, to utilize and direct the earth's resources to the glory of God. This mandate has not been withdrawn from fallen man. But only regenerate individuals—that is, Christians who truly love the Lord—can understand and carry out its implications.

Christians are called to apply God's revelation to all areas of life and to all disciplines. Unfortunately, what we have been witnessing in the last century is the non-Christian's usurpation of the cultural mandate against the terms of the Bible. When exercised contrary to the principles of the Bible, the cultural mandate becomes a pretext to manipulate man and his environment. Adam's delegated authority did not include the power to manipulate others, for Adam himself was under the law as expressed by God.

Adam was told by God that he could eat of all the trees of the garden but one: the tree of the knowledge of good and evil. If he ate that fruit, the penalty was death. Adam heard God's command. Thus he had received the law as revealed by God, and understood at least in principle the difference between right and wrong in absolute terms: in terms of life and death. Having a free will, he could do either of two things: keep God's law or, breaking it, assume an autonomous attitude and thus formulate his own laws without reference to God. Adam chose the latter, thus becoming the first humanist.

This deliberate disobedience we call the Fall. Christian theism holds that man is flawed in his total being: There is no part of man that was not tainted by the Fall. Simultaneous with Adam's fall, nature was blighted. Moreover, the flawed character of Adam was subsequently passed on to all humans. This points to man's tremendous significance: One man's act not only affected him but also extended to all his descendants and to the world surrounding him.

Christian theism explains the present abnormality of man in terms of the flaw caused by the Fall. The humanist thinkers of the Renaissance had no answer for the fact that man's noble attributes are vitiated by selfishness, cruelty, and vice. They tended to close their eyes to man's flaws and dwell on his virtues. Modern man, more deeply aware of the flaws, sometimes sees himself as absurd and futile.

Christian theism provides the answer in the atoning work of Christ. The fatal infection of sin is cured, though symptoms and effects remain. The Christian is substantially healed by Christ's work, but he is never perfect in this life. Therefore, Christian man is in need of the absolutes of the Bible to order and direct his fallen nature.

Christian theism teaches that man is held accountable to his Creator. Absolute standards exist by which all moral judgments of life are to be measured. With the Bible, there is a standard of right and wrong. These fundamental principles made up the Reformation world view. They were passed on in substance and without significant alteration to the American colonies through the influence of a book written by Samuel Rutherford, *Lex, Rex, or the Law and the Prince* (1644).

Government under Biblical Law

Lex, Rex challenged the fundamental principle of seventeenth-century political government in Europe: the divine right of kings. This doctrine held that the king or state ruled as God's appointed regent. Therefore, the king's word was law. (Although Scripture was seen as normative, it was the king alone who interpreted and embodied that norm.)

Counterbalanced against this position was Rutherford's assertion that the basic premise of government and therefore of law must be the Bible, the Word of God, rather than the word of any man. All men, even the king, Rutherford argued, were *under* the law and not above it. This religious concept was considered both heresy and treason and punishable as such.

Lex, Rex created an immediate controversy. It was banned in Scotland and was publicly burned in England. Rutherford, a Presbyterian minister who was one of the Scottish commissioners at Westminister Abbey in London and rector of St. Andrew's Church in Scotland, was placed under house arrest and summoned to appear before the Parliament at Edinburgh where probable execution awaited him. He died shortly before he could be made to comply with the order.

But Rutherford's ideas lived on to influence later generations. His basic presupposition of government based upon the absolutes of the Bible was finally realized in colonial America through the influence of two sources: John Witherspoon and John Locke.

Witherspoon, a Presbyterian minister who had been educated at Edinburgh University, brought the principles of *Lex, Rex* into the writing of the Constitution. The only clergyman to sign the Declaration of Independence, Witherspoon was a member of the Continental Congress from 1776 to 1779 and from 1780 to 1782. He played a key role on a number of the committees of the first Congress. Witherspoon's students, profoundly influenced by him, also reached positions of eminence in the Constitutional Convention and in early United States history. They included a president, James Madison; a vice president, Aaron Burr; ten cabinet officers; twenty-one senators; thirty-nine congressmen; and twelve governors, as well as other public figures.[2]

James Madison was particularly influenced by Witherspoon. Columbia University professor Richard B. Morris writes in *Seven Who Shaped Our Destiny:* "Most influential in shaping Madison's . . . outlook was Princeton's president, John Witherspoon, a leading empiricist of his day . . . whose expositions of the doctrines of resistance and liberty quickly established him throughout the continent as an imposing intellectual."[3] The Witherspoon influence later played a major role in the drafting of the Constitution. In fact, Madison has been labeled "The Father of the Constitution" for his contribution in writing the founding document.

Two principles enunciated in *Lex, Rex* were drawn upon by the colonists in declaring their independence from Great Britain in 1776. First, there was the concept of the covenant or constitution between the ruler and God and the people. This covenant, Rutherford argued, could not grant the state absolute or unlimited power without violating God's law. Taking the cue from Rutherford, the colonists asserted that King George had violated his covenant with God by transgressing their God-given rights.

Rutherford's second principle declared that all men are created equal. Since all men are born sinners, Rutherford reasoned that no man is superior to any other man. He established the principle of equality and liberty among men, which was later written into the Declaration of Independence.

Although John Locke secularized the Reformed tradition, he nevertheless drew heavily from it.[4] He elaborated fundamental concepts such as unalienable rights, government by consent, the social compact (a constitution between the people and the government), separation of powers, and the right to resist unlawful authority. The biblical base for these concepts is set forth in Rutherford's *Lex, Rex*. As Francis Schaeffer has noted, many "of the men who laid the foundation of the United States Constitution were not Christian in the [full] sense, and yet they built upon the basis of the Reformation either directly through the *Lex, Rex* tradition or indirectly through Locke."[5]

It is important to understand that our political institutions have their base in this Reformation thinking. When we contrast this fact with the increasingly arbitrary nature of our modern civil government, we see that we have, in effect, come full circle. Today, in many ways, our "democratic" institutions reflect the governmental viewpoints of those absolute monarchists who condemned Samuel Rutherford. There is one vital difference. The monarchs of that day acknowledged the sovereignty of God, at least in theory. The Bible was held in high respect, and to challenge the monarch's prerogatives on biblical grounds—as Rutherford did in *Lex, Rex*—was considered a dangerous threat as well as heresy. If *Lex, Rex* were published today it might very well be ignored and labeled another irrelevant Christian statement in a society that respects neither the Bible nor the church.

The Influence of Blackstone

The renowned eighteenth-century English jurist William Blackstone also played a leading role in forming a Christian presuppositional base to early American law. Because the American colonists and Blackstone shared the same background of Reformation thinking, Blackstone's ideas on law were readily accepted in the colonies.

Blackstone, who was a lecturer at law at Oxford, embodied the tenets of Judeo-Christian theism in his *Commentaries on the Laws of England,* published betwen 1765 and 1770. The *Commentaries* were popular in Great Britain, but by 1775, more copies of the *Commentaries* had been sold in America than in all England.[6] So influential were the *Commentaries* that historian Daniel Boorstin writes: "In the first century of American independence, the Commentaries were not merely an approach to the study of the law; for most lawyers they constituted all there was of the law."[7]

Blackstone, a Christian, believed that the fear of the Lord was the beginning of wisdom. Thus he opened his *Commentaries* with a careful analysis of the law of God as revealed in the Bible. He defined law as a rule of action which is prescribed by some superior and which the inferior is bound to obey. To illustrate this definition Blackstone expressed the presuppositional base for law as he saw it:

> The doctrines thus delivered we call the revealed or divine law, and they are to be found only in the holy scriptures. Upon these two foundations, the law of nature and the law of revelation, depend all human laws; that is to say, no human laws should be suffered to contradict these.[8]

Blackstone took it as self-evident that God is the source of all laws, whether they were found in the Holy Scriptures or were observable in nature. His presuppositions were thoroughly Christian, founded upon the belief that there existed a personal, omnipotent God who worked in and governed the affairs of men. In consequence, man was bound by those laws, which were in turn a system of absolutes. Why? Because man is a derivative being. Blackstone wrote:

> Man, considered as a creature, must necessarily be subject to the laws of his Creator, for he is entirely a dependent being. . . . And, consequently, as man depends absolutely upon his Maker for everything, it is necessary that he should in all points conform to his Maker's will.[9]

Blackstone argued that the cultural mandate given to Adam and Eve in Genesis 1 is the basis for man's possession of property. This divine mandate was the only true basis for the right to hold private property or, for that matter, any right. In Blackstone's view, and in the eyes of those who founded the United States, every right or law comes from God, and the very words *rights, laws, freedoms,* and so on are meaningless without their divine origin.

Blackstone's influence is clearly expressed in the Declaration of Independence. The colonists argued that it is "the Laws of Nature and of Nature's God" that entitled them to independence and to an equal station among nations. Blackstone had some years earlier written that the "will of Maker is called the law of nature."[10] And in echoing *Lex, Rex* the colonists proclaimed that "all men are created equal."

In seeking independence from Great Britain the colonists declared to the world their belief in a personal, infinite God—"their Creator"—who endowed them with "certain unalienable" or absolute rights. To the men of that time, it was self-evident that if there were no God there could be no absolute rights. Unlike the French revolutionaries a few years later, the American colonists knew very well if the unalienable rights they were urging for were not seen in the context of Judeo-Christian theism, they were without content.

The Declaration of Independence, therefore, is structured upon a Judeo-Christian base in two fundamental ways. First, it professes faith in a "Creator" who works in and governs the affairs of men in establishing absolute standards to which men are held accountable. Second—and even more fundamentally, since all Western nations of that era professed a belief in the Creator—there is the idea that man is a fallen creature and, hence, cannot be his own lawgiver and judge. In the end it is God to whom the appeal must be made. In this sense, the law cannot be simply what a judge or a führer says it is. It is what God says it is.

"The Christian Idea," Notes

1. James W. Sire, *The Universe Next Door: A Basic World View Catalog* (Downers Grove, Ill.: InterVarsity Press, 1976), p. 31.

2. Rousas J. Rushdoony, *This Independent Republic* (Fairfax, Va.: Thoburn Press, 1964), p. 3.

3. Richard B. Morris, *Seven Who Shaped Our Destiny* (New York: Harper & Row, Publishers, 1973), p. 192.

4. Schaeffer, *How Should We Then Live?*, p. 109.

5. Schaeffer, *How Should We Then Live?*, p. 110.

6. Perry Miller, *The Life of the Mind in America: From the Revolution to the Civil War* (New York: Harcourt, Brace, Jovanovich, 1970), p. 115.

7. Daniel Boorstin, *The Mysterious Science of the Law* (Magnolia, Mass: Peter Smith, 1958), p. 3. Although thoroughly accepted in basic espousal of Christian theism, Blackstone, on the eve of the war with Great Britain, was criticized by various American colonial leaders, chief of whom may have been the Virginian, Thomas Jefferson (1743-1826). The criticism stemmed from the sovereignty Blackstone placed in the English Parliament. Shortly before the war, Blackstone remarked: "If the Parliament will positively enact a thing to be done which is unreasonable, I know of no power in the ordinary form of the Constitution that is vested with authority to control of it." Perhaps Blackstone, as a loyal Englishman, in his defense of

the British Parliament, was only echoing a sentiment of the times. On the other hand, Blackstone may have been saying—which was true—that in the "ordinary" form what Parliament enacted was law. Extraordinarily, if the enactment were "unreasonable" one might resort to "extraordinary" forms for recourse. This the colonists did. No matter the flaw (if it were indeed a flaw) in his thinking on this subject, Blackstone's real contribution was the foundation he laid for law and government in America, and his contributions were strongly felt up to the mid-nineteenth century.

8. William Blackstone, *Commentaries on the Law of England,* Chitty ed., p. 28.

9. William Blackstone, *Commentaries on the Law of England,* Tucker ed. (1803), p. 39.

10. Blackstone, *Commentaries* (Tucker ed.), p. 39.

2. In Defense of Religious America

Terry Eastland

"Religion in American life, Mr. Cadwell. We need it." That is the concluding line of a radio commercial which for some perhaps providential reason I have had occasion to hear several dozen times over the past year. It is not an advertisement for any particular religion, just religion itself, which presumably could be Christian or Jewish or Muslim or Hindu or—though I think the commercial's sponsors did not quite have this in mind—the Reverend Sun Myung Moon's. It is an innocuous ad, so ecumenical as to be able to effect no conversion to anything. But concerned as it is with religion in American life, the message serves beautifully as a kind of theme song for our times. It implicitly raises the question brought up by the activities of so many others in the past year, from Jerry Falwell to the American Civil Liberties Union: What should be the place of religion in American life? What, that is, should be the place of religion, not so much in the life of any one individual American as in American civil society?

Discussion of this question has not been especially enlightening. It has centered almost exclusively on the First Amendment, and the reflections on the First Amendment have themselves been unhelpful. Columnists and politicians have been content to repeat the mythology most famously (though not originally) articulated by Chief Justice Earl Warren when he said that the First Amendment "underwrote the admonition of Thomas Jefferson that there should be a wall of separation between church and state." The Chief Justice had a way with history, but for the sake of accuracy—and much else besides—it should be noted that Jefferson said what he said in 1802, when he was President, in a letter to the Danbury Baptists. However interesting Jefferson's thoughts may be, and however much we may wish today to regard his views as authoritative on church-state matters, this letter is simply not relevant to a consideration of the framing of the First Amendment and its original intention—unless of course Jefferson had been sitting in

Congress in the summer of 1789 (in fact he was in Europe as Secretary of State and would not return until the autumn).

The invocation of Jefferson obscures history by implying that the Founding Fathers were hostile to religion, since in today's usage the idea of a wall connotes antagonism and suspicion between the two sides thus separated. As a matter of historical fact, the Founding Fathers believed that the public interest was served by the promotion of religion. The Northwest Ordinance of 1787, which set aside federal property in the territory for schools and which was passed again by Congress in 1789, is instructive. "Religion, morality, and knowledge being necessary to good government and the happiness of mankind," read the act, "schools and the means of learning shall forever be encouraged."

It is only from history, not from clichés about history, that we can understand what we once were as a nation in regard to religion, and what we have since become. Let me therefore start with these propositions: that there was a principal religion in American life from 1620 until roughly 1920; that this religion was Protestant Christianity; and that Protestant Christianity has been our established religion in almost every sense of that phrase.

The one sense in which Protestant Christianity was *not* established, of course, was as our national religion. There never has been a Church of the United States, complete with a bishop and supported by tax revenues, as in England. Nor can there be one: the First Amendment to the Constitution did make sure of that. But nothing more than that.

The intention of the framers of the First Amendment was not to effect an absolute neutrality on the part of government toward religion on the one hand and irreligion on the other. The neutrality the framers sought was rather among the sects, the various denominations. Accordingly, as Michael J. Malbin has shown, although there could be no national establishment of a sect, there could be state aid to religious groups so long as the assistance furthered a public purpose and so long as it did not discriminate in favor of some or against others; all sects, in other words, would have to be benefited.[1]

The perspective of colonial history in the period dating from the Great Awakening makes it all the more clear that the First

Amendment could not have been meant to enforce neutrality by government as between religion and irreligion. The Society for the Propagation of the Gospel, a sort of missionary arm of the Church of England, had been in business in America since 1701. For three quarters of the eighteenth century, and especially in the years just prior to the Revolution, a widespread religious attitude in America was fear—fear that the Crown would establish the Anglican religion. The principle of non-establishment of a particular denomination was a product of this historical period, and the First Amendment applied this principle at the national level. Throughout the late eighteenth and early nineteenth centuries the principle was similarly applied at the colonial and, later, the state levels. As at the national level, so at the state level: no one denomination was to be given state support; there had to be neutrality among sects.

Thus, if Anglicanism could not reign in a given colony or state, neither could Congregationalism. The Anglican establishments in Maryland, South Carolina, North Carolina, and Georgia were wiped out before 1776, and Virginia's died finally in 1802. Congregationalism held on long past 1791 in Massachusetts, Connecticut, and New Hampshire, but by 1833 had lost its privileged status in all of these states.

It should be noted that although these establishments were of different sects, they belonged to the same religious family tree—that of Protestant Christianity. This is hardly surprising. The original colonies were English, and their English settlers were primarily Protestant. The non-English minorities—the Scots, the Scotch-Irish, the French, the Dutch, the Swedes, the Germans—were also mostly Protestant. There were only a few Catholics, mostly in Maryland, and even fewer Jews. This relative mix would endure until well past the middle of the nineteenth century.

The heavily Protestant orientation of the churchgoers of early America should not obscure the fact that many if not a majority of Americans were unchurched in the eighteenth century. But with a very few exceptions these unchurched were not freethinking atheists or agnostics. Hence, while the principle of non-establishment could be extended to prohibit the establishment of one particular religion (and not just the sects within a religion), few people were sufficiently bothered, as a practical or theoretical matter, to make this extension. The prominent exception was Madison, who believed that Christianity should not be favored over any other religion. Yet even Madison agreed on the general proposition that so far as the public interest was concerned, religion itself was better than irreligion.

State Support of the Protestant Faith

The particular sects, then, had been disestablished at the state level by 1833. But Christianity had not been, and would not be, until much later. In the early part of the nineteenth century, states set up both constitution and statute provisions declaring it the duty of all men "to worship the Supreme Being." States also regulated membership in Christian denominations, imposed fines for failure to fix the worship hour on Sundays, and even mandated that elected officials believe in "the Christian religion."[2]

State courts did their part to support the Protestant faith. In 1811 the New York state court upheld an indictment for blasphemous utterances against Christ, and in its ruling, given by Chief Justice Kent, the court said, "We are Christian people, and the morality of the country is deeply engrafted upon Christianity." Fifty years later this same court said that "Christianity may be conceded to be the established religion."

The Pennsylvania state court also affirmed the conviction of a man on charges of blasphemy, here against the Holy Scriptures. The Court said: "Christianity, general Christianity is, and always has been, a part of the common law of Pennsylvania . . . not Christianity founded on any particular religious tenets; nor Christianity with an established church and tithes and spiritual courts; but Christianity with liberty of conscience to all men."

States also required the teaching of the Christian religion in state colleges and universities, and in prisons, reformatories, asylums, orphanages, and homes for soldiers. Furthermore, public aid was given to church-run hospitals and orphanages. Last, but certainly not least, many states required Bible reading and prayers in the elementary and secondary public schools.

Religion was far more integrated into the actual curriculum than these religious exercises might suggest. Textbooks referred to God without embarrassment, and schoolteachers considered one of their major tasks the development of character—an aim quite consistent, as we shall see, with America's brand of Protestant Christianity. The influence of William Holmes McGuffey (1800-1873), a Presbyterian educator and philosopher, was remarkable. His *Eclectic Readers* were published in 1836, and from that year until 1920—two years after Mississippi became the last state to institute a public-school system—his books sold more than 120 million copies, a total that put them in a class with only the Bible and Webster's Dictionary. McGuffey's *Readers* stressed, as the Northwest Ordinance did, "religion, morality, and knowledge," in that order.

Protestant Christianity Established by Culture

As with the public schools, so with almost every area of American life. The establishment of Protestant Christianity was one not only of law but also, and far more important, of culture. Protestant Christianity supplied the nation with its "system of values"—to use the modern phrase—and would do so until the 1920s when the cake of Protestant custom seemed most noticeably to begin crumbling. But before coming to that moment we should reflect on the content of the particular religion that held sway in American life for the better part of 300 years, and remark more precisely on the significance of its "cultural" establishment.

As a general metaphysic, Protestant Christianity was understood in ways Catholics and Jews and deists could accept. Not only Protestant Christians but most people agreed that our law was rooted, as John Adams had said, in a common moral and religious tradition, one that stretched back to the time Moses went up on Mount Sinai. Similarly, almost everyone agreed that our liberties were God-given and should be exercised responsibly. There was a distinction between liberty and license.

Beyond this it is possible to be much more specific. Protestant Christianity was Reformed in theology, Puritan in outlook, experiential in faith. It was also evangelical in its orientation toward the world. These propositions held true of not only the denominations of Puritan origin (such as the Congregational, Presbyterian, and Baptist churches) but also those with more highly qualified views on the issue of predestination (such as the Methodist church) and those we might today consider "High Church" (such as the Episcopal church). Almost everyone drank from the same Reformation well, which happened to be the Westminster Confession of 1643. Reformation theology placed emphasis on the sovereignty of God and the depravity of man. It was a religion of the book—the Bible—that demanded the individual conversion of man and, in consequence, the living of a changed life.

This point had enormous social and political consequences. It is unlikely that a predominantly Catholic or Jewish America would have given birth to the type of society that eventually evolved by the late eighteenth century. The reason is that neither would have emphasized to the degree the American Puritans did the importance of personal development in the moral (and for them spiritual) sense of character formation. The Westminster Confession describes the preaching of the word as "an effectual means of driving them [sinners] out of themselves" and "of strengthening them against temptation and corruption, and of building them up in grace."

That is doctrine that will shape a man, and the shaping, molding emphasis of the American Puritans, the character-building emphasis, can even today be seen—literally seen—in needlework shops where samplers bearing the old, straightforwardly didactic Protestant American messages can be found. Often such messages take the form of unedited Bible verses (from the King James version). Scripture was not incidental to the Puritan American. It was to be considered, meditated upon, learned by heart. "As a man thinketh in his heart," says the Bible, "so is he." The Puritans did not think only with their heads.

The American Protestant characteristically was driven out of himself, not only into Christ but also into the world. Hence the description—"this-worldly ascetic"—so often applied to individuals in Reformed communities. The change in the history of Christianity that this phrase suggests is seismic. After Luther it was no longer necessary to withdraw from the world (and into a monastery) to serve God. A man could serve God in the secular world. ("What is the chief and highest end of man?" asks the first question of the Larger Catechism of the Westminster Confession. "Man's chief and highest end is to glorify God and fully to enjoy Him forever.") Every job had a purpose, every man a calling, a vocation, no matter how lowly or how exalted. Working in *this* world, furthermore, men could transform the society about them, as the New England Puritans tried to do in their Bible Commonwealths. Though these societies failed according to their own ideals, the impulse to change society remained and would manifest itself in numerous ways, including the voluntarism of the nineteenth century, which became such a mainstay of American life.

The Virtues of Protestantism

American Protestantism not only taught spiritual values but also the less heroic ones of sobriety, honesty, prudence, temperance, and diligence. In the context of these virtues, as Irving Kristol has often pointed out, capitalism made ethical sense. Protestantism was understood to tame and direct a man's interests, including his economic ones, toward worthy ends. Man was understood to be a steward upon earth, and he was to use his liberty and his talents responsibly (and diligently; there was to be no idleness, no sloth). There may be no more interesting text on this than Question 141 of the Larger Catechism of the Westminster Confession, which even as late as 1844 was described by Philip Schaff, a German writing on America's religious life, as "the reigning theology of the country." The question refers to the Eighth Commandment ("Thou shalt not steal") and asks what duties it requires:

> The duties required . . . are: truth, faithfulness, and justice in contracts and commerce between man and man; rendering to everyone his due; restitution of goods unlawfully detained from the right owners thereof, giving and lending freely, according to our abilities, and the necessities of others; moderation of our judgments, wills, and affections, concerning worldly goods; a provident care and study to get, keep, use, and dispose of those things which are necessary and convenient for the sustentation of our nature, and suitable to our condition; a lawful calling, and diligence in it; frugality; avoiding unnecessary lawsuits, and suretyship, or other like arrangements; and an endeavor by all just and lawful means to

procure, preserve, and further the wealth and outward estate of others, as well as our own.

This answer offers much to reflect on; there is, for instance, the implicit approval of both commerce and the creation of wealth, even of one's own wealth. But the principal concern is man's duty, which is to have moderating effects upon his commercial activities. Tocqueville observed that the law allowed the American people to do everything, but that there are things which their religion prevented them from imagining and forbade them to dare. Religion—the Protestant religion here described—was thus a major source of the virtues a nation conceived in liberty always would need. It shaped the society and the individuals within it. Protestant Christianity helped answer the oldest of political questions: What kind of people, having what kind of character, does a society produce?

Tocqueville therefore was right to say that religion was America's "foremost political institution." It was the branch of government that the Constitution, based on self-interest and envisioning a commercial Republic, obviously could not create. Yet it was the branch essential to the maintenance of the Republic. It provided a check on the liberty guaranteed by our conventional political institutions. It was responsible for the character of the people. And as this "informal" branch of government, as our "foremost political institution," Protestant Christianity enjoyed its most significant form of "establishment."

The Decline of Protestantism

In the past sixty years, we have witnessed the disestablishment of this religion. One could argue that it was bound to happen. Good American theory—as given by Madison—holds that the more factions the better for the Republic's chances of survival. This theory applies not only to economic interests but also to religious ones. Despite the fact that the nation had been settled by Protestants, other religious peoples could settle here, too, and eventually they did. The great immigrations from Southern and Eastern Europe after the Civil War brought millions of Catholics to the United States, and by the end of the nineteenth century a sizable number of Jewish and Eastern Orthodox communities were also flourishing.

Meanwhile, something was happening to the old Protestantism itself. Evangelical Protestant Christianity (revitalized by the Second Awakening in the early years of the Republic) had held on strongly throughout the first half of the nineteenth century, but after the Civil War the tendencies toward Arminianism—i.e., the belief in divine sovereignty *and* human freedom—that had been present even in the eighteenth century became far more pronounced.

On the one hand, a liberal variety of Protestantism developed. Liberal theology had little interest in Original Sin; indeed sin to it was nothing more than mere error. Liberal Protestantism emphasized instead man's freedom and his natural goodness. Dogma and the sacraments were slighted, and there was immense optimism about the human race. Influenced by Kant, liberal Protestants reduced Christianity to morality; they had no prophetic voice to speak of (or with). Liberal Protestantism was an accommodation to culture. H. Richard Niebuhr perhaps best described its God as One "without wrath" Who "brought men without sin into a kingdom without judgment through the ministrations of a Christ without a cross."

Liberal Protestantism was not the only accommodation to culture. More conservative Protestants—the keepers of the old religious flame—proved to be poor stewards of it. The old Protestantism descended into revivalistic orgies, as brought to us most sensationally by Billy Sunday. Christianity was presented as something dulcet and sentimental, and as often as not it was allied to the pursuit of profit. Frequently the old Protestantism was served up as a civil religion—a heresy, as Jonathan Edwards, but not Billy Sunday, would have recognized. Here too, and not surprisingly, dogma was neglected. A remark by Dwight Moody perhaps best captures this. "My theology!" he exclaimed, when asked about it. "I didn't know I had any."

In the 1920s H. L. Mencken would acidly but correctly assert that "Protestantism is down with a wasting disease." One of the deepest reasons for its condition was that the Enlightenment had finally made its way to America. By the end of the nineteenth century the higher biblical criticism had disturbed the Protestant theologians' confidence in their ultimate authority, the Bible. So had the modern sciences, not only the physical sciences (especially biology in the form of Darwinism) but also the newer social sciences. Truth no longer seemed absolute but relative to time and place, and the insights into personality and society provided by psychology and sociology seemed at least as plausible as those found in the Bible.

The half-decade following the Civil War had been the great age of urbanization. The rise of the city had also seen for the first time in American history the development of an intellectual class, and it was not kind to the old Protestant faith. By the 1920s it had become intellectual fashion not to believe in God and, if one were a writer, to attack "Puritanism."

The Disestablishment of Protestantism

With the great immigrations, the decline of the old Protestant religion, and the rise of an intellectual class not merely indifferent but hostile to religion, the stage had been set by the 1920s for the cultural disestablishment of the old faith. Indeed, it had begun earlier. The end of World War I in 1918 had inaugurated a period of laxity in morals and manners. This is typically what happens after wars, but the decade of the 20s eventually would prove to be a dramatic break from the past. For it was not followed by a recovery of the old morals and manners, as also typically happens after social upheavals; the Victorian era stayed firmly in the past. Church attendance declined throughout the 20s. People lost their fear of Hell and had less interest in Heaven. They made more demands for material fulfillment.

Such demands, of course, are as American as the Declaration of Independence, which after all sanctified the idea of the pursuit of happiness. That idea owed more to the Enlightenment than to the Bible; certainly it did not sail to America aboard the Mayflower. Since the Declaration of Independence America had held its commitments to liberty and to virtue in tension. By the 20s it was clear the tension had begun to resolve itself in favor of liberty. Americans now insisted, as William Leuchtenburg has noted, not only on the right to pursue happiness but also on the right to possess it. The 20s saw the beginnings of the installment-buying plan; it is impossible to imagine such a purchasing scheme in the American culture of 200 or even 100 years earlier.

Since the 20s the disestablishment of the old Protestant religion has taken place most obviously in the intellectual, governing, bureaucratic, and cultural classes, and to a lesser but no less real and increasing degree in the rest of society. Today the disestablishment is perhaps most easily detected on the college campus. Logical positivism may have long ago fallen out of favor among philosophers, but as a cultural attitude among intellectuals and academics it is still going strong. God-talk (the literal meaning of theology) is not fashionable, not even, it sometimes seems, in a college chapel.

The campuses of the old Protestant culture emphasized the importance of the Christian faith. Now their chapels still stand, but university policies have changed. There is probably no more striking instance of this than at Princeton University, over which both Jonathan Edwards and John Witherspoon once presided. Last year Princeton went looking for a new Dean of the Chapel. A Presbyterian of deep commitment and faith had retired, and his retirement provided the occasion for the reevaluation of the Dean's function. A trustee report came forth with a new job description: Henceforth the Dean should be a person of "deep religious faith" but "above all, he or she must be personally gracious and open, and his or her own religious commitment must include sensitivity to the vulnerability of human finitude and the particularity and relativity of the views he or she espouses." The clauses following "above all" say everything that needs to be said about the distance Princeton has traveled.

Other evidences of disestablishment abound. Today the old idea that law has its roots in the Judeo-Christian ethic, as was believed at the Founding and throughout most of American history, is no longer much discussed, let alone believed in by many American legal philosophers and judges. The public philosophy of America, as Harold Berman has pointed out, has in the past two generations "shifted radically." Law is in theory no longer religious but secular; no longer moral but political and instrumental; no longer communitarian but individualistic. (People increasingly engage in "unnecessary lawsuits.") It is no wonder that Aleksandr

Solzhenitsyn, at Harvard for the commencement address three years ago, left his audience stunned when he spoke of law in a religious context.

From Liberty to Libertine

Meanwhile, liberty, like law, has been severed from its religious basis. What Jefferson once called the "firm conviction" in the minds of Americans that their liberties derive from God is hardly so firm anymore, certainly not among political scientists, columnists, television personalities, and others who influence public opinion. Having been given its own existence, ontologically speaking, liberty fairly runs riot now. The distinction between liberty and license transmitted to us by the old Protestant culture has faded almost completely among the educated classes. Consider again the college campus, where the old doctrine of *in loco parentis* is out of fashion. Administrators now run their campuses as if there is no God, since virtually everything is permitted. Probably the most libertine societies in America today exist on those very campuses that were originally the creations of the old Protestant culture.

To be sure, many other parts of America are closing fast on the campuses. It is the style nowadays not only among the college-educated but also among many blue-collar workers to be economically conservative but socially and morally liberal. This, translated, means balance the budget but decriminalize marijuana and cocaine and let us have abortion on demand. If the liberalism of the 60s has a definite legacy, it is found in the far more liberalized and hedonistic lives many Americans, including many older Americans, and indeed many political conservatives, now lead.

The "Me-Decade" has been well chronicled. Perhaps less obvious, but no less significant, is the change in ethical *thinking* that has occurred throughout society. A book could be written on what has happened to the idea of character. People in authority—teachers, parents, and even ministers—resist the fact that they are in authority. They will not "impose" their values; the idea is to let the young "clarify" *their* "values" (now considered as relative as any matter of taste). More education is no longer rooted in the virtues of courage, temperance, prudence, and the like. It is full of form but empty of content. What matters is that you feel sure the "option" you have chosen for yourself is the right one for you. I have seen a course in "values clarification" offered to adults in a Presbyterian Sunday school curriculum—and as an "option," no less!

Perhaps because the old imperative of "America the Beautiful"—"confirm thy soul in self-control"—has become too hard to follow, ethical teaching, while studiously neutral about personal life, is assiduously assertive in social matters. Where once the major emphasis was on tidying up the individual soul, on making it conform to reality, now the focus has shifted to the external world, to tidying up the laws that regulate the public lives of man and man (or woman). Where people, whether of secular or religious disposition, seem to feel most comfortable, and certainly most confident, is in talking about "social injustice" or "racism" or "poverty" or "exploitation." Recently I joined a panel at a major university on the subject of religion and virtue. A participant who was a professor of theology centered most of his remarks on "corporate sin." I don't recall his once mentioning the idea of virtue, let alone any particular virtue. Sometimes it is hard to find a difference between what ministers and theologians say and what many secular intellectuals say.

Trends within the Supreme Court

This, then, is the picture so far of an America that has experienced the cultural disestablishment of its old religion, the dissolution of its once "foremost" political institution. Consideration of a few trends within the Supreme Court will help complete the picture.

In 1947 the Supreme Court, in *Everson v. Board of Education of Ewing Township,* said the First Amendment "requires the state to be neutral in its relations with groups of religious believers and non-believers." This new doctrine of neutrality not only would seem to forbid the establishment of a religion—as Madison would have had it—but also the establishment of religion in general over non-religion and thus irreligion.

With its doctrine of neutrality, the Court has denied substantial public aid to elementary and secondary church-related schools. And by striking down prayers and Bible readings and now even the posting of the Ten Commandments in the public schools, it has acted according to an implicit doctrine that the public schools should be secular—and "value-free."

In 1961, in *Torcaso v. Watkins,* the Court so enlarged the definition of religion that an observer might say irreligion had now become a religion. The Court decreed that neither a state nor the federal government can "constitutionally pass laws nor impose requirements which aid all religions based on a belief in the existence of God as against those founded on *different beliefs*" (emphasis added). A footnote listed "Ethical Culture" and "Secular Humanism" among other examples of "religions" founded on "different beliefs."

In other contexts the Court has said that virtually anything may qualify as a "religion" so long as the "religious person" believes in whatever he believes in with, as Justice Black put it, "the strength of traditional religious conviction." This definition of religion celebrates individual conscience. It is hardly surprising that in cases involving "privacy" the Court has reduced public restrictions on private choice (as with its abortion decision in 1973). The legal trend here, like the cultural trend, has been toward a pronounced individualism in matters of religion and morals.

These trends of the Court round out the portrait. We are all "pluralists" now. And it should be stipulated that this is not altogether a bad thing. I doubt that any serious religious believer would wish a return to the days of intolerance that were an admitted ill of the old Protestant culture. But people who take religion seriously—and I mean here religion that has social and historical dimension, not merely something you might believe with "the strength of traditional religious conviction" in the midst of a Saturday night drunk—will find much in this picture that is disturbing. For the disestablishment of the old Protestantism has meant defeats not only for Protestants but for Catholics and Jews as well.

By contradicting the historical meaning of the establishment clause of the First Amendment, the Court has said, in effect, that promotion of religion is not in the public interest. Daniel P. Moynihan has correctly written that the recent decisions based on the establishment clause are "an intellectual scandal," and it is perhaps not too much to hope that the Court will one day reverse itself on this matter. Meanwhile, however, the severing of both law and liberty from their historic rooting in religion has serious and more immediate implications. Instrumentalists may argue that obedience to law can be brought about solely through the threat of coercive sanctions, but, as Berman has written, what is far more important is "the tradition of being law-abiding, which in turn depends upon a deeply or passionately held conviction that law is not only an instrument of secular policy but also part of the ultimate purpose and meaning of life."

As for the loss of the religiously-grounded distinction between liberty and license, we have all witnessed the proliferation of rights with no concomitant responsibilities that has been the result. With traditional religion now pushed to the margin of our public life, not only thanks to the Court's doctrines of neutrality and secularism but also, and more important, thanks to the pedagogy of school and college teachers alike, religion is less able to exercise its historic role as a political counterweight, as the voice of constraint and responsibility.

The shift in ethical thinking away from character formation toward personality adjustment and values clarification on the one hand, and social problems on the other, is perhaps the most disturbing change of all. The emphasis on virtues that the old Protestant culture provided was precisely what the Founding Fathers acknowledged their new Constitution could not provide. And yet the Founders also knew that just these virtues were what the best thinkers in antiquity had thought necessary to the maintenance of a republican order. If the old evangelical Protestantism had a special fire in it that burned the ancient virtues into the souls of men, the virtues themselves were not special to that faith. For these were virtues agreeable to Catholic and rabbinical tradition, to the Deists of the Founding period, to the Greeks and Romans. The old Protestant religion understood, as ancient philosophy did, that politics is ultimately about the cultivation of character. It is unclear today that our modern culture even understands this point, let alone wants to deal with it.[3]

Even so, it is answered, by default if not by design. Protestant Christianity is no longer America's "foremost political institution," but this fact does not obviate the need for a system of values in which Americans can move and live and have their commercial (and now leisure) being. If our morality is not engrafted upon Protestant Christianity, it will be engrafted on something else—God only knows what. The brilliance of the Founding Fathers did not anticipate this situation, but surely they did not believe that any institution could ever be "value-free." We are all the time engrafting our way of life upon *some* set of values.

The Trends of the Future

If we are today a secular society, we are still also a liberal society. And in the current groping toward what inevitably will be our public philosophy, the religious person is entitled, if not to prevail, at least to be heard. The religious person can expect to be allowed a voice in matters of public policy. He can expect that his religion will not disqualify him from speaking on political matters, and that if he offers a religious or ethical justification for his position on a public issue, it will not *ipso facto* be considered out of the bounds of public discourse. The question here is ultimately one of where you get your basic beliefs. If, as Michael Novak has written, we should be willing to let people get their politics as much from the Bible as from Gloria Steinem, then biblical or religious values should be permissible in public debate. Unless the free exercise of religion, vouchsafed in the First Amendment, is to mean only trivial whispers, something practiced in the closet, then it must mean a voice equal to that of anyone who is not religious.

The trends go against even the minimal kind of free exercise of religion. It has been argued by serious public philosophers that only a rational, utilitarian morality should ever be enforced by law, and that this morality by definition would exclude any influenced by or grounded in religious considerations. Today this argument, spoken by non-philosophers, is used against the Moral Majority and their kind. You cannot legislate morality, it is said, meaning you cannot legislate a particular kind of morality—the kind having to do with religion as traditionally conceived.

History is not irreversible, but the trends for the past hundred years suggest that traditional religion will have an increasingly marginal influence on our public life. America is still one of the most religious countries in the world, and yet church affiliation

(40 percent of Americans profess one) continues to decline, as Seymour Martin Lipset and Earl Raab noted.[4] These are just the circumstances to expect in a country to which the Enlightenment came late. The much-touted religious renaissance of recent years does not promise to change this state of affairs, at least not soon. Lacking is what has been lacking in much of American religious life for the past hundred years—solid theological content—and on this score the seminaries that have brought us the "death of God," "liberation theology," and other similar inspirations cannot inspire hope. As for the turning of a few scientists toward God, this is hardly a full-blown theological revolution. To postulate, as Sir John Eccles has done, that the brain is the product of evolution but that only God could have created the mind may prove an invaluable service to religion. But we are still a long way from any *Summa,* and a longer way from a great cultural movement.

One need not hold a brief for Jerry Falwell, nor for his cousin evangelists who appear on the television screen in the shank of the evening, to acknowledge what they have done, which at the least has been to flush the anti-religious bias out into the open. The early reaction to Falwell was dominated by comments from civil libertarians who implied, ironically enough, that Falwell had no right to speak out on public issues. Such was not the reaction when the Reverend Martin Luther King wrote his letter from a Birmingham jail, but the hypocrisy is less interesting, I think, than the secular bias that produced it.

If someday people with traditional religious views should be effectively banned from public debate, not only will the free exercise of religion have been denied but a new religion will have been culturally established as our "foremost political institution." It would no doubt look very much like what the Supreme Court alluded to in its *Torcaso* ruling—the religion of "secular humanism." God save us from that.

"In Defense of Religious America," Notes

1. Michael J. Malbin, *Religion and Politics: The Intentions of the Authors of the First Amendment* (Washington, D.C.: American Enterprise Institute for Public Policy Research, 1978).

2. For this and following references, see Harold Berman, "The Interaction of Law and Religion," *Humanities in Society* (Spring 1979).

3. Can a government, asks Francis Canavan, "committed to absolute neutrality among 'religions' . . . be capable of educating anyone? . . . The right questions were raised, but not answered, by Justice Jackson in his dissenting opinion in *Everson* where he said: 'Our public school . . . is organized on the premise that secular education can be isolated from all religious teaching so that the school can inculcate all needed temporal knowledge and also maintain a strict and lofty neutrality as to religion. The assumption is that after the individual has been instructed in worldly wisdom he will be better fitted to choose his religion. Whether such a disjunction is possible, and if possible whether it is wise, are questions I need not try to answer' " ("The Impact of Recent Supreme Court Decisions on Religion in the United States," *Journal of Church and State,* vol. 16, no. 2, 1974).

4. Seymour Martin Lipset and Earl Raab, "The Election and the Evangelical," *Commentary* (March 1981).

3. Religion and the Legitimation of the American Republic

Robert N. Bellah

Civil Religion, Term and Concept

In 1967 I published an essay I have never been allowed to forget.[1] In it I suggested there is such a thing as civil religion in America. My suggestion has roused passionate opposition as well as widespread acceptance. The opposition to the idea has shown little unity. Some of my opponents say there is no such thing; I have invented something that does not exist. Some say there is such a thing but there ought not to be. Some say there is such a thing but it should be called by another name, "public piety," for example, rather than civil religion. Unfortunately for me, my supporters are in even greater disarray. The term "civil religion" has spread far beyond any coherent concept thereof, or at least beyond anything I ever meant by the term. Perhaps the commonest reaction is a puzzled, "Yes, there seems to be something there, but what exactly is it?" Among the professional specialists in American studies there is another reaction: "We knew it all the time. What Bellah says is nothing new." And then there is perhaps a vague reference to Tocqueville. But, with one or two exceptions, little in the way of conceptual clarity has been forthcoming from the specialists. I would like to try once again to clarify this most troublesome problem. The burden of what I want to say is that the confusion about civil religion is rooted in a confusion about the nature of the American republic and that genuinely to clarify the nature of American civil religion would involve a reform of the American republic.

I must admit I am partly to blame for the confusion by my choice of the term "civil religion," which turned out to be far more tendentious and provocative than I at first realized. I think now the choice of the term was fortunate and the controversies it generated are fruitful. More neutral terms such as "political religion" or "religion of the republic" or "public piety" would not have churned up the profound empirical ambiguities "civil religion," with its two thousand years of historical resonance, inevitably did.

On the face of it, what would be more natural than to speak about civil religion, a subject that has preoccupied theorists of republican government from Plato to Rousseau? The founders of this republic had read most of those theorists and were concerned with the problem, even though they did not use the term.[2] The difficulty arises because for most of those two thousand years there has been a profound antipathy, indeed an utter incompatibility, between civil religion and Christianity. There is even a question, which I cannot explore here, whether there has not been a historic antipathy between republican government and Christianity. Most Christian political theorists down through the ages have considered monarchy the best form of government (Christian religious symbolism would seem to be much more monarchical than republican) and the great republican theorists—Machiavelli, Rousseau, even Tocqueville—have wondered whether Christianity can ever create good citizens.[3] Augustine in the opening books of the *City of God* denounced Roman "civil theology" as the worship of false gods and the Roman Republic as based on false ideals and therefore as finally no commonwealth at all. Rousseau, in arguing for the necessity in a republic of a civil religion other than Christianity, wrote, "Christianity as a religion is entirely spiritual, occupied solely with heavenly things; the country of the Christian is not of this world. . . . imagine your Christian republic face to face with Sparta or Rome: the pious Christians will be beaten, crushed, and destroyed. . . . But I am mistaken in speaking of a Christian republic; the terms are mutually exclusive. Christianity preaches only servitude and dependence. Its spirit is so favourable to tyranny that it always profits by such a regime. True Christians are made to be slaves, and they know it and do not much mind: this short life counts for too little in their eyes."[4] And yet at the beginning of our history we were that mutually exclusive thing, a Christian Republic. (Samuel Adams even called us a Christian Sparta.) Or were we? Christianity was never our state religion, nor did we have in Rousseau's strict sense a civil religion, a simple set of religious dogmas to which every citizen must subscribe on pain of exile. What did we have? What do we have now? That indeed is the question.

Religion and Politics

Tension between church and state lies deep in Christian history. The idea of a nonreligious state is very modern and very doubtful. Through most of Western history some form of Christianity has been the established religion and has provided "religious legitimation" to the state. But under that simple formula lie faction, intrigue, anguish, tension, and, on occasion, massacre, rebellion, and religious war. Through much of history the state has dominated a restless church, exploited it, but never destroyed its refusal of final allegiance. On occasion the church has mastered the state, used it for its own ends, and temporalized its spiritual loyalties into a kind of religious nationalism. In all this Christianity is no different from other religions I have characterized as being at the historic stage.[5] Even religions that seem to be much more intrinsically political, such as Islam or Confucianism, have for most of their histories been involved in uneasy and unhappy alliances with state power. Relative to the first four caliphs all Muslim rulers have been viewed as at least faintly illegitimate by the religious community. Relative to the ancient sage kings all the Chinese emperors have lacked fundamental legitimacy in the eyes of the Confucian scholars.

The very spirituality and otherworldliness of Christianity has provided a certain avenue for reducing the tension not always open to other historic religions: the differentiation of functions, the division of spheres. Yet no solution has ever dissolved the underlying tensions described by Augustine and Rousseau. The tendency has been for every solution to break down into religion as the servant of the state or the state as the servant of religion.

Yet there have been great periodic yearnings in Western history to overcome the split, to create a society that would indeed be a Christian republic, where there would be no split in the soul between Christian and citizen. Savonarola had such a dream in fifteenth-century Florence, as did the Anabaptists in sixteenth-century Germany and some of the sectarians during the civil war in seventeenth-century England. Most of these experiments were highly unstable and illustrated rather than refuted Rousseau's argument for mutual exclusiveness. Yet John Calvin in sixteenth-century Geneva created a city that was Christian and republican in an organic way that had few precedents (and that stood curiously behind Rousseau's own republican theorizing). Church and state were not fused; indeed, formal distinctions were sharply maintained. Yet Christian and citizen were finally two ways of saying the same thing. Even more to the point, the New England colonies in the seventeenth century were Christian republics in a comparable sense. In Massachusetts, for example, only Christians could be citizens, though the church did not control the state and both church and state were governed by their members. Even though the reality of this experiment had evaporated by the early eighteenth century, the memory was still strong in the minds of the founders of the republic.

The civil theology of the youthful Hegel in Germany during the decades after the French Revolution shows the yearning for the union of Christian and citizen was still vigorous at the end of the eighteenth century.[6] These youthful speculations stand behind Hegel's mature political theory as well as, curiously, behind the thought of Marx about man and citizen.

Could there be a sense in which the American republic, which has neither an established church nor a classic civil religion, is, after all, a Christian republic, or should I say a biblical republic, in which biblical religion is indeed the civil religion? Is that what it means to say we are "a nation with the soul of a church"?[7] The answer, as before, is yes and no. The American solution to the problem of church and state is unprecedented, unique, and confused. I shall turn from external speculation and from the introduction of tendentious terms like "civil religion" to the way the tradition has understood itself.

The Work of the Founders

Today the almost Pavlovian response applied to all problems in this area is "the separation of church and state." That phrase, especially when it is intensified with the unfortunate Jeffersonian image of the "wall of separation," is pernicious precisely to the degree it seems to offer a clear solution when in fact it creates more difficulties than it eliminates. The first thing to remember is that the phrase "separation of church and state" has no constitutional standing. The first clause of the first amendment states, "Congress shall make no law respecting an establishment of religion." That clause has a long history of interpretation that I shall not review here, but it certainly does not mean and has never meant the American state has no interest in or concern for religion, or churches either, for that matter, and it certainly does not mean religion and politics have nothing to do with each other.[8] To the extent the "wall of separation" image leads to those conclusions it distorts the entire history of the American understanding of religion and leads to such absurd conclusions as that religious congregations should have no tax exemption and legislative bodies should not be opened with prayer. To attribute such intentions to the founders of the republic is not only a historical error but a political error about the nature of the republic. Inspection of the second clause of the first amendment, "or prohibiting the free exercise thereof," should begin to dispel the distortions of the extreme separationist position.

The Constitution, while prohibiting a religious establishment, protects the free exercise of religion. It is this second clause to which that other common phrase, "religious freedom," refers, a phrase that has often been used to sum up the American teaching about religion. This phrase too has a significant Jeffersonian source, for Jefferson pointed to his authorship of a bill for "establishing religious freedom" in Virginia as one of the three things he most wanted to be remembered for. The phrase "establishing religious freedom," which is not constitutional but which explicates the free exercise clause, suggests the positive institutionalization in this area. Indeed, religious freedom or free exercise is the controlling idea. The prohibition of the establishment of a particular religion is required because it would be an infringement on religious freedom. Even so, today it is not uncommon for the religious freedom concept to be swallowed up in the separation concept because freedom here as elsewhere is interpreted in purely negative terms, as the liberal philosophical tradition tends to treat it. Religious freedom becomes then merely the right to worship any God you please or none at all, with the implication that religion is a purely private matter of no interest or concern to political society. I will argue that "establishing religious freedom" means something much more than that, indeed, that it has a powerful positive political significance. But the difficulty of interpretation is not entirely in the mind of the analyst. It is not just a question of reading late twentieth-century ideas about religion into the minds of the founders, though there is much of that. The difficulty is rooted in certain fundamental unclarities about the American political experience and the nature of the American regime, unclarities that go back to the formative period of the republic.

The basic unclarity rests on whether we are a republic in recognizable relation to the republics of classical and modern times and dependent on that inner spirit of republican character and mores that make for republican citizenship, or whether we are a liberal constitutional regime governed through artificial contrivance and the balancing of conflicting interests. What we wanted was to have our cake and eat it too, to retain the rhetoric and spirit of a republic in the political structure of a liberal constitutional state. In so doing we blurred every essential political consideration, including the place of religion in our public life. Indeed, we artfully used religion as a way of evading the incompatibilities in our political life. For as the religious bodies remained vital and central in our public life, the evasion was (at least partially) successful. Today when religion, more even than our other institutions, is uncertain about itself, the evasion is no longer tenable. But I am getting ahead of myself.

The great political philosophers from Aristotle to Machiavelli to Montesquieu (who had such an influence on the founders of the republic) all believed a political regime is an expression of the total way of life of a people, its economics, its customs, its religion. The way of life correlates with the type of person the society produces and the political capacities that inhere in that person. As Montesquieu said, a despotic society will have despotic customs—the arbitrary use of power, dependence of inferiors on superiors, slavery—that will produce a person primarily motivated by fear, just the right kind of subject for a despotic polity. But a republic will have republican customs—public participation in the exercise of power, the political equality of the citizens, a wide distribution of small and medium property with few very rich or very poor—customs that will lead to a public spiritedness, a willingness of a citizen to sacrifice his own interests for the common good, that is, to a citizen motivated by republican virtue. It would be as absurd to expect a people long inured to despotism to create a successful republic as for a republican people to tolerate a despotic regime. And yet these patterns are not fixed. There is indeed constant flux and a tendency toward degeneration—good customs become corrupted and republican regimes become despotic. Since republics go against gravity, so to speak, it is essential if a republic is to survive that it concern itself actively with the nurturing of its citizens, that it root out corruption and encourage virtue. The republican state therefore has an ethical, educational, even spiritual role, and it will survive only as long as it reproduces republican customs and republican citizens.[9]

But the much newer form of political organization, which I am calling liberal constitutionalism though it grew in the very seedbeds of modern republicanism, developed a markedly different idea of political life, partly in response to a newly emerging economic order. Though formulated by some of the toughest minds in the history of modern philosophy—Hobbes, Locke, Hume, and Adam Smith—this tradition gave rise to what would appear to be the most wildly utopian idea in the history of political thought, namely, that a good society can result from the actions of citizens motivated by self-interest alone when those actions are organized through the proper mechanisms. A caretaker state, with proper legal restraints so that it does not interfere with the freedom of the citizens, needs to do little more than maintain public order and allow the economic market mechanisms and the free market in ideas to produce wealth and wisdom.

Not only are these political ideas, republicanism and liberalism, different; they are profoundly antithetical. Exclusive concern for self-interest is the very definition of the corruption of republican virtue. The tendency to emphasize the private, particularly the economic side of life in the liberal state, undermines the public participation essential to a republic. The wealth the liberal society generates is fatal to the basic political equality of a republic. And yet the American regime from the beginning has never been a pure type of either. The republican moment emerged first, however, out of the revolutionary struggle and crystalized in a document, the Declaration of Independence. The liberal moment emerged second, during the complex working out of interests in the new nation, and crystalized in the Constitution. Even that division is too simple, for there are liberal elements in the Declaration of Independence and republican elements in the Constitution, but it does suggest from the very beginning the balance has never been very easy or very even. The Declaration of Independence has several central references to God and the Constitution has none at all. It is time, then, to turn to religion as a means of mediating the tensions within the American regime.

Religion in the Early Republic

In the early republic religion had two vital locations: in the superstructure and in the infrastructure of the new political regime. It is to the superstructural location of religion that the Declaration of Independence points. By superstructural I mean a locus of sovereignty taken to be above the sovereignty of the state. Perhaps the most striking recognition of this superordinate sovereignty comes from the hand of Madison in 1785 during the debate on the bill establishing religious freedom in Virginia: "It is the duty of every man to render to the Creator such homage, and such only, as he believes to be acceptable to him. This duty is precedent both in order of time and degree of obligation, to the claims of Civil Society. Before any man can be considered as a member of Civil Society, he must be considered as a subject of the Governor of the Universe: And if a member of Civil Society, who enters into any subordinate Association, must always do it with a reservation of his duty to the general authority; much more must every man who becomes a member of any particular Civil Society, do it with a saving of his allegiance to the Universal Sovereign." Here Madison confines himself to the superordinate sovereignty of God over the individual citizen, which precedes the sovereignty of political society over him.

The Declaration of Independence points to the sovereignty of God over the collective political society itself when it refers in its opening lines to "the laws of nature and of nature's God" that stand above and judge the laws of men. It is often asserted that the God of nature is specifically not the God of the Bible. That raises problems of the relation of natural religion to biblical religion in eighteenth-century thought that I do not want to get into here, but Jefferson goes on to say, "We hold these truths to be self evident, that all Men are created equal, that they are endowed by their Creator with certain unalienable Rights, that among these are Life, Liberty and the pursuit of Happiness.—That to secure these rights, Governments are instituted among Men, deriving their just Powers from the consent of the governed.—That whenever any Form of Government becomes destructive of these ends, it is the Right of the People to alter or abolish it." We have here a distinctly biblical God who is much more than a first principle of nature, who creates individual human beings and endows them with equality and fundamental rights.

It is significant that the reference to a suprapolitical sovereignty, to a God who stands above the nation and whose ends are standards by which to judge the nation and indeed only in terms of which the nation's existence is justified, becomes a permanent feature of American political life ever after. Washington and Jefferson reiterate, though they do not move much beyond, the language of the Declaration of Independence in their most solemn public addresses, such as their inaugural addresses or Washington's Farewell Address. The existence of this highest-level religious symbolism in the political life of the republic justifies the assertion that there is a civil religion in America. Having said that, I must also say American civil religion is formal and in a sense marginal, though very securely institutionalized. It is formal in the sparsity and abstraction of its tenets, though in this it is very close to Rousseau's civil religion. It is marginal in that it has no official support in the legal and constitutional order. It is in this connection that I must again point out the absence of any reference to God, and thus of any civil religion, in the Constitution of the United States. Belief in the tenets of the civil religion are legally incumbent on no one and there are no official interpreters of civil theology. Indeed, because of the formality I have just pointed out, there was very little civil theology to interpret, although we did produce at a critical juncture in our history at least one great civil theologian, Abraham Lincoln.

The marginality of the American civil religion is closely connected with the liberal side of our heritage and its most important expression, the Constitution. This side has led many to deny there is a civil religion or there ought to be in America. And indeed, from the point of view of the liberal political idea there need not and perhaps ought not to be. The state is a purely neutral legal mechanism without purposes or values. Its sole function is to protect the rights of individuals, that is, to protect freedom. And yet freedom, which would seem to be an irreducible implication of liberalism on etymological grounds alone, no matter how negatively and individualistically defined, does imply a purpose and a value. Since I believe a pure liberalism is a *reductio ad absurdum* and a sociological impossibility, I would locate here at least one of the reasons a pure liberal state has never existed and why in America the rhetoric and to some extent the substance of republicanism has always existed in uneasy tandem with liberalism.

Precisely from the point of view of republicanism civil religion is indispensable. A republic as an active political community of participating citizens must have a purpose and a set of values. Freedom in the republican tradition is a positive value that asserts the worth and dignity of political equality and popular government. A republic must attempt to be ethical in a positive sense and to elicit the ethical commitment of its citizens. For this reason it inevitably pushes toward the symbolization of an ultimate order of existence in which republican values and virtues make sense. Such symbolization may be nothing more than the worship of the republic itself as the highest good, or it may be, as in the American case, the worship of a higher reality that upholds the standards the republic attempts to embody.

Yet the religious needs of a genuine republic would hardly be met by the formal and marginal civil religion that has been institutionalized in the American republic. The religious superstructure of the American republic has been provided only partially by the civil religion. It has been provided mainly by the religious community entirely outside any formal political structures. Here the genius and uniqueness of the American solution is to be found. At the 1976 Democratic convention Barbara Jordan called for the creation of a national community that would be ethical and even spiritual in content. That is what Talcott Parsons calls the "societal community." It is what might be called in Europe the nation as opposed to the state. It is in a sense prepolitical, but without it the state would be little more than a mechanism of coercion.

The first creation of a national community in America, it is now widely recognized, preceded the revolution by a generation or two. It was the result of the Great Awakening of the 1740s, a wave of religious revivalism that swept across the colonies and first gave them a sense of general solidarity. As the work of Professor Nathan Hatch has shown, this religious solidarity was gradually given a more political interpretation from within the religious community in the 1750s and 1760s with the emergence of what he has called "civil millennialism," namely, the providential religious meaning of the American colonies in world history.[10] It is the national community with its religious inspiration that made the American Revolution and created the new nation. It is the national community that was, in my sense of the term, the real republic, not the liberal constitutional regime that emerged in 1789.

The liberal regime never repudiated the civil religion that was already inherent in the Declaration of Independence and indeed kept it alive in our political life even though the Constitution was silent about it. From the point of view of the legal regime, however, any further elaboration of religious symbolism beyond that of the formal and marginal civil religion was purely private. From the point of view of the national community, still largely religious in its self-consciousness, such elaboration was public even though lacking in any legal status. Here we can speak of public theology, as Martin Marty has called it, in distinction to civil religion. The civil millenialism of the revolutionary period was such a public theology and we have never lacked one since.

As a number of scholars have begun to recognize, the problems of creating a national community in America did not decrease with the establishment of the constitutional regime but in a sense became more severe. With the formation of the new nation the centrifugal forces that were restrained during the revolutionary struggle came to the fore and a sense of national community actually declined. To some extent a national community in the new nation was not fully actualized until after the trauma of the Civil War, though that event set in motion new problems that would later create even greater difficulties in maintaining a genuine national community. But, as Perry Miller has pointed out, to the extent we began to create a national community in the early national period it was again religious revivalism that played an important role.[11] I would not want to minimize the role of enlightenment thought in complicated relation with the churches that Sydney Mead has so brilliantly emphasized. From my point of view enlightenment religion and ethics were also a form of public theology and played a significant role. Yet Jefferson's hope for a national turn to Unitarianism as the dominant religion, a turn that would have integrated public theology and formal civil religion much more intimately than was actually the case, was disappointed and public theology was carried out predominantly in terms of biblical symbolism.

Even though I have argued that the public theology that came out of the national community represented the real republic, I do not want to idealize it. As with all vigorous young republics it had an element of self-intoxication that has had ominous consequences for us ever after. The "chosen people" or "God's new Israel" symbolism that was pretty well eliminated from the formal civil religion was common in the public theology, though it also had its critics. The public theology provided a sense of value and purpose without which the national community and ultimately even the liberal state could not have survived, but it was never entirely clear what that value and purpose was. On the one hand it seemed to imply the full realization of the values laid down in the Declaration of Independence but certainly not fully implemented in a nation that among other things still legalized slavery. On the other hand it could imply a messianic mission of manifest destiny with respect to the rest of the continent. It may be a sobering thought, but most of what is good and most of what is bad in our history is rooted in our public theology. Every movement to make America more fully realize its professed values has grown out of some form of public theology, from the abolitionists to the social gospel and the early socialist party to the civil rights movement under Martin Luther King and the farm workers' movement under Caesar Chavez. But so has every expansionist war and every form of oppression of racial minorities and immigrant groups.

The clearest and probably the purest expression of the ethical dynamism I have located in the realm of the public theology broke through at one crucial moment in our history into the civil religion itself in the person of our greatest, perhaps our only, civil theologian, Abraham Lincoln. Basing himself above all on the opening lines of the Declaration of Independence, in the Gettysburg Address he called us to complete "the great task remaining before us," the task of seeing that there is a "new birth of freedom" and that we make real for all our citizens the beliefs upon which the republic is based. In the Second Inaugural Address Lincoln incorporated biblical symbolism more centrally into the civil religion than had ever been done before or would ever be done again in his great somber tragic vision of an unfaithful nation in need above all of charity and justice.

It has not been my purpose here to evaluate the whole checkered story of civil religion and public theology in our national history but only to point out they have been absolutely integral to one aspect of our national existence, namely, our existence as a republican people. But so far I have spoken only of what I have called the superstructural role of religion in the republic. Now I would like to turn to the infrastructural role.

Religion and the Creation of Citizens

As I have already pointed out in describing the classical notion of a republic, there is a necessity in such a regime not only for asserting high ethical and spiritual commitments but also for molding, socializing, and educating the citizens into those ethical and spiritual beliefs so they are internalized as republican virtue. Once again, however, when we look at the liberal constitutional regime we will see a complete lacuna in this area. The state as a school of virtue is the last thing a liberal regime conceives itself to be. And yet here too what the liberal regime could not do the national community as the real republic could.

The problem was partly handled through federalism. What would not be appropriate on the part of the federal government could appropriately be done at lower jurisdictional levels. Just as religion was much more open and pervasive at local and even state levels through most of our history than it ever was at the federal level, so the state as educator, and educator in the sphere of values, was widely accepted at lower jurisdictional levels. Robert Lynn has brilliantly shown how the McGuffey readers purveyed a religious and republican ideology, including a powerful stress on the common good and the joys of participation in the public life, during much of the nineteenth century.[12]

And yet, as important as the public schools have been, the real school of republican virtue in America, as Alexis de Tocqueville saw with such masterful clarity, was the church. Tocqueville said religion is the *first* of our political institutions. It was a republican and a democratic religion that not only inculcated republican values but gave the first lessons in participation in the public life. More than the laws or the physical circumstances of the country, said Tocqueville, it was the mores that contributed to the success of the American democracy, and the mores were rooted in religion. As a classic theorist of republican government would, Tocqueville saw that naked self-interest is the surest solvent of a republican regime, and he saw the commercial tendencies of the American people as unleashing the possibility of the unrestrained pursuit of self-interest. But he saw religion as the great restraining element that could turn naked self-interest into what he called "self-interest rightly understood," that is, a self-interest that was public spirited and capable of self-sacrifice. In this way Tocqueville showed how religion mitigated the full implications of American liberalism and allowed republican institutions to survive. Late in his life he began to doubt that such a compromise would really work in the long run, and his doubts have been all too fully confirmed by our recent history. Yet for its time and place Tocqueville's analysis was undoubtedly right. It gives us an essential clue to understand this strange, unique, and perhaps finally incoherent society in which we live.

What Tocqueville saw about the role of religion in such a society as ours was well understood by the founders of the republic. It is significant, for example, that John Adams, during his first year as our first vice-president under the new liberal constitutional regime, said, "We have no government armed with power capable of contending with human passions unbridled by morality and religion. Our constitution was made only for a moral and a religious people. It is wholly inadequate to the government of any other."[13] And Washington in his Farewell Address wrote, "Of all the suppositions and habits which lead to political prosperity Religion and morality are indispensable supports. In vain would that man claim the tribute of Patriotism, who should labour to subvert these great Pillars of human happiness, these firmest props of the duties of Men and citizens. The mere Politician, equally with the pious man ought to respect and cherish them." Perhaps the recognition by our first and second presidents of the necessity of religion and morality, of the basis in the mores and religious beliefs of a people, for a successful republic, in the rather negative, circuitous, and almost apologetic terms of the quotations, expresses the uneasy compromise between republicanism and a liberal regime I am arguing was characteristic of the new nation. But it also suggests the founders of the republic fully understood the relation between the way of life of a people and their form of political organization.

The Corruption of the Republic

It is inevitable, having celebrated only several years ago the two hundredth anniversary of our republic, that we should look around us to see how well our heritage is understood and how much of it is still operative in our public life. We might have hoped that a political campaign for the presidency in that bicentennial year or the recent 1980 campaign would have been educative in the high republican sense of the term. We have had such campaigns in the past. In the Lincoln-Douglas debates the deepest philosophical meaning of our republic and of our history was plumbed by two men of enormous intelligence and sensitivity to the crucial issues. Alas, we did not get that in 1976 or in 1980. Perhaps the Illinois farmers who drove into the towns from miles around to hear the Lincoln-Douglas debates were a different kind of people from the millions in their living rooms in front of the television screen. Perhaps there were other reasons. But in recent campaigns what we got were vague and listless allusions to a largely misunderstood and forgotten past and an attitude toward the present that seemed to be determined, above everything else, not to probe beneath the thinnest of surfaces. And yet the great themes I have been probing here were present, not in any articulate form but present in the uncertainty, the groping, the yearning for something that has so slipped out of memory as to be almost without a name. It is the ethical purpose of our republic and the republican virtue of our citizens, or rather the loss of them, that has haunted our recent political life.

Our rhetoric speaks in the terms of another day, another age. It does not seem to express our present reality. And yet our politicians and those to whom they speak are surprised and troubled by the lack of it, concerned less to find a new rhetoric than to find an easy formula to make the old rhetoric apt again. Such an easy formula is the assertion that we must restrain, control, and diminish government, as though the enormous growth of our government were some fortuitous thing and not a sign and symptom of the kind of society in which we live.

To ask the questions the 1976 and 1980 campaigns did not ask is to ask whether under the social conditions of late twentieth-century America it is possible for us to survive as a republic in any sense continuous with the historic meaning of that term. If we discover the republican element in our national polity has been corroded beyond repair, we must consider whether a liberal constitutional regime can survive without it, a question it seems to me not too difficult to answer, but I am prepared to listen to contrary arguments. Finally we must ask, if we have the courage, if both our republic and our liberal constitutional regime lack the social conditions for survival, what kind of authoritarian regime is likely to replace them, remembering that republican and liberal regimes have been in the history of the planet few and brief. Perhaps we can even discern, beneath the battered surface of our republican polity, the form of despotism that awaits us. Of course, I would hope to discover how to do what Machiavelli says is that most difficult of all political things, reform and refound a corrupt republic. But we must not flinch from whatever reality is to be discovered.

I have mentioned corruption. Corruption is a great word, a political word with a precise meaning in eighteenth-century discourse even though its use has become narrowed and debased with us. Corruption is, in the language of the founders of the republic, the opposite of republican virtue. It is what destroys republics. It might be well for us today to remember what Franklin said on the last day of the Constitutional Convention, 17 September 1787. Old, sick, tired, he had sat through that long hot Philadelphia summer because his presence was crucial to the acceptance of the new document. He was the very symbol of America. He rose on that last day to call for unanimous consent in hopes that that too might help the document be accepted, and he said, "In these sentiments, Sir, I agree to this Constitution with all its faults, if they are such; because I think a general government necessary for us, and there is no form of Government but what may be a blessing to the people if well administered, and believe further that this is likely to be well administered for a course of years, and can only end in Despotism, as other forms have done before it, when the people shall have become so corrupted as to need despotic Government, being incapable of any other."[14] Can we not see in those words the sentiments of an old republican, aware of the compromises contained in the new Constitution but hoping almost against hope that the republican virtue of the people would offset them, at least for a time?

Corruption, again using the eighteenth-century vocabulary, is to be found in luxury, dependence, and ignorance. Luxury is that pursuit of material things that diverts us from concern for the public good, that leads us to exclusive concern for our own good, or what we would today call consumerism. Dependence naturally follows from luxury, for it consists in accepting the dominance of whatever person or group, or, we might say today, governmental or private corporate structure, that promises it will take care of our material desires. The welfare state—and here I refer to the welfare that goes to the great corporations, to most above the median income level through special tax breaks, and to the workers whose livelihood depends on an enormous military budget as much as to the welfare that goes to the desperately poor to keep them from starving—in all its prolixity is the very type of what the eighteenth century meant by dependence. And finally ignorance, that is, political ignorance, is the result of luxury and dependence. It is a lack of interest in public things, a concern only for the private, a willingness to be governed by those who promise to take care of us even without our knowledgeable consent. I would need to explore throughout our society the degree and extent to which corruption in these forms has gone in order to assess whether there is strength enough in our republic for its survival.

Sources of Revival

I would also need to look at religion, following today the brilliant sociological analysis Tocqueville made of the role of religion in our public life, a role all the founders of the republic discerned. To what extent do our religious bodies today provide us with a national sense of ethical purpose? Certainly here there are some notable recent examples. The religious opposition to the Vietnam War was certainly more effective than the opposition of those who spelled America with a "k." And if we have made some significant progress with respect to the place of racial minorities in our society in the last twenty years, it is due mostly to religious leadership. Yet is the balance of American religious life slipping away from those denominations that have a historic concern for the common good toward religious groups so privatistic and self-centered that they begin to approach the consumer cafeteria model of Thomas Luckmann's invisible religion? And to what extent is the local congregation any longer able to serve as a school for the creation of a self-disciplined, independent, public-spirited, in a word, virtuous citizen? Have not the churches along with the schools and the family, what I have called the soft structures that deal primarily with human motivation, suffered more in the great upheavals through which our society has recently gone than any other of our institutions, suffered so much that their capacity to transmit patterns of conscience and ethical values has been seriously impaired? I am not prepared to say the religious communities, among whom I would include the humanist communities, are not capable even today of providing the religious superstructure and infrastructure that would renew our republic. Indeed, I would look to them, as always before in our history, for the renewing impulse, the "new birth" any ethical institution so frequently needs. But the empirical question as to whether the moral capacity is still there on a sufficient scale seems to me open.

If we look to my own community, the scholarly community, there is not a great deal to be proud of. We have left the understanding of our basic institutions, as we have left everything else, to the specialists, and with notable exceptions they have not done a very good job of it. Somehow we have never established a strong academic tradition of self-reflection about the meaning of our institutions, and as our institutions changed and our republican mores corroded, even what knowledge we had began to slip away. On the whole it has been the politicians more than the scholars who have carried the burden of self-interpretation. The founders were all political thinkers of distinction. Lincoln's political thought has moments of imaginative genius—his collected works are still the best initiation into a genuine understanding of the regime under which we live. Even as late as Woodrow Wilson and Calvin Coolidge we had presidents who knew our history in intricate detail and understood the theoretical basis of our institutions. In contrast we have never produced a political philosopher of the first rank. The only profound work of political philosophy on the nature of the American polity was written by a Frenchman. Still we have produced works of the second rank that are not without distinction, though they are usually somewhat isolated and eccentric and do not add up to a cumulative tradition. Such works are Orestes Brownson's *The American Republic* and Raymond Croly's *The Promise of American Life*. But in a barren time we must be grateful for such works as we have. If we turn to these works, we will be referred once again to the great tradition with which I began this chapter. Croly quotes the European/American philosopher George Santayana: "If a noble and civilized democracy is to subsist, the common citizen must be something of a saint and something of a hero. We see, therefore, how justly flattering and profound, and at the same time how ominous, was Montesquieu's saying that the principle of democracy is virtue."[15] How ominous indeed! In that context we can understand the bicentennial epigram written by Harry Jaffa, one of the few political scientists who continues the great tradition today: "In 1776 the United States was so to speak nothing; but it promised to become everything. In 1976, the United States, having in a sense become everything, promises to become nothing."[16]

One would almost think the Lord has intended to chastise us before each of our centennial celebrations so we would not rise up too high in our pride. Before the centennial he sent us Grant, before the bicentennial, Nixon (in whom we can perhaps discern the dim face of the despotism that awaits us—not a despotism of swastikas and Brownshirts but a despotism of game plans and administrative efficiency). It is not a time for self-congratulation. It is a time for sober reflection about where we have come from and where we may be going.

"Religion and the Legitimation of the American Republic," Notes

1. Robert N. Bellah, "Civil Religion in America," *Daedalus* 96 (Winter 1967). Reprinted in Robert N. Bellah, *Beyond Belief: Essays on Religion in a Post-Traditional World* (New York: Harper & Row, 1970).

2. Benjamin Franklin came close when he spoke of "Public Religion" in his pamphlet of 1750 entitled *Proposals Relating to the Education of Youth in Pensilvania.* See Ralph L. Ketcham, ed., *The Political Thought of Benjamin Franklin* (Indianapolis, Ind.: Bobbs-Merrill, 1965), p. 55.

3. Tocqueville wrote in a letter to Gobineau on 5 September 1843: "The duties of men among themselves as well as in their capacity of *citizens,* the duties of citizens to their fatherland, in brief, the public virtues seem to me to have been inadequately defined and considerably neglected within the moral system of Christianity." Alexis de Tocqueville, *The European Revolution and Correspondence with Gobineau,* John Lukacs, ed. and trans. (Garden City, N.Y.: Doubleday Anchor, 1959), p. 192.

4. Jean Jacques Rousseau, *The Social Contract,* trans. Willmoore Kendall (Chicago, Ill.: Gateway, 1954), book 4, ch. 8, pp. 204-223.

5. See Robert N. Bellah, "Religious Evolution," *American Sociological Review* 29 (1964), pp. 353-374. Reprinted in Bellah, *Beyond Belief.*

6. See Raymond Plant, *Hegel* (Bloomington: Indiana University Press, 1973), ch. 1.

7. See Sidney E. Mead, *The Nation with the Soul of a Church* (New York: Harper & Row, 1975).

8. It is worth noting that while the Constitution specifically forbade a nonrepublican form of government in any state, the First Amendment did not forbid the states to establish religion.

9. Jean Jacques Rousseau, *The Government of Poland,* trans. Willmoore Kendall (Indianapolis, Ind.: Bobbs-Merrill, 1972), pp. 29-30, is contemptuous of a people who are not ethically prepared for it espousing liberty:

> "I laugh at those debased peoples that let themselves be stirred up by agitators, and dare to speak of liberty without so much as having the idea of it; with their hearts still heavy with the vices of slaves, they imagine that they have only to be mutinous in order to be free. Proud, sacred liberty! If they but knew her, those wretched men; if they but understood the price at which she is won and held; if they but realized that her laws are stern as the tyrant's yoke is never hard, their sickly souls, the slaves of passions that would have to be hauled out by the roots, would fear liberty a hundred times as much as they fear servitude. They would flee her in terror, as they would a burden about to crush them."

10. Nathan O. Hatch, *The Sacred Cause of Liberty* (New Haven, Conn.: Yale University Press, 1977). See especially ch. 1.

11. Perry Miller, *The Life of the Mind in America* (New York: Harcourt, Brace and World, 1965), ch. 1.

12. Robert Wood Lynn, "Civil Catechetics in Mid-Victorian America: Some Notes about American Civil Religion, Past and Present," *Religious Education* 68, no. 1 (1971), pp. 5-27.

13. Quoted in John R. Howe, Jr., *The Changing Political Thought of John Adams* (Princeton, N.J.: Princeton University Press, 1966), p. 185.

14. Ralph L. Ketcham, ed., *The Political Thought of Benjamin Franklin* (Indianapolis, Ind.: Bobbs-Merrill, 1965), p. 401.

15. Raymond Croly, *The Promise of American Life* (New York: Macmillan, 1909), p. 454.

16. Harry V. Jaffa, *How to Think About the American Revolution* (Durham, N.C.: Carolina Academic Press, 1978), p. 1.

Study Questions

1.   What are the fundamental principles of the Christian world view Whitehead argues were passed along to colonial America from the Reformation?

2.   To what extent is the "general metaphysic" described by Eastland consistent with Rutherford's "basic presuppositions of government based upon the absolutes of the Bible" which Whitehead mentions?

3.   Does the "established" Protestant Christianity of which Eastland speaks have the same "content" as the biblical world view that Whitehead claims was finally realized in colonial America?

4.   In your view, what *was* "finally realized" in the founding of America? To what extent was the "established" moral and religious consensus distinctively Christian?

5.   What effect, if any, did the founders' attempt to retain the spirit of republicanism within the structure of liberalism (Bellah's thesis) have on what was finally "established"?

6.   In what ways is Bellah's "republicanism" compatible with Whitehead's "fundamental principles of the Christian world view"? In what ways are they not compatible?

7.   How does Bellah explain the fundamental conflict between Christianity and republicanism? If this conflict exists, how is it that Christianity can be identified with republican virtue?

Part II

Were the
Founders
Christian?

The question whether the founders of our republic were Christian is one which is fraught with pitfalls. What does one mean by Christian? Does it imply a set of beliefs, a general outlook on life, or a particular kind of religious experience? Must we first know the hearts of the founders before we can answer the question? If so, how are we to know *that*? Fortunately, the readings included in Part II are for a far more humble purpose than divining the eternal destiny of persons who lived 200 years ago.

The next three chapters focus on how our forebears' self-proclaimed religious beliefs related to their understanding of politics and government. They touch on questions about how religion influenced the shaping of America's new public order, both generally and particularly. Beginning with a broadly painted picture of the patterns of religious thought held by the founders, the readings move through a discussion of the particular religious faiths of the founders and conclude with a specific description of Jefferson's rationalist faith.

The Early American Social Consensus

Robert Bellah provides us with an interesting historical survey of the sources of America's "myth of origin." He uses myth of origin to refer to that body of widely held common beliefs which shapes the way a people conceives of its beginnings. He finds four sources of myth and symbol for the new American nation: the Bible, with its concepts of conversion and covenant; the English political tradition, with its "rights of Englishmen"; Roman classicism, with its attribute of republican virtue; the Enlightenment ideals, such as individualism and the social contract.

Echoing some of our other authors, Bellah affirms that "biblical imagery has operated powerfully, consciously and unconsciously, to shape the American interpretation of reality." He points out, for example, that "Christianity informed the political as well as the religious structure" of the early Puritan settlements. But to his mind the "remarkable coherence" of America's revolutionary movement, including its successful conclusion in the Constitution, is due "in considerable part to the convergence of the Puritan covenant pattern and the Montesquieuan (Roman) republican pattern."

Bellah considers the pattern of revolutionary America's social consensus to be remarkably coherent because the synthesis or blending together of "Calvinist theology" and pagan "classical philosophy" resulted in a fundamental ambiguity. The synthesis involved two compatible dimensions of differing content: (1) the belief that a society rests upon the deep inner convictions of its people (whether Calvinism's conversion or classicism's republican virtue); and (2) the conviction that government rests upon law derived from a higher source (whether Calvinism's God or classicism's Nature). The shared dimensions of the Puritan and pagan patterns brought coherence to America's early social consensus, but the differing content of those dimensions meant a fundamental ambiguity of meaning within the consensus.

Bellah goes on to point out that there was a third major pattern in addition to the Puritan and pagan ones: a way of thinking grounded in the belief that "the orientations of the natural sciences" could be applied to the social and political sphere. This third pattern resulted in a fundamental tension between those on the one hand who held the traditional religious (Puritan) and philosophical (pagan) views, and those on the other hand who, following the utilitarianism of Hobbes and Locke, accepted the rationalist (liberal) notion that individual self-interest rather than virtue was to be the effective basis of the new American polity.

We recall that in his earlier chapter Bellah argued that the fundamental tension between virtue and self-interest was mitigated until recently by religion, but now that tension is reappearing as a fatal weakness in American civil religion. If Bellah's analysis is accurate, would it be fair to say that those seeking to restore a Christian America seek to reestablish the preeminence of the Puritan-pagan synthesis in the face of a new dominant utilitarianism? What is interesting, of course, is that Bellah believes that utilitarianism was part of the American public consensus (civil religion) from the beginning. While the Puritan-pagan views were espoused by "most articulate Americans" in the 1770s (and were reflected in the Declaration of Independence), he argues that by as early as the 1790s the more utilitarian views "were beginning to prevail" (and were so reflected in the constitution).

Religion and the Founders

In chapter 5 David Gill begins by agreeing with Bellah that "on the ideological level, religion had a powerful and on-going impact" on the founding of America, even though "on the institutional level, religion and the state were carefully separated." Gill's understanding of the religion of the founders is also not altogether inconsistent with Bellah's view that the patterns of religious thought in early America included elements of evangelical (Puritan), classical, and rationalist faith. "The faith of the Founding Fathers," Gill argues, "was a combination of influences from Puritanism and deism."

Gill sketches briefly the main elements of the Puritan (evangelical) and deist traditions, noting their differences and similarities. "Deism," Gill explains, "was essentially the result of the application of the rationalism of the Enlightenment to the Christian religion." Although pointing out how some Puritans (notably Jonathan Edwards) opposed accommodation and compromise with the rationalists and deists, he argues that "deism and [Christian] orthodoxy pointed in the same direction." For example, the rationalist optimism in human reason led to the conviction that human governments derived their just powers from the consent of the governed. But the right to choose one's government could also be powerfully rooted in the Congregational principle of Puritanism. After a close look at the specific faith positions of some of the founders, Gill concludes that "deism held the reins, while the witness of Puritanism continued, nevertheless, to exercise some influence."

Similar to Bellah's position, Gill holds that the religious ideology of both deism and Puritanism underlay the writing of the Declaration of Independence and the Constitution, and the attempt to protect individual rights and liberty was "the fruition of

both Reformation individualism and inwardness and Enlightenment rationalism and dignity."

Anticipating Whitehead's argument in chapter 8, Gill
shows how all the founders "recognized that morality is closely tied
to religion, and that morality and religion have a close relation to
politics and other aspects of the culture." He also makes the same
point that Whitehead and Eastland have already made: "The
Founding Fathers' generation was 'Christian' in the sense that a
general commitment to biblical values and ethical norms was carried over." But how "Christian" is that? James Skillen, in the last
chapter of this section, argues provocatively that to view Christianity chiefly in terms of values and ethics is to capitulate to
rationalism.

Skillen's piece is helpful in at least two ways. First, his discussion of Jefferson's general philosophic outlook gives us a needed
look at the crucial contours of rationalist Enlightenment faith. Second, he introduces us to a unique and, perhaps, useful understanding of the meaning of religion for our society.

Religion and Rationalism

Skillen is convinced that Jefferson held to a rationalist religious faith. He argues that Jefferson was "an Enlightenment
rationalist in his deepest convictions about God, humanity, and the
world." Thus rationalism functioned as a religion for Jefferson.
Within this religious framework, Skillen explains, Jefferson believed in God as a benevolent Creator who preserved humans in life
and judged their moral worth after death. Jefferson saw humans as
sophisticated animals with superior rationality who possessed
Reason and a moral sense or conscience. Jefferson had faith in
human Reason as a moral ideal, and he had faith in its ability
through conscience and common sense to guide people in right obligations to God and their fellows. He believed natural law shaped
the world, and that natural rights endowed individuals by their
Creator were self-evident to Reason and to common sense. But
Jefferson did not consider this Enlightenment faith to be a "religion," Skillen explains; for him it was a rational and universal
philosophy.

Within his broader rationalist faith, Skillen argues, Jefferson understood "religion" principally in terms of morality. Accordingly, Jefferson believed religion (that is, morality) was a thing to be encouraged publicly because it functioned to promote human welfare. This is why Jefferson espoused religion as a social good and supported what he considered to be "universal" religion consisting of moral tenets "on which all sects could be expected to agree."

The point Skillen makes is that Jefferson's religion was, in fact, far more than simply a moral system. His religion actually was a faith in the assumptions of rationalism; as such it included his conviction "that the true religion of morality is a rational and natural religion independent of any special revelation." So, argues Skillen, when Jefferson wrote in support of true, universal religion, he was not, as he supposed, simply reporting self-evident facts about reality. He was actually urging upon others "a specific religious commitment."

Skillen credits Jefferson and his fellow rationalists for being successful evangelists who were able to convert Christians to the rationalist meaning of religion. Skillen explains how virtually all churches and Christian groups bought into the idea of considering themselves as "religious" groups while thinking of Jefferson's principles for a universal morality "as part of a rational philosophy rather than as part of a new religion." Religious freedom then meant that "each religious group would . . . be free to hold its private dogmas without coercive support or impairment, while Jeffersonians would be free to organize the universal order on a common, rational, moral basis." Jefferson's religion came to function as the universal common denominator in the public realm only because other religious groups admitted to its public authority "while remaining satisfied to hold on to their own peculiar dogmas in a limited, private, nonuniversal realm."

Raising a civil religion issue that will be developed further in the next section by John Whitehead and Rockne McCarthy, Skillen accuses Christians and the churches of being responsible for contributing to a fundamentally unfair and destructive "interpretive framework of sacred (religious) and secular (not religious) duality" in which political life was seen as "neutral, rational, and non-religious." Skillen argues that political life cannot be religiously neutral, but is based upon religious assumptions about God, humanity, and the world, and that the founders adopted the religious assumptions of rationalism when constructing their public philosophy. Clearly, Skillen has grave reservations about how fully Christian the founders were (or, for that matter, how consistently biblical the churches were), at least insofar as their public philosophy was concerned.

4. America's Myth of Origin

Robert N. Bellah

Once in each of the last three centuries America has faced a time of trial, a time of testing so severe that not only the form but even the existence of our nation has been called in question. Born out of the revolutionary crisis of the Atlantic world in the late eighteenth century, America's first time of trial was our struggle for independence and the institution of liberty. The second time of trial came not long before the end of the nation's first hundred years. At stake was the preservation of the union and the extension of equal protection of the law to all members of society. We live at present in a third time of trial at least as severe as those of the Revolution and the Civil War. It is a test of whether our inherited institutions can be creatively adapted to meet the twentieth-century crisis of justice and order at home and in the world. It is a test of whether republican liberty established in a remote agrarian backwater of the world in the eighteenth century shall prove able or willing to confront successfully the age of mass society and international revolution. It is a test of whether we can control the very economic and technical forces which are our greatest achievement before they destroy us.

In the beginning, and to some extent ever since, Americans have interpreted their history as having religious meaning. They saw themselves as being a "people" in the classical and biblical sense of the word. They hoped they were a people of God. They often found themselves to be a people of the devil. American history, like the history of any people, has within it archetypal patterns that reflect the general condition of human beings as pilgrims and wanderers on this earth. Founded in an experience of transcendent order, the new settlements habitually slipped away from their high calling and fell into idolatry, as the children of Israel had done before them. Time and again there have arisen prophets to recall this people to its original task, its errand into the wilderness. Significant accomplishments in building a just society have alternated with corruption and despair in America, as in other lands, because the struggle to institutionalize humane values is endless on this earth. But at times the issue grows acute. A period of history hangs in the balance. A people finds that it must decide whether its immediate future will be better or worse, and sometimes whether it will have a future at all.

I wish to examine the history of America's religious self-understanding, the myths that have developed to help us interpret who and what we are in America and to inquire whether they may still have power to help us understand our present situation and know how to deal with it. The present situation has, therefore, influenced the selection I have made from the materials of the past. It has not, I hope, dictated the outcome of my inquiry. We need truth whether it is comforting or whether it is dismaying. While committed to the pursuit of how it has actually been in America, I am not uninvolved in the outcome. I am convinced that in these last years of the twentieth century the republic is in danger. If we believe that it is worth saving, then we must know what it is that we wish to save, not holding with a deathly grip to an unchanging past but seeking the inspiration to undertake that reformation, reconstruction, and reconstitution which are necessary.

This chapter is not primarily about political theory or about ideology, though both are involved, but about religion and myth. In particular I will be reexamining the American civil religion[1] and the mythological structure that supports it. By civil religion I refer to that religious dimension, found I think in the life of every people, through which it interprets its historical experience in the light of transcendent reality. I do not want, at this point, to argue abstractly the validity of the concept "civil religion." I hope to demonstrate its usefulness. In using the word "myth," I do not mean to suggest a story that is not true. Myth does not attempt to describe reality; that is the job of science. Myth seeks rather to transfigure reality so that it provides moral and spiritual meaning to individuals or societies. Myths, like scientific theories, may be true or false, but the test of truth or falsehood is different.

The Origin Time of the American Nation

America's myth of origin is a strategic point of departure because the comparative study of religion has found that where a people conceives itself to have started reveals much about its most basic self-conceptions. At first glance the problem of origin in America seems a relatively simple one. Unlike most historical peoples, America as a nation began on a definite date, July 4, 1776. Thus, in analyzing America's myth of origin, close attention must be paid to the mythic significance of the Declaration of Independence, which is considerable. Or taking a less precise definition of beginning, one might consider the whole period, from the Declaration of Independence to the inauguration of Washington under the new Constitution, as the origin time of the American nation. America began as the result of a series of conscious decisions. The acts embodying those decisions have a kind of absolute meaning-creating significance. As Hannah Arendt says, "What saves the act of beginning from its own arbitrariness is that it carries its own principle within itself, or, to be more precise, that beginning and principle, *principium* and principle, are not only related to each other, but are coeval."[2] We will want to consider the act of conscious meaning-creation, or conscious taking responsibility for oneself and one's society, as a central aspect of America's myth of origin, an act that, by the very radicalness of its beginning, a beginning *ex nihilo* as it were, is redolent of the sacred. The sacredness of the Constitution, which is closely bound up with the existence of the American people, derives largely from that source since it does not, not explicitly at least (and in this it differs from the Declaration of Independence), call upon any source of sacredness higher than itself and its makers.[3]

And yet those datable acts of beginning, radical though they were, and archetypal for all later reflection about America, were themselves mythic gestures which could not but stir up, at the beginning and later, the images and symbols of earlier myths and mythically interpreted histories. In human affairs no beginning is absolutely new and every beginning takes meaning from some counterpoint of similarity to and difference from earlier events. Indeed when we look closely at the beginning time of the American republic we find not a simple unitary myth of origin but a complex and richly textured mythical structure with many inner tensions. One way to begin is to consider the profoundly mythic meaning of "America" long before the founding of the United States, a meaning that was by no means obliterated but in some ways reinforced by the establishment of the new nation.

The Newness of America

The origin myth of America in this broader perspective is origin itself. According to John Locke, "In the beginning all the world was America."[4] America stood for the primordial state of the world and man and was indeed seen, by the first generations of Europeans to learn of it, to be the last remaining remnant of that earlier time. The newness which was so prominent an attribute of what was called the "new" world was taken not just as newness to its European discoverers and explorers but as newness in some pristine and absolute sense: newness from the hands of God. That sense of indelible newness, which has been a blessing and a curse throughout our history, has not evaporated even today. If it gives us a sense that we come from nowhere, that our past is inchoate and our tradition shallow, so that we begin to doubt our own identity and some of the sensitive among us flee to more ancient lands with more structured traditions, it also gives us our openness to the future, our sense of unbounded possibility, our willingness to start again in a new place, a new occupation, a new ideology. Santayana has spoken of "the moral emptiness of a settlement where men and even houses are easily moved about, and no one, almost, lives where he was born or believes what he has been taught."[5] Yet other Europeans have envied our capacity to act without being immobilized by ancient institutions.

The newness of America, so prominent in the consciousness of the early European observers, and which we have still not entirely outgrown even though it is nearly 500 years since Columbus (from the point of view of Europe) "discovered" America, had another important consequence. For the early explorers, and certainly for those in Europe reading their first reports, the specificity and detail of America's native flora and fauna, and even more, its aboriginal Indian cultures, which by 1492 had already completed a long and distinguished history in this hemisphere, were swallowed up in a generalized feeling of newness which replaced that specificity and detail with the blank screen of an alleged "state of nature." Upon that screen they projected certain fantasies, dreams, and nightmares long carried in the baggage of European tradition but seldom heretofore finding so vivid and concrete an objective correlative. Thus America came to be thought of as a paradise and a wilderness, with all of the rich associations of those terms in the Christian and biblical traditions, or, more simply, thus Europeans came to think of America as both a heaven and a hell.

The Dream of Paradise

Locke, who, as we have seen, tended to identify America with the state of nature, defined the latter as "a State of Peace, Goodwill, Mutual Assistance, and Preservation." And he goes on to say, "Men living together according to reason, without a common Superior on Earth, with Authority to judge between them, is *properly the State of Nature.*"[6] This description conforms admirably with Columbus's description of life in his newly discovered West Indies:

> The people of this island, and of all the other islands which I have found and of which I have information, all go naked, men and women, as their mothers bore them, although some women cover a single place with the leaf of a plant or with a net of cotton which they make for the purpose. They have no iron or steel or weapons, nor are they fitted to use them, not because they are not well built and of handsome stature, but because they are very marvellously timorous. They have no other arms than weapons made of canes, cut in seeding time, to the ends of which they fix a small sharpened stick. . . . They are so guileless and so generous with all they possess, that no one would believe it who has not seen it. They never refuse anything which they possess, if it be asked of them; on the contrary, they invite anyone to share it, and display so much love as if they would give their hearts. . . . And they do not know any creed and are not idolators; only they all believe that power and good are in the heavens . . . not . . . because they are ignorant; on the contrary, they are of a very acute intelligence and are men who navigate all these seas.[7]

His description suggests the paradisic imagery which clearly lies just below the surface of this and many other early descriptions of the American Indians, descriptions that quickly catapulted them into the central representatives of Adamic man in the European imagination. The emphasis is, above all, on innocence as expressed in the Indians' nakedness, so striking to the heavily clad Europeans; their freedom about sexual relations; their lack of any discernible government; their communal sharing of property; and their lack of either religious dogmas or priests. And to complete the Edenic picture was their total lack of aggression. Why indeed should anyone be aggressive in a land where fruit was to be had for the picking, game for the trapping, and all good things were abundantly at hand, even including gold?

Even when experience began to render a rather different picture of the land and its people, the search for a literal Eden went on, especially in Latin America. Already Columbus believed he had located the general site where the earthly paradise would be found and imagined that fresh-water currents in the sea off the northern coast of South America actually flowed from it.[8] With literal-minded doggedness others would seek El Dorado, the Seven Cities of Cibola, or the Fountain of Eternal Youth. While the paradisic expectations of the English colonists were not so fully developed as those further South they were strong enough to cause early Maryland to be described as an "Earthly Paradise" and Georgia as "that promis'd Canaan."[9] The Sicilian immigrants who arrived in New York expecting the streets to be paved with gold or the little old ladies who invest their life savings in California land developers' schemes to "make the desert blossom like the rose" are only late incarnations of an old dream about the New World.

The Nightmare of Wilderness

But there was another picture of America, closer to Hobbes than to Locke, that is also present from the beginning. Unlike the paradisic view, it dwelt on scorching deserts and uncrossable mountains, hurricanes and floods, tropical heat and arctic cold. In accordance with this violent and extreme landscape, the second view found the native inhabitants anything but innocent. Instead they were depicted as "horrid savages" devoted to murder, rape, human sacrifice, and cannibalism and prepared to use every ruse of cunning and treachery. Led by cruel and despotic chieftains the Indians were described as spending the time left over from murder, plunder, and rapine in the barbaric worship of a vast array of demons, chief of whom was the devil himself. The Hobbesian image of the American state of nature was not paradise but wilderness, in the most negative sense of the word: unfruitful desert, abode of death.

America was, when first discovered, and to some extent even today, a vast unknown to the Europeans who explored and settled it. It is not surprising that anything so vast, so significant, and so little known as the new world would arouse in those who contemplated it the deepest wishes and the darkest fears. The paradise theme has been more prominent and more conscious, but those who believe that the American dream, the paradisic hope, has but lately turned into a nightmare, suffer from illusion. The nightmare was there from the beginning. There is, of course, an inner affinity between dream and nightmare. It is an old story in history that a dream of paradise can motivate hellish actions, and each new-world El Dorado was won at the expense of nightmarish enslavement or extermination of Indians and often unspeakable internecine brutalities among Europeans.

For all the new European inhabitants of America the Christian and biblical tradition provided images and symbols with which to interpret the enormous hopes and fears aroused in them by their new situation, as I have already suggested in using the terms "paradise" and "wilderness." The English colonists, especially in New England, had a particular version of that interpretation, one that contained a dialectical relationship between wilderness and paradise. That dialectic must be seen against the background of a vast mythic scenario which began to unfold in Europe—providentially, the Puritan fathers thought—just after the discovery of the New World. That scenario was the Protestant Reformation, and it was an informing event in the background not only of the Puritans in New England but of most of the settlers in the middle and southern colonies as well.

The Idea of Reform

The idea of reform[10] is far older than the Reformation and is, in fact, central to Christianity itself. It is related to the idea of conversion, the turning from evil to good, from self to God, which is close to the heart of the biblical message in both testaments. Reformation is a kind of renovation or renewal, making new, particularly stressed in the letters of Paul. In 2 Corinthians 5:17 Paul writes, "If then any be in Christ a new creature, the old things are passed away, behold, all things are made new." The primary reference of the concept of reformation or renewal is the soul of the individual. Renewal is embodied in the sacramental life of the church in the sacrament of baptism, a kind of rebirth which brings the individual into the church, the communion of saints, who, because they are in Christ, share a provisional form of paradise. But the church itself may need renewal, and thus another meaning for the term developed. Monasticism was a kind of reform and could lead to movements of reform more generally in the church, as with Augustine, Benedict, or Bernard of Clairvaux.

Finally, always in the background and occasionally in the foreground, was the notion that the world itself is in need of reform and rebirth. The last book of the New Testament, Revelation, was the bearer of such ideas of millennial renewal, of an age of holiness when Christ would return and rule on earth, ideas that time and again broke out into movements of millennial expectation. The Reformation was a heightening and intensification of all these ideas. It began above all as a reform of the church, but it led to a more rigorous stress on the reform of the individual soul, particularly the lay soul, than had been common in the medieval church, and it also carried overtones of apocalyptic expectation. The Roman Church was identified with the Whore of Babylon and the Protestant Church with the New Jerusalem as they are described in Revelation. In this perspective the Reformation could be interpreted as an event presaging the end of times and the birth of a new heaven and a new earth.

The symbolic connections between the heightened consciousness of renewal and rebirth brought on by the Reformation and the discovery and settlement of a "new" world are obvious enough, but the connections are greatly intensified when we consider how closely the notion of "wilderness" in the Bible is tied in with the renewal theme. Christ's forty days in the wilderness following his baptism by John the Baptist were often interpreted as symbolic of purification and renewal before beginning his ministry, and the monks who withdrew to the desert were in a sense following his example. Following the method of typological interpretation[11] which saw Old Testament events as prefiguring New Testament ones, the forty years that the children of Israel spent wandering in the wilderness of Sinai were interpreted as a figure of Christ's forty days. The Israelites were being tested, purified, and renewed for entering into their inheritance of the Promised Land, as Christ was being prepared for his inheritance at the right hand of the Father.

The wilderness theme was also linked to the millenial imagery in an important passage of Revelation 12:6: "and the woman fled into the wilderness, where she had a place prepared by God, in which to be nourished for one thousand two hundred and sixty days." The "woman" was interpreted to be God's true Church which would have to flee to a prepared place in the wilderness just before the end of times.

Now all of these references and quite a few more, including some in the Song of Songs and in several of the postexilic prophets, were used by the New England fathers to interpret their situation. They saw themselves on a divinely appointed "errand into the wilderness" with profound personal, ecclesiastical, and world-historical meaning. Under the circumstances, wilderness was by no means entirely a negative concept. It was a place of danger and temptation, but the "enclosed garden" that the saints were required to build up in the midst of the wilderness was itself a foretaste of paradise.[12] And as Jonathan Edwards and others came to believe, it was precisely here, in the wilderness of the new world, that God was most likely to begin his new heaven and new earth. A precarious but fruitful balance between hope and fear had been struck.

Biblical Imagery

The Bible was the one book that literate Americans in the seventeenth, eighteenth, and nineteenth centuries could be expected to know well. Biblical imagery provided the basic framework for imaginative thought in America up until quite recent times and, unconsciously, its control is still formidable. The typological or figural interpretation of the Puritans is neither higher biblical criticism nor scientific history. Both of these more recent endeavors have their uses, but the mythical level of human consciousness cannot be satisfied by them. A tradition of living myth is always typological in this sense: it sees connections and analogies between many different elements in the tradition and it interprets current events and predicaments in terms of traditional motifs. When Protestant literalism and enlightenment rationalism became dominant in the late eighteenth and nineteenth centuries, typological interpretation was taken up covertly by the novelists and poets or began to operate at unconscious or semiconscious levels of popular culture and ideology. The split between rational and mythic discourse which has characterized our recent cultural history is very dangerous for it impoverishes both modes of thought.[13] It is one of the possible benefits of the current new appreciation of the meaning and function of myth that we may be able to rescue it from the realm of unconscious fantasy where it always continues to operate, often in dark and devious ways, and restore it once again to its creative role in human consciousness. At any rate it is my purpose to suggest some of the ways in which biblical (and other) imagery has operated powerfully, consciously and unconsciously, to shape the American interpretation of reality and to some extent the actions of Americans in the world.

"A Modell of Christian Charity"

In our search for America's myth of origin we have considered the function the new continent served in the European consciousness and the way in which biblical themes, particularly as heightened by the Reformation, shaped its meaning. We have set the scene and brought in the stage furniture but we have not begun the drama. A myth of origin for America must point to certain events in America, not only to their archetypal foreshadowings in biblical history.

Fortunately we have a document from the earliest period in American history which expresses beautifully the various ideas we have been assembling. The document is a sermon preached by John Winthrop, the first leader of the Massachusetts Bay Colony, on board ship in 1630 even before landing in the new world. It defines the meaning of the new venture and its implications and obligations for the new settlers. Of it Perry Miller has written, ". . . in relation to the principal theme of the American mind, the necessity laid upon it for decision, Winthrop stands at the beginning of our consciousness."[14] The sermon is called "A Modell of Christian Charity."

> Thus stands the cause betweene God and us. Wee are entered into Covenant with him for this worke, wee have taken out a Commission, the Lord hath given us leave to draw our owne Articles, wee have professed to enterprise these Accions upon these and these ends, wee have hereupon besought him of favor and blessing: Now if the Lord shall please to heare us, and bring us in peace to the place wee desire, then hath hee ratified this Covenant and sealed our Commission [and] will expect a strickt performance of the Articles contained in it, but if we shall neglect the observacion of these Articles which are the ends wee have propounded, and dissembling with our God, shall fall to embrace this present world and prosecute our carnall intencions seekeing great things for our selves and our posterity, the Lord will surely brake out in wrathe against us, be revenged of such a perjured people and make us knowe the price of the breache of such a Covenant.
>
> Now the onely way to avoyde this shipwracke and to provide for our posterity is to followe the Counsell of Micah, to doe Justly, to love mercy, to walke humbly with our God. For this end, wee must be knitt together in this worke as one man, wee must entertaine each other in brotherly Affeccion, wee must be willing to abridge ourselves of our superfluities, for the supply of others necessities, wee must uphold a familiar Commerce together in all meeknes, gentlenes, patience and liberallity, wee must delight in each other, make others Condicions our owne, rejoyce together, mourne together, labour

and suffer together, allwayes haveing before our eyes our Commission and Community in the worke, our Community as members of the same body, soe shall wee keep the unitie of the spirit in the bond of peace, the Lord will be our God and delight to dwell among us as his owne people and will commaund a blessing upon us in all our ways, soe that wee shall see much more of his wisdome, power, goodnes and truthe than formerly wee have beene acquainted with. Wee shall finde that the God of Israell is among us, when tenn of us shall be able to resist a thousand of our enemies, when hee shall make us a prayse and glory, that men shall say of succeeding plantacions: the lord make it like that of New England: for wee must Consider that wee shall be as a Citty upon a Hill, the eies of all people are uppon us: soe that if wee shall deale falsely with our God in this worke wee have undertaken and soe cause him to withdrawe his present help from us, wee shall shame the faces of many of Gods worthy servants, and cause theire prayers to be turned into Cursses upon us till wee be consumed out of the good land whither wee are goeing: And to shutt upp this discourse with that exhortacion of Moses, that faithful servant of the Lord in his last farewell to Isreall, Deut. 30. Beloved there is now sett before us life, and good, deathe and evill in that wee are commaunded this day to love the Lord our God, and to love one another, to walke in his wayes and to keepe his Commandments and his Ordinance, and his lawes, and the Articles of our Covenant with him that wee may live and be multiplied, and that the Lord our God may bless us in the land whither we goe to possess it: But if our heartes shall turne away soe that wee will not obey, but shall be seduced and worship . . . other Gods, our pleasures, and proffitts, and serve them; it is propounded unto us this day, wee shall surely perishe out of the good Land whither wee passe over this vast Sea to possess it;

> Therefore lett us choose life,
> that wee, and our Seede,
> may live; by obeyeing his
> voice, and cleaveing to him,
> for hee is our life, and
> our prosperity.[15]

The Deuteronomic formula of the blessing and the curse is John Winthrop's way of summing up the meaning of immense hopes and fears of the colonists in the face of the unknown land that lay ahead. He turned the ocean-crossing into a crossing of the Red Sea and the Jordan River and held out the hope that Massachusetts Bay would be a promised land. Most of the colonists were men and women who had been profoundly converted, inwardly reformed and renewed, and who felt uneasy and unhappy about continuing to live in an England where they felt much was corrupt in the church and state. But even before they had freed themselves from the bonds of English society, they had undertaken an "Agreement" in Cambridge, England, the year before and bound themselves to a new covenant with obligations both to God and one another.[16] The "Agreement" of the Massachusetts Bay Colony was a beginning that contained its own principle, just as, as we have seen, the acts establishing the new republic did. But here the archetypes that the mythic gestures of beginning point to are much more explicit. Here too is one of those mythic precursors to which, explicitly or not, the act of the founding of the republic itself inevitably pointed.

Christian Commonwealth

In his contrast between charity and the worship of pleasure and profit Winthrop echoes Augustine's great contrast of *caritas* as the principle of the City of God and *cupiditas* as the principle of the earthly city.[17] Augustine in turn was elaborating the New Testament contrast between Babylon, the city of the beast, the principalities and powers of this world, and the New Jerusalem, the Heavenly City where the saints would be gathered after the apocalypse. Of course neither in the New Testament nor in

Augustine did the New Jerusalem appear as a political community in this world. For Augustine even the church was but a foreshadowing of the Heavenly City which remains invisible on this earth, since the visible church contains many who will in the end turn out not to be citizens of the Heavenly City. Political society he saw largely in negative terms, at best a punishment and correction of sin, at worst a nightmare of corruption in which the strong eat up the weak and the stronger eat up the strong. Although the Augustinian note is evident in Winthrop and the New England Puritans, and although Winthrop also saw the new colony not as the New Jerusalem itself, which would be brought about only by God's direct intervention, but only as a foretaste of it, Winthrop was fundamentally more positive toward the political order than Augustine had been. Winthrop was, unlike Augustine, the leader of a total society in which the church and state, though different, were closely connected and in which Christianity informed the political as well as the religious structure.

John Calvin, the great European predecessor of the New England Puritans, working carefully from a basically Augustinian starting point, had argued that a well-ordered nonmonarchical church could operate symbiotically with a well-ordered polity, namely the city-republic of Geneva, to create an ethical social order. He had managed to restore much of the dignity of the classical conception of political order and to combine Christian charity with civic virtue. The Calvinist Christian commonwealth would not be the City of God on earth but it could be a worthy harbinger of it. It was this conception that the New England Puritans brought to America where it was enhanced by the millennial expectations of which we have spoken.

There was, then, a strongly social, communal, or collective emphasis in early New England political thought. That collective emphasis, that understanding of man as fundamentally social, was derived from the classical conception of the *polis* as responsible for the education and the virtue of its citizens, from the Old Testament notion of the Covenant between God and a people held collectively responsible for its actions, and from the New Testament notion of a community based on charity or love and expressed in brotherly affection and fellow membership in one common body. This collective emphasis did not mean a denigration of the individual because the Calvinist synthesis of the older traditions maintained a strong sense of the dignity and responsibility of the individual and especially stressed voluntaristic individual action. But Calvinist "individualism" only made sense within the collective context. Individual action outside the bounds of religious and moral norms was seen in Augustinian terms as the very archetype of sin.

Liberty and Duty

This dual emphasis on the individual and on society can be traced in the dialectic of conversion and covenant that was continuously worked over in the colonial Protestant Churches and came to provide a series of feelings, images, and concepts that would help shape the meaning of the new republic. To the early Puritans, conversion was an intensely personal and individual experience of salvation and the prerequisite of church membership. A public account of such a personal experience, subject to inquiry and examination and the confirmation of goodly moral character, was required from each prospective member. While the Puritans were aware that members of the church, conceived as the Covenant of Grace, were ultimately known only to God and that it was almost certain that there were hypocrites in the visible church, they tried as far as possible to maintain a church of the converted. In addition to the inward covenant there was also the outward or national covenant to which all New Englanders were conceived of as belonging or at least to which they were subject. This was the basis of civil society. Ideally, individual conversion and external covenant should go together and there were those who tried to blur the distinction in practice as well, but there was also a long tradition of concern over the tension that usually exists between the two.

Conversion, following traditions deeply rooted in both testaments of the Bible, was felt to be a form of liberation. To be converted was to be freed from the bondage of sin and death, emancipated from slavery to the world, the flesh, and the devil. The Reformation emphasized that the converted man is a free man, in certain respects answerable only to God. Evangelical preachers in the eighteenth century often expatiated on the theme of the "sweets of liberty."[18] But conversion as a liberating experience was always balanced by the coordinate concept of covenant, which implied a definite set of obligations between God and man and between man and man. Much of the controversy of colonial piety emerged from the effort to keep a balance between conversion and covenant. The long struggle over whether a conversion experience was essential for church membership was an argument over whether the converted could share in the covenant relation with the converted and attain at least some of the worldly and spiritual advantages of church membership. The Great Awakening, the wave of religious revivals that swept through all the colonies in the 1740s, aroused the passionate involvement of Jonathan Edwards and others who shared his opposition to a church based on the external covenant alone. They hoped the Awakening would serve as a channel of grace through which most or all of the community could be converted and thus share fully in the obligations and rewards of the covenant.

But the Awakening raised the specter of unbalance in the other direction. Some of those carried away by the emotional enthusiasm of the revival interpreted their new spiritual liberation as freedom from any law whatsoever. Others, less obvious than the open antinomians, interpreted their inner emotional experience as guarantees of their salvation without any further need for action in the world. Edwards, in his *Treatise Concerning Religious Affections,*[19] is at pains to counter both of these errors. He developed a scheme of twelve signs indicative of the genuineness of the conversion experience. Among the most important of them were a genuine and permanent transformation in the nature of the convert, that is of his whole personality in relation to his environment; and the last and most fully described sign, the actual practice, both religious and ethical, which the genuine convert would show in his subsequent life. The strong note of social responsibility struck in Winthrop's conception of the covenant continued in the line of Calvinist and evangelical thought in the eighteenth century. Conversion was not just an act of purely private piety. The liberty flowing from it did not mean escape from social obligations. Covenant liberty was seen as profoundly social as in the following quotation from the leading eighteenth-century Baptist Isaac Backus:

True liberty of man is, to know, obey and enjoy his Creator, and to do all the good unto, and enjoy all the happiness with and in his fellow creatures that he is capable of; in order to which the law of love was written in his heart, which carries in it's nature union and benevolence to Being in general, and to each being in particular, according to it's nature and excellency, and to it's relation and connexion with the supreme Being, and ourselves. Each rational soul, as he is part of the whole system of rational beings, so it was and is, both his duty and his liberty, to regard the good of the whole in all his actions.[20]

The juncture of liberty and duty in Backus's last sentence is the key to the Protestant conception of liberty in relation to conversion and covenant. Opposed to external compulsion in religion and, as the decades passed, ever more explicitly in politics as well, they retained a profound sense of obligation both to higher law and to "the good of the whole." Edwards noted with disapproval the common "notion of liberty" as "a person's having the opportunity of doing as he pleases." And Isaac Backus noted that all government "in the imagination of many, interferes with such liberty."[21] But if the evangelical leaders recoiled from antinomianism and anarchy, they recoiled equally from a cold "external covenant." Genuine covenant obligations to God and other men were to be joyfully accepted in the warm hearts of the converted. The restraint of a purely exterior law involving no inner assent was to them not much better than no law at all. And indeed they stood ready to exhort their fellows to throw off such involuntary external constraint when the hour came to do so.

Nonbiblical Symbols for the Republic

So far we have confined our investigation to biblical events and images, elaborated in the colonial experience, and how they came to provide a structure of mythic meaning for the great founding events of the republic. But the Bible was not the only source of myth and symbol for the new nation.

The English political tradition was the major influence on colonial thought and institutions, and references to it were copious. In the mounting controversy that preceded the Revolution, references to the British Constitution and "the rights of Englishmen" were innumerable. In many respects the unprecedented degree of self-government existing in the colonies almost from the beginning was due to specifically English political and constitutional development and would not have been tolerated by any other major colonial power. And yet there is remarkably little to show of English influence in the new republic at the level of myth and symbol. Even granted that this is mainly due to hostility toward Britain generated by the Revolution itself ("The British," said Jefferson, "are in our bowels and we must expel them"),[22] it might well have been possible to turn to some earlier period in English history—Magna Carta, say, or the Protectorate under Cromwell—to provide a body of legitimating symbols for the new nation. But the only major body of nonbiblical symbols that we find in the words and acts of the founding fathers is not English but Roman.

For several centuries before the American Revolution the history of the Roman republic had figured prominently in the imagination of educated Europe. Modern political theory from Machiavelli to Montesquieu had been preoccupied with understanding its greatness and its decline. Latin literature was at the core of humanistic education in America as well as Europe. Virgil's Aeneid even fitfully rivaled the Exodus of the Children of Israel as an archetypal story of flight into the wilderness in order to found a new city. Just as Winthrop thought of Moses so Captain John Smith thought of Aeneas in what Howard Mumford Jones calls the "prose Aeneid" that he composed to recount his establishment of the English Colony in Virginia.[23] But it was not so much Latin myth or legend that dominated the minds of educated Americans in the late eighteenth century as it was the history of Roman liberty. It was this history which served as both archetype and warning. As Joseph Warren wrote in 1772 in commemorating the second anniversary of the Boston massacre: "It was *this* noble attachment to a free constitution, which raised ancient Rome from the smallest beginnings to that bright summit of happiness and glory to which she arrived; and it was the loss of *this* which plunged her from *that* summit into the black gulph of infamy and slavery."[24]

It is not surprising then that Roman classicism dominated

the surface symbolism of the new republic. Its very terminology was latinate, the words "republic," "president," "congress," and "senate" being Latin in origin and clearly distinct from the terminology for their British counterparts. The great seal of the United States bears two Latin mottos, *E pluribus unum* and *Novus ordo saeclorum* (new order of the ages), though even the Virgilian reference of the latter should not blind us to the biblical level of meaning that it also carries. George Washington, the Cincinnatus of the West, went to his inauguration by passing under arches of laurel. Greco-Roman classicism dominated the architecture and much of the art of the early republican period.[25]

At a deeper level, the Roman attribute that preoccupied the imagination of the founders of the new nation was republican virtue, especially as it was interpreted by Montesquieu, the great forerunner of modern sociology and one of the political thinkers most influential on late eighteenth-century America. According to Montesquieu, in his tripartite scheme of despotism, monarchy, and republic, each type of society has its own principle of social life which provides the spring of action for its members. For despotism that principle is fear. For monarchy it is honor: the spirit of emulation, what today we might call status seeking. For a republic, and especially for its democratic rather than aristocratic form, the principle of social life is virtue, which James Sellers has recently paraphrased in more modern languages as "willed initiative."

> In a democracy there is no prince furnished with an army to maintain the laws by force. And since the people are established on the basis of parity, there is no pride of rank to exploit. If there is any will or motivation to see that the laws are obeyed and that justice is done, it must come out of the hearts of the citizenry, from the will and ability of the people to act on behalf of the greater community. It is this quality rather than fear or ambition, that makes things work in a democracy. This quality is *la vertu.* . . . It conveys the idea that the citizen of a republic finds the beginning of his participation in governance in his own inner spirit, but that this spirit takes the form of action, and especially that kind of action that expresses willingness: initiative.[26]

In Montesquieu's analysis, a republic will stand only so long as its citizens love it. If it needs external coercion its principle is lost. And Montesquieu, echoing many a hero of the early Roman republic, tells us that only frugality and the absence of luxury can keep the public interest in the minds of the citizens and make possible that renunciation of self which is so difficult but without which no republic can long survive. The agrarian ideal of Jefferson and others in the early republic—the ideal of a nation of frugal independent husbandmen ready to serve at their community's call—owes much to this notion of republican virtue. Although from a different starting point, the evangelical version of the Protestant Ethic led to an identical conclusion.

In the end the Roman archetypes proved less profound and less lasting than the biblical ones, for Latin culture was more confined to the elite than biblical culture. The great image for the founding of the nation was Exodus, not Aeneid. Even the classicist Jefferson proposed a picture of Moses leading Israel across the Red Sea for the Great Seal of the United States. And in his second inaugural address he said, "I need, too, the favor of that Being in whose hands we are, who led our forefathers, as Israel of old, from their native land, and planted them in a country flowing with all the necessaries and comforts of life; who has covered our infancy with his providence, and our riper years with his wisdom and power."[27]

We might wonder at the choice of Israel and Rome as the archetypes of the new nation, in view of the long history of suffering of the former and the decline and fall of the latter. We may wonder that our ancestors overlooked the darker days of those early nations. They did not. They hoped to construct a republic on principles so sound that it might avoid their fate. But they were certain that if we should decline in piety and public virtue we would meet the inexorable fate of the nations, which are as but dust in the hands of God.

The Influence of Thomas Hobbes

But there was another tradition of political thought also beginning to seep into the American colonies in the early eighteenth century, one related to Calvinist theology and classical philosophy in curious patterns of attraction and repulsion. This was a relatively new trend of thought originating in the first attempt to apply the attitudes and orientations of natural science to the social and political sphere when, in the seventeenth century, natural science began to take on the prestige that it has characteristically maintained ever since. The truly innovative figure here was Thomas Hobbes, although it was the more modest and conciliatory thought of Hobbes's follower and critic, John Locke, that had most influence in America. As many scholars have pointed out, there is a remarkable resemblance between Hobbes's state of nature and Augustine's *civitas terrena*. Both assume that natural man is fundamentally selfish and greedy, eager to satisfy his own desires and ready to dominate or destroy any who stand in his way. The *bellum omnium contra omnes* is Hobbes's phrase, but it is an apt description of Augustine's picture of man without God. Just as Augustine's *cupiditas* as the principle of the earthly city is an appropriate term for Hobbes's conception of fundamental human motivation. The critical difference between the two theorists—and it is important because it will distinguish Calvinist from utilitarian in eighteenth-century America—becomes evident when we consider how each of them explained such order and peace as does prevail in worldly society.

For both Augustine and Hobbes the *bellum omnium* is a marginal case, illustrative of certain truths about human nature but not, except in situations of exceptional breakdown, actually descriptive of normal human existence. For Augustine, of course, God is lord of the earthly city as well as the heavenly one. His providence, even though inscrutable, orders human history. Among other things, he often chooses to send kings and tyrants, including unjust ones, as a scourge to the wicked and a trial to the saints, and such kings maintain a semblance of peace. But essential to Augustine's political thought is the idea that even fallen man retains some "image" or "impression" of divine truth and justice, without which there could be no political order.[28]

What distinguishes Hobbes from the classical and Christian traditions and their modern continuers is the absence of any notion of God or the Good and a corresponding radical theoretical individualism. For Hobbes the marginal case of the war of all against all is not escaped through any semblance or trace of divine justice but through a social compact made by individuals to maximize their self-interest. In order to evade the natural state of anxiety, fear, and suffering, men appoint a monarch over themselves to whom they cede their natural liberty in return for peace and security. But for Hobbes, and here Locke is his true disciple, social concord is still based not on divine justice, not even on a shadow of *caritas,* but on self-interest, on *cupiditas* alone. The idea that society could be based on a mere coagulation of individual interests, that the pursuit of private vice could result in public virtue, was a radically new idea in the seventeenth and eighteenth centuries and one that did not sit well with other still powerful traditions.

The Fusion of Covenant and Republican Patterns

The remarkable coherence of the American revolutionary movement and its successful conclusion in the constitution of a new civil order are due in considerable part to the convergence of the Puritan covenant pattern and the Montesquieuan republican pattern. The former was represented above all by New England, the latter by Virginia, but both were widely diffused in the consciousness of the colonial population. Both patterns saw society resting on the deep inner commitment of its members, the former through conversion, the latter through republican virtue. Both saw government as resting on law, which, in its positive form, was created by the active participation of those subject to it, yet ultimately derives from some higher source, either God or Nature. When Jefferson evoked at the beginning of the Declaration of Independence the "laws of nature and of nature's God" he was able to fuse the ultimate legitimating principles of both traditions. And when in concluding it he wrote, "And for the support of this declaration, with a firm reliance on the protection of divine providence, we mutually pledge to each other our lives, our fortunes, and our sacred honor," he was not only invoking a republican formula for the establishment of a civil compact but echoing the formula of the Puritan covenant. Only the confluence of these two patterns can help us understand the fusion of passion and reason that, with such consistency, seems to have motivated the major actors in the revolutionary drama.

Liberty was the great theme of American revolutionary emotion. As early as 1770 one observer noted that "the minds of the people are wrought up into as high a degree of Enthusiasm by the word liberty, as could have been expected had Religion been the cause."[29] Liberty meant liberation from British tyranny and from the rule of kings. It is hard for us to realize the psychological exhilaration of the overthrow of monarchy in that day when, except for a few small and declining republics, monarchy was universal. In view of the fact that Parliament more than George III was tyrannizing over the Americans it is remarkable that it was George who became the very symbol and incarnation of the restraint the Americans were overthrowing. In the imagination of some New England preachers George even became the Antichrist, the "horrible wild beast" of the thirteenth Book of Revelation.[30] The intensity of the rejection of the king, considering the fact that he was a constitutional monarch and, in any dispassionate use of the term, no tyrant, is only to be explained as the rejection of a whole conception of authority, that is of authority as external, arbitrary constraint, for which a king is a much better image than a parliament.

In the first months of the war a spontaneous unity swept through the colonies. David Ramsay in his history of the revolution published in 1791 looked back at the spirit of 1775 as one that "calmer seasons can scarcely credit." He wrote:

> The Governor of the Universe, by a sacred influence on their minds, disposed them to union. From whatever cause it proceeded, it is certain, that a disposition to do, to suffer, and to accommodate, spread from breast to breast, and from colony to colony, beyond the reach of human calculation.[31]

The "brotherly affection," the willingness to "abridge ourselves of our superfluities, for the supply of other necessities," that Winthrop spoke of in the early Puritan covenant seemed again to live in the revolutionary ranks. The liberation from external restraint and the emergence of "the blessed unison of the whole American harpsichord, as now set to the tune of liberty," as it was described in 1775, must indeed have inspired the millennial expectations that were never far below the surface in colonial America.[32]

Yet the difficult years of 1777 and 1778 saw much falling away, doubting, and hardness of heart. One Calvinist minister was led to produce a sermon called "The American States Acting Over the Part of the Children of Israel in the Wilderness and Thereby Impeding Their Entrance into Canaan's Rest."[33]

The Spirit of 1775 that Alan Heimert has compared so convincingly to that of the Great Awakening had not been able to survive genuine adversity or overcome the selfish proclivities or inordinate demands of individuals. Even in 1775, John Adams recounted, ". . . a common horse jockey . . . who was always in the law, and had been sued in many actions at almost every court," came up to him and said, "Oh, Mr. Adams what great things have you and your colleagues done for us! We can never be grateful enough to you. There are no courts of justice now in the province, and I hope there never will be another."[34] Adams's distress at this homegrown anarchism that Edwards and Backus had noticed earlier was motivated at least in part by class anxieties and concern for the protection of property, though he was also moved by larger purposes. But the dissenting Protestants of all classes were equally alarmed after 1776 about the absence of governmental regularity. They repeatedly requested the Massachusetts General Court, for example, to establish a constitution so that the people of the commonwealth would not be left "in a state of nature," by which they meant, with Jonathan Edwards, "*Hobbes's* state of war," where men "would act as the wild beast of the desert; prey upon and destroy one another."[35] We are not surprised to learn that Alexander Hamilton said, "We may preach till we are tired of the theme the necessity of disinterestedness in republics, without making a single proselyte." But Jefferson did not much disagree when he wrote at the end of the war, "They will forget themselves, but in the sole faculty of making money, and will never think of uniting to effect a due respect for their rights."[36]

The Conflict of Virtue and Interest

To some extent this tension between concern for the common cause and concern for one's selfish interest was reflected at the theoretical level in the tension between utilitarians and those who held the traditional religious and philosophical views. There were some Americans in the eighteenth century fully aware of the underlying conflict. In his *Two Discourses on Liberty* of 1774, Nathaniel Niles, the Calvinist preacher and follower of Jonathan Edwards, attacked Locke's view of the origin and purpose of government. The notion that government arises out of a contract for the mutual defense of private property "is the maxim on which pirates and gangs of robbers live in a kind of unity," he wrote. He correctly pointed out that the utilitarian conception of society, lacking even the Augustinian trace of divine order, would inevitably collapse into chaos:

> God cements mankind into society for their greater good, while each, consenting to submit his exercise of the several powers with which he is vested to the cognizance of the whole body, agrees to deny himself such gratifications as are deemed incompatible with the felicity of the rest. . . . Just so far as his affection is turned on private interest, he will become regardless of the common good, and when he is detached from the community in heart, his services will be very precarious at best, and those will not be expected at all which imply self-denial.[37]

The conscious conflict between the civil (Calvinist classical) and utilitarian views came to a head, then, over the issue of whether virtue or interest was to be the effective basis of the new American polity. In the 1770s most articulate Americans chose virtue. In arguing against a property qualification for holding office, an anonymous tract of 1776 argued:

> So sure as we make interest necessary in this case, as sure we root out virtue; and what will then become of the genuine principle of freedom. This notion of an interest has the directest tendency to set up the avaricious over the head of the poor, though the latter are ever so virtuous.[38]

Samuel Adams, who hoped America would be a "Christian Sparta," expressed the general view when he wrote:

We may look up to Armies for our Defense, but Virtue is our best Security. It is not possible that any State shd long remain free, where Virtue is not supremely honored.[39]

But by the 1790s, as Gordon S. Wood has shown, quite other views were beginning to prevail. Instead of lamenting the fact that Americans seemed to be more intent on individual happiness than upon public good, some began to argue that just such a principle was the basis of the new American system. The new Constitution, it was felt, harnessed individual acquisitiveness to public order. As James Wilson wrote, in America there was introduced "into the very form of government, such particular checks and controls, as to make it advantageous even for bad men to act for the public good." Wood sums up these views as follows:

America would remain free not because of any quality in its citizens of spartan self-sacrifice to some nebulous public good, but in the last analysis because of the concern each individual would have in his own self-interest and personal freedom.[40]

Wilson and others entranced with the new system argued that it would be immune to the corruptions of the classical republics and that it would not suffer a collapse into tyranny. John Adams, who believed virtue was essential in a republic but saw awfully little of it in his countrymen, adopted a very somber view of America's future and interpreted the Constitution largely in negative terms as an effort to slow the inevitable descent.[41] Just as Locke did not displace Calvin in the seventeenth century, so the newer view did not eliminate the older one in the late eighteenth century. Washington's Farewell Address, published in 1796, restated the older moral position when he argued that Providence connects "the permanent felicity of a Nation with its virtue," and the early nineteenth century would see a revival of those sentiments in both religious and political form. The struggle of the two positions has never ceased and the conflict between them is a central theme of this chapter.[42]

The founding fathers as they moved from heroic acts of liberation to the constituting of liberty were aware of the difficulty of maintaining revolutionary zeal as the basis for civil responsibility. Revolution and constitution are as necessarily interlinked as are conversion and covenant, their lineal predecessors, but the tension between them seems as inevitable in the one case as in the other. The Constitution could not take for granted that its citizens would all be motivated by civic virtue and so its concern was as much to protect individuals and groups from abuse at the hands of the government and their fellow citizens as it was to involve all its citizens in genuine participation. Indeed many delegates at the Constitutional Convention feared the active participation of the ordinary citizens far more than their lack of zeal. The Constitution, therefore, was a kind of "external covenant" uniting convinced republicans with the lukewarm—as perhaps it had to be.

The men who consciously felt themselves to be "founding fathers" had a profound conviction of the solemnity and significance of their role as lawgivers. John Adams wrote that he was grateful to have "been sent into life at a time when the greatest lawgivers of antiquity would have wished to live."[43] The time, care, and enormous intelligence expended on the process of producing the constitution expressed not only the traditional culture of a covenant- and compact-making people, perhaps unique in that respect in human history, but also a sense of the meaning of their act on the world stage. John Adams, even ten years before the Revolution, could write: "I always consider the settlement of America as the opening of a grand scheme and design in Providence for the illumination of the ignorant and the emancipation of the slavish part of mankind all over the earth."[44] At the end of the seventeenth and the beginning of the eighteenth centuries Americans had wavered about claiming to be a city set on a hill with the eyes of the world upon it. But by the end of the eighteenth they were certain once more. In Washington's first inaugural address, occurring at the event that completed, as it were, the constituting of the new nation, he said: "The preservation of the sacred fire of liberty and the destiny of the republican model of government are justly considered, perhaps, as *deeply,* as *finally,* staked on the experiment intrusted to the hands of the American people." They created a structure that, within limits we will have to consider, did protect the liberty of the people and did provide a space for popular initiative. In that, the founding fathers were not deluded in their conviction of the importance of their acts.

Perhaps it would be well to make more explicit the analogy between revolution and constitution on the one hand and conversion and covenant on the other that underlies this whole discussion. Revolution, like conversion, is an act of liberation, a leaving of old structures, a movement away from constraint. Both revolution and conversion open up the deepest levels of the psyche, touch the springs of our deepest hopes and fears. If these acts of liberation did not contain elements of antinomianism and anarchism they would not be genuine, for the old authority must be radically broken before the new order can be born. But unless the free act of liberation moves rapidly toward an act of institution or constitution, an act not of throwing off the past but of establishing the future, then even the liberation itself turns into its opposite. Conversion that does not move toward covenant becomes a new hardness of heart. Revolution that does not move toward constitution quickly becomes a new despotism, as we have seen with so many nineteenth- and twentieth-century "revolutions." It is in this sense that the American Revolution succeeded, where so many others failed.

And yet the success it had was at best partial. The Constitution was after all an external covenant. To Jefferson and the evangelicals, perhaps those most concerned that the element of liberation not be lost in the act of institution, the establishment of the Constitution was only the beginning instead of the end of the struggle. Jefferson, as is well known, believed that every generation had the right "to begin the world over again," and that: "Nothing is unchangeable but the inherent and unalienable rights of man," and it was he that felt it would be a good thing to have a revolution every twenty years.[45] He was contemptuous of those who "look at constitutions with sanctimonious reverence, and deem them like the ark of the covenant, too sacred to be touched."[46] The evangelicals, in the revival of 1800 that was intimately connected with the electoral victory of Jeffersonian republicanism called for a "SECOND REVOLUTION, which is inward and spiritual."[47] Like Edwards they wanted everyone in a full covenant and would be satisfied with nothing less. For the Jeffersonians and evangelicals a constitution too quickly becomes cold and external, a shell for the pursuit of self-interest rather than a space for the exercise of free initiative in the public interest.

Thus the tensions that had long operated in America's religious life were transferred into American political life. A structure of liberty, necessary as it is to prevent liberation from destroying itself, nevertheless contains within it new forms of external constraint and new bulwarks for private interest. It requires therefore, again and again, just as religious life requires reformation and revival, a new birth of freedom.

"America's Myth of Origin," Notes

1. See also the following articles of mine on this subject: "Civil Religion in America," *Daedalus* (Winter 1967); "Evil and the American Ethos," in *Sanctions for Evil,* ed. Nevitt Sanford and Craig Comstock (San Francisco: Jossey-Bass, 1971); "American Civil Religion in the 1970s," *Anglican Theological Review,* Supplementary Series 1 (July 1973); "Reflections on Reality in America," *Radical Religion,* vol. 1, no. 3, 1974; "Religion and Polity in America," *Andover Newton Quarterly,* vol. 15, no. 2, 1974.

2. Hannah Arendt, *On Revolution* (New York: Viking Compass, 1965), p. 214.

3. On this point Hannah Arendt has the following to say: "The great measure of success the American founders could book for themselves, the simple fact that the revolution here succeeded where all others were to fail, namely in founding a new body politic stable enough to survive the onslaught of centuries to come, one is tempted to think, was decided the very moment when the Constitution began to be 'worshiped,' even though it had hardly begun to operate." Arendt, *On Revolution,* p. 199.

4. John Locke, *The Second Treatise of Government,* 49, 1.

5. Quoted in James Sellers, *Public Ethics* (New York: Harper & Row, Publishers, 1970), p. 169. It is interesting to note, in passing, that Santayana described in 1920 as a permanent feature of the American character what some observers today mistakenly believe is only characteristic of the current younger generation.

6. Locke, *Second Treatise,* 2, 4-9.

7. Howard Mumford Jones, *O Strange New World* (New York: Viking Compass, 1967), pp. 15-16.

8. George H. Williams, *Wilderness and Paradise in Christian Thought* (New York: Harper Bros., 1962), p. 101.

9. Mircea Eliade, *The Quest: History and Meaning in Religion* (Chicago: University of Chicago Press, 1969), p. 94.

10. In this section I am very much dependent on Gerhart B. Ladner, *The Idea of Reform* (New York: Harper & Row, 1967).

11. On typological interpretation in early Christianity and the Middle Ages see the classic article of Erich Auerbach, *Scenes from the Drama of European Literature* (New York: Meridian Books, 1959), pp. 11-76. For the Puritan use of this mode of interpretation see Robert Middlekauff, *The Mathers* (New York: Oxford University

Press, 1971), pp. 106-111. A contemporary use of the method with effervescent results is Norman O. Brown's *Love's Body* (New York: Random House, 1966).

12. See George H. Williams, *Wilderness and Paradise*, p. 101.

13. For an extraordinarily suggestive effort to link symbol, myth, and reflective thought see Paul Ricoeur, *The Symbolism of Evil* (New York: Harper & Row, 1967). See also Mircea Eliade, *Images and Symbols* (New York: Sheed and Ward, 1969); and my forthcoming *The Roots of Religious Consciousness*.

14. Perry Miller, *Nature's Nation* (Cambridge, Mass.: Harvard University Press, 1967), p. 6.

15. *Winthrop Papers,* vol. 2, The Massachusetts Historical Society, pp. 294-295.

16. For a discussion of Winthrop's covenant theory see Perry Miller, *Errand into the Wilderness* (Cambridge, Mass.: Harvard University Press, 1956), pp. 148-149.

17. There are many places in Augustine's writings where this contrast appears. One of the most central is *City of God*, XIV, 28.

18. Alan Heimert, *Religion and the American Mind* (Cambridge, Mass.: Harvard University Press, 1966), p. 454.

19. *The Works of Jonathan Edwards,* vol. 2 (New Haven, Conn.: Yale University Press, 1959).

20. Heimert, *Religion and the American Mind,* p. 459. On this interesting figure see William G. McLoughlin, *Isaac Backus and the American Pietistic Tradition* (Boston: Little, Brown & Co., 1967).

21. Heimert, *Religion and the American Mind,* p. 458.

22. Quoted in Erik Erikson, *Dimensions of a New Identity,* Jefferson Lectures, 1973, (New York: W. W. Norton, 1974), p. 89.

23. Jones, *O Strange New World,* p. 238.

24. Jones, *O Strange New World,* p. 254.

25. Jones, *O Strange New World,* pp. 251-265.

26. Sellers, *Public Ethics,* pp. 72-73.

27. Saul K. Padover, ed., *The Complete Jefferson* (Duell, Sloan & Pearce, 1943), p. 414.

28. "If the image of God and the law of God were completely obliterated from man's soul by sin, if no 'faint outlines' of the original remained, men would have no conception of justice, righteousness, or peace to use as the foundation of the human standards of equity, fair-dealing, and order that are the pillars of civilized society. . . ." Herbert A. Deane, *The Political and Social Ideas of St. Augustine* (New York: Columbia University Press, 1963), p. 96.

29. Heimert, *Religion and the American Mind,* p. 21.

30. Heimert, *Religion and the American Mind,* p. 411.

31. Heimert, *Religion and the American Mind,* p. 401.

32. Ruth Bloch in an unpublished paper, "Millennial Thought in the American Revolutionary Movement," 1973, has provided copious evidence for a connection I had only surmised.

33. In Conrad Cherry, *God's New Israel: Religious Interpretations of American Destiny* (Englewood Cliffs, N.J.: Prentice-Hall, 1971), p. 67.

34. Arendt, *On Revolution,* p. 300.

35. Heimert, *Religion and the American Mind,* pp. 303-304.

36. Heimert, *Religion and the American Mind,* pp. 518-519.

37. Heimert, *Religion and the American Mind,* pp. 516-517.

38. Heimert, *Religion and the American Mind,* p. 521.

39. Clinton Rossiter, *The Political Thought of the American Revolution,* (New York: Harvest Books, 1963), p. 200.

40. Gordon S. Wood, *The Creation of the American Republic, 1776-1787* (New York: W. W. Norton, 1972), p. 612.

41. On Adams see Wood, *Creation of the American Republic,* ch. 14; and Paul K. Conkin, *Puritans and Pragmatists* (New York: Dodd, Mead, 1968), ch. 4.

42. A long, reflective, and in my opinion profound essay on the basic tension in American culture that was published too recently to be taken fully into account in this chapter is Wilson Carey McWilliams, *The Idea of Fraternity in America* (Berkeley: University of California Press, 1973).

43. Arendt, *On Revolution,* p. 204.

44. Heimert, *Religion and the American Mind,* p. 15.

45. Erickson comments on Jefferson's words, "God forbid that we should ever be twenty years without . . . a rebellion," as follows: "Why twenty years? Did he, maybe, refer not only to history but also to the life cycle: God forbid anyone should be twenty years old without having rebelled?" Erickson, *Dimensions,* p. 72.

46. Arendt, *On Revolution,* p. 235.

47. Heimert, *Religion and the American Mind,* p. 548.

5. Faith of the Founding Fathers?

David Gill

Barely a generation after the Founding Fathers got the United States off the ground, a French visitor to the new country, Alexis de Tocqueville, wrote in his famous *Democracy in America*:

> On my arrival in the United States the religious aspect of the country was the first thing that struck my attention; and the longer I stayed there, the more I perceived the great political consequences resulting from this new state of things.[1]

The reality of a carefully separated church and state existing in a mutually influential and positive relationship was unforgettable for de Tocqueville. The history of Europe had been in many ways the story of a continuing and often ugly battle for power between the church and state. Here at last appeared to be the much sought-after happy relationship of a healthy church and a progressive, enlightened state.

Modern anthropologists have taught us at least two things about religion: first, every culture in every time and place has religion; and second, whatever that religion may be, it is *functionally* interrelated with other parts of the culture and significant. Understanding the religious part is essential to understanding the cultural whole. Sociologists have debated the specific nature of the role played by religion in society somewhat inconclusively. At this point it seems that the best approach is an eclectic one. Religion has both a personal, individualistic side and a corporate, group aspect; it functions as a cause of social events and yet is itself affected by other influences; it has both transcendent and immanent sources and objectives; it can be revolutionary or conservative. The day of one-sided theoretical ax-grinding is hopefully over and the greater complexity and richness of the religion/society relationship can be appreciated.

What the anthropologists, sociologists, and historians of religion have told us in general is amply demonstrated in particular by the generation of America's Founding Fathers. De Tocqueville's observations were neither selective nor accidental: the relationship between religion and society or church and state in early America was real, vital, and fruitful. It is not necessary to commit the fallacy of calling this a "Christian country" or resort to idolatrous and blind adulation of the United States to recognize that, in spite of weakness and errors, the early leadership of the country came up with an admirable solution to the age-old problem of church/state relationships.

Whatever the faith of the Founding Fathers may have been specifically (and I will return to that subject in some detail) they protected the liberty to practice and advocate any religion (or no religion) for the citizenry. First the federal government, then eventually all the state governments, removed the fact and the possibility of an established religion. The first article of the faith of the Founding Fathers should probably be identified as the voluntary nature of true religious commitment. Religion is not an affair of coercion, but rather one of persuasion.

Religious influences functioned significantly among the Founding Fathers. From Founding Father John Adams to contemporary historian of the ideological origins of the American Revolution, Bernard Bailyn, the consensus is that as far back as the 1730s or earlier, the Revolutionary ideology was already formed. Sidney Ahlstrom's recent and masterful *A Religious History of the American People* argues that:

> No factor in the "Revolution of 1607-1760" was more significant to the ideals and thought of colonial Americans than the Reformed and Puritan character of their Protestantism; and no institution played a more prominent role in the molding of colonial culture than the church.[2]

It is clear that a double movement took place in the founding of this country: on an institutional level, religion and state were carefully separated; on the ideological level, religion had a powerful and ongoing impact.

At the time of the Revolution, the ecclesiastical situation in the colonies increasingly reflected the ethnic and sectarian divisions in Europe. The American colonies were inhabited by people from virtually every Christian species in Europe. When the war for independence required unity, it was unity without easing the religious distinctions. There were common themes but first we will look briefly at the diversity.

By the time of the Revolution the Congregational churches were the most numerous and characteristically "American." They were the direct bearers of the Puritan tradition and were centered in Massachusetts and New England. They were gradually dividing between the more rationalistic, deistic, Unitarian types, and the "consistent Calvinist" conservative types, but those theological divisions had no demonstrable connection with the degree of patriotic or revolutionary fervor. Some of the more conservative theologically were among the most radical politically!

The Anglican church had representation along most of the seaboard but its strength was in Virginia and the aristocratic South. The Anglicans had Reformed, Calvinistic influences in their theology and history and thus were not wholly distinct from the theology of Puritan Congregationalism, but in general the Anglicans were more "latitudinarian" and rationalistic. As with Congregationalism, there is no way to make a causal correlation between theological radicalism and political radicalism: two-thirds of the signers of the Declaration of Independence were nominal Anglicans yet most of the 70,000 or so Loyalists who left the colonies were Anglicans and included nearly all the clergy!

Two groups which later became much larger than the Congregationalists and Anglicans had certain affinities to them. The Presbyterians were mainly of Scotch-Irish origin and centered in western Pennsylvania. Their theology was unabashedly Calvinistic, and it was mainly the question of denominational vs. independent congregational government that kept them apart from the Puritans, not any major ideological differences. The Methodists were an Anglican group until after the Revolution. In 1784 the Methodists organized separately from the Anglican (Episcopal) church in America, and in the nineteenth century became the largest church in America for a time. Their emphases on personal religious experience, doctrinal simplicity, holiness of life, and their circuit/district/class organization made Methodism appealing and adaptable to the American frontier more than any other religious group.

The Quakers were important for their "holy experiment" in Pennsylvania: a nonviolent, open, liberated state run by Christians for seventy years until 1756 when their pacifist convictions led them to step out of civil government rather than get involved in the frontier Indian violence provoked by the Scotch-Irish and others living on the frontier. More by example and witness than by direct political involvement, Quakerism influenced those in favor of religious liberty, opposed to slavery, and involved in other humane projects. Baptists, Catholics, Lutherans, Dutch Reformed, Mennonites, Dunkers, and other sects completed the religious panorama in Revolutionary America but were not a particularly significant influence at this point in United States history, except in the general sense of adding to the pluralistic and general Protestant, Reformed character of colonial religion.

A visitor to the new country would have observed a real diversity of church affiliations, although probably two-thirds or more of the population were of the Calvinistic-Reformed tradition in some way. On listening to the sermons and reading the publications of all these groups the most visible division of opinion would probably be between those vigorously holding to the old orthodoxy and those moving with the Enlightenment toward a more rationalistic sort of deism. This division crossed virtually all denominational barriers. The faith of the Founding Fathers was a combination of influences from Puritanism and deism. It is to those major "faiths" we now turn.

The Puritan Tradition

In spite of the fact that scholars have not held the view for many years, many people in our era continue to think of prudishness, sexual prohibitions, and witchhunts, of uptight, grim, religious spoilsports, when they hear the word *Puritan*. Clearly there were excesses and mistakes made by Puritans, and the early years of Massachusetts Bay Colony required a severity and discipline for mere survival which today's affluent society finds repulsive and hard to understand. But Puritanism's essence was not in any of the above, but in a revolutionary and powerful relationship with the sovereign God. It was a religious relationship that radically affected all aspects of human existence every day of the week. To give you an idea of the contrast between that popular superstition and the direction of recent serious study of Puritanism, one of the most significant recent studies is Michael Walzer's *Revolution of the Saints: A Study in the Origins of Radical Politics.*[3] As the subtitle indicates, Walzer argues that the Puritans of seventeenth-century England were the first "active, ideologically committed political radicals."

As followers of the theology of John Calvin, the leader of Geneva's Reformation in the sixteenth century, the Puritan theology began and focused on an understanding of God as Sovereign Creator, Sustaining Providence, Electing Redeemer, Returning King. All authority came from the Sovereign God or it was illegitimate. Holy Scripture served as the revelation of God's will for man's affairs and was therefore centrally important and authoritative. Church and state were two different spheres but both were equally under the authority of the Sovereign God, and never under the authority of a human compact or contract. Of particular importance for us was the Puritan sense of human sinfulness. Man was fallen, totally depraved, and therefore in need of God's mercy. In the mystery of God's inscrutable electing will, however, some were not elected. The inward grace of God was not enough to control humanity: human government was instituted by God to restrain evildoers. Later on, this Puritan notion of human sinfulness, complemented by the Hobbesian notion of human selfishness, was to underlie the careful balancing of powers in the United States Constitution.

Puritanism also emphasized the idea of man's "calling" or "vocation," that is, one's work is not to be viewed as a matter of indifference or purely out of practical concerns; rather, even one's secular work is a "calling" to service for God. Sidney Ahlstrom argues that this concept was extremely influential in breeding a people who were serious, purposeful, and responsible in civil and economic roles. He also points to the great emphasis placed by Puritans on law (divine, natural, moral, and statutory). Law restrained, humbled, guided, ordered; it transmuted the ideology (or theology) into secular impulses.

> Puritanism . . . helped create a nation of individualists who were also fervent "moral athletes" with a strong sense of transcendent values which must receive ordered and corporate expression in the commonwealth.[4]

A further aspect of Puritanism which became a significant factor in the founding of this country was the congregational form of church government the Puritans sustained. This type of church government strengthened the average American's desire for a voice in political government and gave him some practical experience. Inadvertently, ecclesiastical localism prepared the way for a social compact as the only viable basis for a political unity broader than a local unit. Massachusetts Bay Colony itself was essentially a federation of towns or churches.

Finally, the Puritan was committed to the view that Christian conversion was supremely a matter of inward experience. Ahlstrom suggests that this heavy Puritan emphasis on inward experience helped prepare the way for the internalizing of European "natural law" theories into American "natural rights" theories. This is, of course, a subtle distinction, but an important one as it turns the focus more on man than cosmic orderliness, more on liberty than order and obedience, more on the individual than the nation.

Historically, Puritanism began in the 1620s and 1630s with the Pilgrims and then Puritans of Massachusetts Bay Colony. Its heyday was the seventeenth century as the colony became a model of a hard-working, successful, God-fearing society, a "city set upon a hill." As early as 1662, however, an important compromise was allowed: The Halfway Covenant allowed a kind of secondary membership (but membership nonetheless) to parents and children without the "inward experience." In simple terms, rather than risk losing the less spiritual children of the earlier generation now grown successful, the Puritan leaders compromised. By the end of the seventeenth century, further compromises of the early vision were made, at least by certain of the leaders. The principle of congregational autonomy, which all Puritans held dear, made effective discipline impossible.

Essentially, the influences which increasingly worked on a segment of Congregationalism during the late seventeenth and then the eighteenth centuries were those of Enlightenment rationalism. In religious garb this came in the form of deism and then Unitarianism, and will be described in the next section. A second influence which served to undermine the force of the original Puritan vision was simply the growing wealth and comfort, the success, of Puritan merchants and businessmen.

In the first half of the eighteenth century, especially in the 1730s and 1740s, a powerful religious movement, the Great Awakening, swept across the colonies, including the Puritan north, having a substantial impact in pre-Revolutionary America. The renewal was begun by English evangelists George Whitefield and John Wesley (the founder of Methodism). Americans, such as the Dutch Reformed pastor Theodore Frelinghuysen, Presbyterians William Tennent and Samuel Davies, and above all Congregationalist Jonathan Edwards, soon played major roles in spreading and sustaining the revival. Theologically, the Arminians (such as John Wesley) allowed more room for human freedom of the will in conversion than did old-line Calvinists (such as George Whitefield or even Jonathan Edwards). All of the revivalists, however, had an unashamedly supernaturalistic viewpoint, a high view of a sovereign God, a fear of hellfire and brimstone—in general, a real reverence and awe for the living God.

The Great Awakening thus "reawoke" certain important themes in America's Puritan and Reformed heritage. It also was significant in that the leaders of the revival were probably the first "American" public figures, and the first to plan their activities in explicitly intercolonial terms. A certain tying together of the colonial religious population was a product of the Awakening. The movement also broke out of the confines of the sometimes stiff and traditional formal structures of colonial churches. The implication was clear: people's willingness to stand up against authorities, break out of structural restraints, question old, well-established practices, were all encouraged by the revival. Their loyalty to the transcendent God and even to the intercolonial Christian movement challenged traditional and provincial ties.

Jonathan Edwards (1703-58) deserves special mention here for several reasons. He is acknowledged to be the most brilliant mind produced in the history of the American colonies; he was certainly the most important theologian in colonial America; his role in the Great Awakening was central, and his 1741 sermon "Sinners in the Hands of an Angry God" is a classic. Edwards was a powerful opponent of the accommodated, compromised version of Christian faith which he felt began with the 1662 Halfway Covenant and now was epitomized in the "fashionable new divinity" of the rationalists and deists. Edwards was thus important for reviving Puritan orthodoxy. At the same time, however, it is interesting to note that he was not only familiar with Locke and Newton, both of whom were claimed by the deists and rationalists as favorable to their position, but Edwards liked the work of both giants and brought the spirit of the Age of Reason into contact with the faith of orthodoxy without sacrificing either. Edwards was able to find the elusive point where truth stands in integrity and openness, without being prostituted for the approval of the age or buried by fearful conveyers of the old order.

Puritanism, then, was the first of two major traditions in the faith of the Founding Fathers. Its heyday was the seventeenth century, but it was revived by the Great Awakening just a generation before 1776; its center was Massachusetts, but its spirit and message were shared by most other parts of the colonial population to some significant degree. Its emphases included human fallenness and consequent need for law and restraint by a government, the government itself protected by limited and balanced powers, the equality of men as sinners (though election introduced another class) and of churches as congregations, the importance of law and institutions and serious participation by the citizens, and the influence of inwardness on "natural law" theories. These influences are to be seen in the Declaration of Independence but even more in the Constitution with its limited and balanced powers.

The Deistic Tradition

The second tradition in the faith of the Founding Fathers was deism. In fact, if we have to pick one word to describe their religious faith it would be deism, not Puritanism. The Puritan and evangelical influences were more subtle and covert; the deism was pretty explicit, especially on the part of leaders such as Thomas Paine, Thomas Jefferson, Ethan Allen, Benjamin Franklin, and

John Adams. If the seventeenth century was the Puritan era, the eighteenth century was the deistic era, at least among a large percentage of the educated and ruling classes.

Deism was essentially the result of the application of the rationalism of the Enlightenment of the Christian religion. That is, man's reason was made to sit in judgment on all truth. The conclusion was (negatively) a rejection of miracles, biblical revelation, the special divinity of Christ, and (positively) a belief in the inherent goodness and perfectibility of man, an optimism in man's reason and capability of achieving happiness in this world and the next, and the inevitability of progress due to the fact that the truth is self-evident to reasonable man. In 1695 John Locke's *The Reasonableness of Christianity* stated essentially this position.

John Locke (1632-1704), who also authored the *Essay Concerning Human Understanding* and *Two Essays on Government,* the latter of which was especially important in colonial political thought, was shifting the ground of religion from revelation to reason. Although Locke himself was not necessarily unorthodox in his conclusions as far as what he confessed to be true Christian faith, he nevertheless paved the way for thoroughgoing rationalists to discard the supernatural core of Christian faith. Isaac Newton (1642-1727) was the other forefather of the deistic position, accepting as true only knowledge that was based on observation and experimentation.

We have already noticed that some orthodox Christians, notably Jonathan Edwards, believed that any truth that Locke or Newton discovered would serve the Christian faith without undermining its cardinal principles and affirmations. Others were not so generous to orthodoxy. John Wise in 1710 is considered the first Puritan, Congregationalist pastor to radically depart from the historic faith. He argued for a rationalized religion based on natural law. Max Savelle, in his fine study of the colonial mind, argues that Wise "marked a step in the gradual turning of religion, in the America of the 18th century, away from . . . the glory of God toward . . . the happiness of man."[5]

Among the important religious leaders who followed John Wise in turning from orthodoxy to rationalistic religion, Jonathan Mayhew and Charles Chauncy must be mentioned. Both of them contributed to the development of deism and Unitarianism. Deism was attacked by Puritan orthodoxy for two main reasons: First, deism was at least Arminian (man is free and participates in his salvation) and usually even Pelagian (man is not inherently sinful) with respect to their doctrine of man. Second, deism had an Aryan view of Christ: He was great but inferior to God. This latter issue led to a rejection of traditional trinitarian Christianity, hence Unitarianism. God was the God of a Newtonian universe, governed by law, orderliness, natural goodness, the "best of all possible worlds."

The political implications of deistic faith and rationalistic optimism in human reason and progress were seen especially in the Declaration of Independence with its talk of "inalienable rights" including "the pursuit of happiness" (as opposed to the Puritan "pursuit of God's glory"). If men were free and independent, rational beings, human governments were derived from the consent of the governed and were concerned with natural rights, not cosmic order. Thomas Clap, the President of Yale and defender of orthodoxy, observed concerning the rationalists:

> If every particular Person has a Right to judge for *himself,* then surely *publick Bodies* and *Communities of men* have a Right to judge *for themselves,* concerning their own publick state and Constitution.[6]

Clap did not necessarily express the fears of other Puritan orthodox, of course, for the right to choose one's government could even more powerfully be rooted in the Congregational principle of government. Deism and orthodoxy pointed in roughly the same direction, but for different reasons: one was optimistic about man, the other pessimistic.

Faith of the Founding Fathers

A close look at the specific positions taken by some of the generation of the Founding Fathers will enable us to see the way deism held the reins, while the witness of Puritanism continued, nevertheless, to exercise some influence. The Founding Fathers were heirs of both Puritanism and Enlightenment rationalism. They were what I would call "chastened deists"—that is, their optimism in the powers and progress of human reason was qualified by a vivid sense of human sinfulness that was not often acknowledged by the mainline deists and Unitarians.

Although it was very much a minority position among the Founding Fathers, evangelical orthodoxy was represented by some of the leaders of the Revolutionary and Constitutional generation. For all of their political radicalism, Samuel Adams of Massachusetts, Roger Sherman of Connecticut, and Patrick Henry of Virginia were staunch evangelical believers. John Witherspoon represented another strong voice for orthodoxy in Revolutionary America. He had come from Scotland in 1768 to become president of Princeton and sat as a member of the Constitutional Convention. So these four and a few others of lesser note represented a strict orthodox faith among the Founding Fathers, but a strong Puritan/Calvinist or Anabaptist/Arminian evangelicalism was simply not the dominant "faith" of that generation.

Two of the more important leaders of the Revolution were Ethan Allen and Thomas Paine. Allen was the hero of Ticonderoga and a self-educated rebel from the Great Awakening. He was the only American deist to write a full-length, systematic outline of his deist faith. His *Reason: The Only Oracle of Man* (1784) attacked the Bible along with "priestcraft" and enthroned reason and natural revelation in their place. Allen said, "I have invariably endeavored to make reason my guide through the whole contents of the system."[7] Thomas Paine, the greatest pamphleteer of the war effort, also became one of the era's most important proponents of deism and rationalism. His *Age of Reason* (1794-96) was an important attack on orthodoxy and a defense of deism.

George Washington's religious affiliation throughout his life was with the Anglican (Episcopal) church. His speeches are liberally salted with references to "Deity" or God in one figure of speech or another. It would be unfair to pass those references off as mere political rhetoric of the kind we have come to expect from presidents (the required references to religion and God in certain political and diplomatic situations, etc.). Washington's personal theology was never systematically stated. In his inaugural addresses and his Farewell Address he argued that the "invisible hand" of a "great and glorious Being" ought to be acknowledged, invoked, and thanked—hardly ringing statements of Christian faith, but fine as far as they went! In his Farewell Address he reminded the people that "reason and experience both forbid us to expect that national morality can prevail in exclusion of religious principle."[8] Washington had a real appreciation for religion and faith and even prayer, but the God to whom he makes reference resembles the deistic providence more than the God of Israel who was in Christ reconciling the world to himself.

John Adams, the second president, remained a religious rationalist throughout his life and gradually moved into Unitarian Congregationalism. In 1813 he wrote, "The human understanding is a revelation from its maker which can never be disputed or doubted. There can be no skepticism . . . or incredulity, or infidelity here. No prophecies, no miracles are necessary to prove the celestial communication."[9] Adams was certain that religion was good and even essential as a basis for the principles of freedom and morality, but it was a religion of human reason, not divine revelation.

Benjamin Franklin read the English deists as a teenager and from that point on was a supporter of the moderate-to-radical deistic position. He openly admired his friend, evangelical revivalist George Whitefield, but does not seem to have absorbed any of his theology! Max Savelle has referred to Franklin's faith as a kind of "religious pragmatism." In his later life Franklin summarized his faith as follows:

> I believe in one God, creator of the Universe. That he governs it by his Providence. That he ought to be worshipped. That the most acceptable Service we render to him is doing good to his other children. That the soul of Man is immortal, and will be treated with Justice in another Life respecting its Conduct in this. These I take to be the fundamental Principles of all sound Religion, and I regard them as you do in whatever Sect I meet with them. As to Jesus of Nazareth, my Opinion of whom you particularly desire, I think the System of Morals and his Religion, as he left them to us, the best the World ever saw or is likely to see; but I apprehend it has received various corrupting changes, and I have, with most of the present Dissenters in England, some Doubts as to his Divinity.[10]

Franklin's faith was a common summary of moderate deism during his time: a benevolent and wise Creator and Providence, doing good as the essence of true religion; Jesus as the great Teacher of morals; some sort of immortality of the soul—these themes were the core of the faith of most of the Founding Fathers.

Thomas Jefferson, author of the Declaration of Independence and third president of the United States, was an outspoken and thoroughgoing deist. "Do we want to know what God is? Search not the book called Scripture, which any human hand might make, but the scripture called creation."[11] Jefferson spent a part of his life editing out forty-six pages of "unacceptable" parts of Jesus' teaching from the Gospels. What was left he called "the most sublime and benevolent code of morals which has ever been offered to man."[12] But Jefferson was very much a materialist (i.e., he denied the idea of a "spiritual reality" outside of nature), very much an opponent of not only his contemporaries in the clergy but of most interpreters of Jesus all the way back to Paul, for whom he had a special dislike. Jefferson's rationalism comes out in his writing of the Declaration of Independence in its references to natural and inalienable rights as the ground of political authority (vs. the Puritan grounding in the sovereignty of God).

In concluding this sample of the Founding Fathers' religious positions, Sidney Ahlstrom's recent comment is worth quoting at some length:

> Only an extensive essay could clarify the religious differences of the major Founding Fathers. They were all inhabitants of that "lost world" which Daniel Boorstin has delineated—a brief and beautiful flowering of confidence in man, education, and political institutions which Americans for over a century fervently and uncritically appropriated, and which all still honor even after seeing how far the country fell short of its founding principles.[13]

Faith and the Foundation of America

Religious faith had a substantial impact on the foundation of this country. First, the religious ideology of Puritanism and deism underlay the writing of the Declaration of Independence and the Constitution. In other words, much of what was institutionalized in law and political institutions reflected certain religious themes. The attempt to guard individual rights and liberty can be seen as the fruition of both Reformation individualism and inwardness and Enlightenment rationalism and dignity. The necessity and the potential of written law and constitutions had roots in the Puritan emphasis on human sinfulness as well as deistic optimism in man's ability to progressively order his life in compliance with rational and self-evident propositions. The form of representative institutions reflected the religious government of Congregationalism to a significant degree.

Second, the religious faith of the Revolutionary generation was almost universally acknowledged to be the essential rootage for morality and freedom. In spite of legal sanctions and constraints, man cannot be made "moral" or "ethical" nor can freedom be preserved without a religious (transcendent) referent. The Founding Fathers all recognized that morality is closely tied to religion, and that both morality and religion have a close relation to politics and other aspects of the culture (as de Tocqueville observed). Deism had sacrificed the theological affirmation of the meaning of Jesus Christ as God, Savior, and Redeemer, while retaining Jesus as Moral Teacher. The Founding Fathers' generation was "Christian" in the sense that a general commitment to biblical values and ethical norms was carried over.

The Founding Fathers would have disagreed with Karl Marx's argument that religion is always "superstructure"—a reflection of a social reality. For them religion was "substructure" and foundation for morality and society. The religious weakness of the Founding Fathers was their general trend toward rationalism: Human reason became the filter through which all acceptable religion had to pass. The misplaced arrogance of the Enlightenment thinker blinded him to the dynamic, supernatural redeeming God and King who came into our history in Jesus Christ. The rationalistic reductionism of deism undermined biblical revelation by its a priori presuppositions and cracked the foundation of both the religion and morality which they wished to retain.

We should not be too hard on the Founding Fathers in this area, though, for it is inherently impossible to institutionalize either religious faith or morality. Religion becomes a sham and a hypocrisy when its forms are enforced without regard to its spirit, which only operates voluntarily. We are living in an age characterized by the "loss of absolutes." Everything is relative, including religion, ethics, and even political means and ends. There is no intrinsic morality or purpose within the American political system. Where will the moral and ethical guidance for the political arena come from? Who will choose the ends and the means to which American resources will be devoted?

It is in the area of ends and means, of morality, that Christians can and must exert their influence. Pure pragmatism, technical efficiency—those "unvalues" will govern political action unless and until groups of people raise their voice sufficiently loud and clear and dare to live their convictions. Christians have a revolutionary loyalty to the Kingdom of God and its values. We are not subject to the caprice of what is "popular" or "efficient" but committed to what is godly, humane, loving, and just. From our position of loyalty to God and faithful witness to our earthly political habitat, we need to give modern de Tocquevilles ample evidence that American Christians are playing a critical role in her politics.

"Faith of the Founding Fathers?" Notes

1. Alexis de Tocqueville, *Democracy in America,* 2 vols. (New York: Vintage Books, 1945) 1:319.

2. Sidney Ahlstrom, *A Religious History of the American People* (New Haven, Conn.: Yale University Press, 1972), p. 347.

3. Michael Walzer, *Revolution of the Saints: A Study in the Origins of Radical Politics* (New York: Atheneum, 1968).

4. Ahlstrom, *Religious History,* p. 348.

5. Max Savelle, *Seeds of Liberty: The Genesis of the American Mind* (Seattle: University of Washington Press, 1965), pp. 29-30.

6. Thomas Clapp, cited in Savelle, *Seeds of Liberty,* p. 46.

7. Ethan Allen, cited in Savelle, *Seeds of Liberty,* p. 43.

8. George Washington, cited in Edwin Scott Gaustad, *A Religious History of America* (New York: Harper & Row, 1966), p. 126.

9. John Adams, cited in Gaustad, *Religious History,* p. 128.

10. Benjamin Franklin, cited in Savelle, *Seeds of Liberty,* pp. 41-42.

11. Thomas Jefferson, cited in C. Gregg Singer, *A Theological Interpretation of American History* (Philadelphia: Presbyterian and Reformed Publishing Co., 1964), p. 39.

12. Thomas Jefferson, cited in Gaustad, *Religious History,* p. 129.

13. Ahlstrom, *Religious History,* p. 368.

6. The Republican Vision of Thomas Jefferson

James W. Skillen

The historical events of the Revolutionary period in America were also the events that laid the foundation for the civil-religious and educational patterns of American life that exist today. The key historical events were the Revolutionary War itself, the confederation of the independent states, the eventual federation of the republic under the constitution of 1789, and the internalizing of democratic ideals in the early national period. One of the central figures in this period was Thomas Jefferson, whose vision of the republic, of freedom, and of education is at the center of the contemporary understanding of the place and meaning of schools in America. To understand American education and civil religion we must understand Jefferson.

Jefferson's General Philosophic Outlook

Thomas Jefferson, the botanical expert, architectural designer, experimental inventor, political leader, and intellectual enthusiast, is not usually remembered as a religious philosopher. His thinking about God and religion was, in fact, neither original nor unique. Nevertheless, as Robert Healey points out, "Jefferson's belief that a particular kind of God had created a particular kind of universe and a particular kind of man is the logical basis of the rest of his thought."[1]

What kind of thinker was Jefferson? Without doubt he was an Enlightenment rationalist in his deepest convictions about God, humanity, and the world, and the chief outlines of his thought provide an adequate summary of Enlightenment faith.

First of all, Jefferson returned to the classical Latin philosophers, especially to the Stoics, for his outlook on life. Not that Jefferson was a classical scholar, but as he matured he left behind the orthodox Christianity of his youth and built up a moralistic, patriotic religion of personal goodness and dedication to public duty, very similar to the religion of Cicero. Peter Gay summarizes Jefferson's stance as an Enlightenment figure this way:

> Machiavelli and Bolingbroke confirmed [for Jefferson] what he had learned in Cicero's *Tusculan Disputations:* contempt for the fear of death, contempt for "superstition," admiration for sturdy pagan self-reliance. It was from Bolingbroke that he copied this sentence: while the system of Christ is doubtful and incomplete, "A system thus collected from the writings of ancient heathen moralists, of Tully, of Seneca, of Epictetus, and others, would be more full, more entire, more coherent, and more clearly deduced from unquestionable principles of knowledge." Nothing displays the family resemblance among all branches of the Western Enlightenment more strikingly than this earnest entry in a young colonial's commonplace book; the heathen sentiment from Bolingbroke, intellectual parent to Voltaire as much as to Jefferson, went back like many such sentiments, to a common root: classical Latinity.[2]

Jefferson's religion was essentially a moral philosophy. God functioned in this moral philosophy, not as the historical Lord of Abraham, Isaac, and Jacob, not as the father of Jesus Christ, head of the church and Lord of the world, but as the benevolent creator who preserves humans in this life and judges the moral worth of each person after death. The center of gravity in such a world is not God but the moral life of human beings. Jefferson could advise his nephew, Peter Carr, for example, to take up the critical reading of the Bible, not in order to learn a specially revealed truth from God, but to see how much of this rather "human" book could pass the rational and moral test for truth. "Do not be frightened from this inquiry," advised Uncle Thomas, "by any fear of its consequences":

> If it ends in a belief that there is no God, you will find incitements to virtue in the comfort and pleasantness you feel in its exercise, and the love of others which it will procure you. If you find reason to believe there is a God, a consciousness that you are acting under his eye, and that he approves you, will be a vast additional incite-

ment; if that there be a future state, the hope of a happy existence in that increases the appetite to deserve it; if that Jesus was also a god, you will be comforted by a belief of his aid and love.[3]

The satisfaction of such a religion, as one can see here, is in the "incitement to virtue," the feelings of "comfort and pleasantness," the "appetite" for doing good that a person can obtain from the rational conclusions of a careful empirical inquiry. Whether or not God exists, whether or not Jesus is a God—these are incidental questions whose solutions have value only in terms of their usefulness for the moral life of human beings. In an important sense such questions need not even be answered; or at least it is relatively inconsequential whether they are answered positively or negatively. As Jefferson wrote to John Adams, my religion "is known to my God and myself alone. Its evidence before the world is to be sought in my life; if that has been *honest* and *dutiful* to society, the religion which has regulated it cannot be a bad one."[4]

Another important feature of Jefferson's "enlightened" view of life is his understanding of human life as animal life. Human creatures constitute a unique species of animal "whose humanity lay in . . . physical needs and physical attributes." The needs must be satisfied while the attributes are developed; "from these propositions Jefferson derived his doctrine of man."[5] Jefferson's anthropology, which regards humans as sophisticated, physical animals, stands in the line of modern thinkers from John Locke through the Enlightenment rationalists and Common Sense philosophers.[6] Moreover, the physical needs and attributes of the human animal require a special kind of adaptation and ingenuity in order to enable individuals of the same species to live and work together. This species has to create a social life designed to facilitate the satisfaction of every person's needs. For Jefferson nothing could be clearer than that the creator who made human beings with needs "intended all men to achieve satisfaction of their needs in the world in which He had placed them."[7] Thus humans came to accept the moral responsibility of creating a social arrangement capable of satisfying the physical needs of each individual.

Jefferson's view of human nature combines a physical, biological explanation of the world (including many species of animals, one of which is human) with a strong doctrine of human moral responsibility. This understanding of life is Jefferson's philosophy—a philosophy shared with many others of his day. This philosophy was also his religion; it provided the framework and the content of his belief in and relationship to the author of nature.

One of the linchpins of Jefferson's moral philosophy was his faith in "reason." Certainly Jefferson had no faith in abstract reason or in speculative reason—reason as a source of truth and ideas in itself. But Jefferson did put his trust in experimental, empirical reason, the kind of intellectual faculty that worked carefully with the "facts." Reason, for Jefferson, was even the ultimate judge of true religion, because in the deepest sense reason was Jefferson's religious guide and Lord. In his *Notes on the State of Virginia* Jefferson confessed, "Reason and free inquiry are the only effectual agents against error. Give a loose to them, they will support the true religion by bringing every false one to their tribunal, to the test of their investigation. They are the natural enemies of error, and of error only."[8] Jefferson's advice to nephew Peter Carr includes the challenge to "Fix reason firmly in her seat, and call to her tribunal every fact, every opinion. Question with boldness even the existence of a God; because, if there be one, he must more approve of the homage of reason, than that of blindfolded fear."[9]

It is striking here that Jefferson appears supremely confident in reason and its ability to be the self-sustaining judge of truth, even if God does not exist. At the same time, if God *does* exist, Jefferson is supremely confident of knowing exactly the "rational" preferences and desires of that God. Once again we are confronted directly with the *faith* of an Enlightenment rationalist. As Carl Becker observes, "The eighteenth century did not abandon the old effort to share in the mind of God; it only went about it with greater confidence, and had at last the presumption to think that the infinite mind of God and the finite mind of man were one and the same thing."[10] Whether or not God exists, reason is supreme and one can be rational if one chooses. The finite mind, then, can be in touch with, and is an expression of, that which is the supreme and ultimate order of the universe. To be rational is to be certain, to be right, to be human, to be moral, to be in touch with the true order of nature and nature's God. Jefferson's writings, consequently, always stress the contrast between reason or rationality and an opposite something that is wholly unacceptable. "Opinion," "superstition," "fear," "novelty," "fraud"—all of these are clearly the opposite of reason and her offspring.[11] To be fully human, one must follow reason, not opinion or superstition or novelty.

Reason, which supposedly uncovers the factual truth of the universe, is thus at the heart of Jefferson's faith. But despite Jefferson's practical empirical rationalism, his faith rests in more than scientific or intellectual reason. Rationality, for Jefferson, is also a *moral* ideal. Reason guides people in the direction that they *ought* to go. Rationality is the source of and guide to social order and harmony. Reason does not simply describe the "facts" of the physical universe; it also prescribes what ought to be and how human beings ought to live as nature's moral agents.

John Dewey emphasized this point years ago. Jefferson's view of life is moral through and through, observed Dewey. And morality to Jefferson indicates what is rational and natural: "To put ourselves in touch with Jefferson's position we have therefore to translate the word 'natural' into *moral*."[12] In other words, when Jefferson talks about nature or the laws of nature or nature's God, or about reason and the rational order of the universe, he is not talking about the physical, biological, psychological world alone; he is also talking about a moral universe in which the human animal *ought* to learn to live by reason in order to live in tune with the dictates of nature for the human species.

Another key term in understanding Jefferson's Enlightenment faith is *conscience* or the *moral sense*. Conscience is the human faculty by means of which nature and conviction authoritatively impress upon the individual the demands of duty to God and to fellow humans.[13] Of course, conscience or the moral sense should testify to what is rational. Jefferson, however, believes that the moral sense is autonomous, since not everyone does in fact think rationally or understand the dictates of nature and reason. Even though reason is the only sure guide to truth, Jefferson believes that every person (not just the philosopher) can "sense" or "feel" what is morally right by a direct, unreflective intuition. Thus, he treats conscience as a sixth "sense," independent of thinking, an intuitive receptor of moral guidance that no one can escape. In a letter to Thomas Law, Jefferson expresses his surprise that so many people could have differing opinions about the nature of the common moral sense which the creator implanted in all human creatures, making it "so much a part of our constitution as that no errors of reasoning or of speculation might lead us astray from its observation in practice."[14]

On the one hand, therefore, Jefferson starts from the observed "fact" that people do not all think rationally and correctly according to his assumed standard of what is rational. They do not all agree about the true order of nature or share the same opinions. It is necessary, in Jefferson's view, to be able to count on some sense within human nature by which everyone will "feel" what is universally right and good. On the other hand, Jefferson is confident that some people (including himself) can know what the rational foundation of morality really is. The truly rational person not only shares the universal moral sense with everyone else but also is able to rise above the clash of conflicting opinions, superstitions, and novel thoughts that belong to the minds of the mass of humankind in order to discover the unity and congruence of reason, conscience, and nature. In fact, the morally sensitive, rationally disciplined person is in a position to help shape and discipline the moral habits and consciences of others in accord with the truth.[15]

Within the context of Jefferson's thinking about God, humanity, and nature we can now give a brief account of the feature of his general philosophy that is perhaps most important for his social and political ideas. This is the doctrine of "natural rights."

The ancient Stoics conceived of the order of the universe as an eternal, rational, moral law-order. Human beings, in other words, could find and understand their place and identity in the world by coming to an understanding of the rational *natural law*. This philosophy was revived and enjoyed great influence between the Renaissance and the Enlightenment, and it had a tremendous impact on Jefferson by way of John Locke and Scottish Common Sense philosophy. Becker provides a valuable background description of this development, pointing to the general influence of Locke as a transmitter of the modernized Stoic outlook:

Locke, more perhaps than any one else, made it possible for the eighteenth century to believe what it wanted to believe: namely, that in the world of human relations as well as in the physical world, it was possible for men to "correspond with the general harmony of Nature"; that since man, and the mind of man, were integral parts of the work of God, it was possible for man, by the use of his mind, to bring his thought and conduct, and hence the institutions by which he lived, into a perfect harmony with the Universal Natural Order. In the eighteenth century, therefore, these truths were widely accepted as self evident: that a valid morality would be a "natural morality," a valid religion would be a "natural religion," a valid law of politics would be a "natural law." This was only another way of saying that morality, religion, and politics ought to conform to God's will as revealed in the essential nature of man.[16]

Even Garry Wills (who challenges Becker's assumption that Locke's general influence on the Enlightenment is sufficient to explain Jefferson's political philosophy) does not try to prove that Locke was not influential on Jefferson. Wills argues simply that the impact of Scottish Common Sense philosophy on Jefferson must be considered preeminent.[17]

Jefferson saw important connections combining the will of God, the order of nature, and the essential nature of human beings. God is rational; nature is rational; humans are rational. God's will is revealed not through any special unnatural revelations but simply through human nature and the rest of the universe. What a person discovers about himself and his natural, rational morality is the whole truth about human nature, just as one's scientific discovery of the order of nature is the whole truth about the nonhuman world. But if a rational explanation of everything is sufficient, if it provides an exhaustive account of all that exists, then there is no other "will of God" that could possibly transcend or remain hidden from human beings. The consequence of this line of thought is that nature, including its human beings, becomes deified; or to put it the other way around, God is fully rationalized and naturalized.[18]

By Jefferson's time, therefore, the old Stoic natural law philosophy had become a natural rights doctrine. It was a tenet of Enlightenment faith that nature's laws for human beings actually inhere in each individual and in the moral sense as a natural right. Take, for example, those familiar phrases of the Declaration of Independence penned by Jefferson:

> We hold these truths to be self-evident, that all men are created equal; that they are endowed by their Creator with certain unalienable rights; that among these are life, liberty and the pursuit of happiness. That, to secure these rights, governments are instituted among men, deriving their just powers from the consent of the governed.

Jefferson's appeal here (for a ground of firm truth and authority) is neither to God nor to God's eternal law nor to the Bible. It is simply to what is "self-evident" within the mind and common conscience of humanity; it is an appeal to the universal, rational/moral essence of human nature that corresponds to the true order of nature, which is God's will.

The universal testimony of the truth within a person is not merely that of an external order of nature but is the testimony of each person's inalienable rights. These *natural rights,* understood through simple, intuitive self-evidence without any need to appeal beyond the inner testimony of conscience and reason, are the sole basis for the powers and obligations of a government, according to Jefferson. The creator endows individuals with rights; he does not have anything to do with the creation of government or with the defining of its normative structure, limits, and tasks.

With nature, reason, conscience, and natural rights on such a firm footing, surely it is easy to understand how Jefferson could have been relatively unconcerned about the existence or nonexistence of a traditional deity. His deepest faith was in human reason and conscience as the judge of the truth. If nature has a God, fine; he will know his place. If reason does not find sufficient evidence for God's existence, fine; the self-sufficient world of nature and reason are enough to give firm direction to human moral life.

The Meaning of Religion for Jefferson

The place and meaning of religion in Jefferson's thought presents two aspects. On the one hand Jefferson appears quite irreligious. He remained unconvinced about a number of Christian doctrines; he was an Enlightenment materialist and naturalist; he was quite willing to base morality on natural reason and the moral sense without feeling an absolute necessity for belief in God; he was a moral philosopher, not a theologian or churchman in the traditional sense. On the other hand, we have seen that Jefferson approached nature and reason quite religiously. He had faith in reason; he did believe in nature's God; and morality was religion for Jefferson. Obviously then, we must come to a sharper definition of "religion" in Jefferson's thought if we are to understand his political philosophy, which included the principle of religious freedom.

In a letter written in 1809, Jefferson makes the following statement that substantially clarifies his religious position and circumscribes the nature of the problem we have just raised:

> Reading, reflection and time have convinced me that the interests of society require the observation of those moral precepts only in which all religions agree . . . and that we should not intermeddle with the particular dogmas in which all religions differ, and which are totally unconnected with morality. . . . The practice of morality being necessary for the well-being of society, he [the Creator] has taken care to impress its precepts so indelibly on our hearts that they shall not be effaced by the subtleties of our brain.[19]

First, note that Jefferson's idea of the purpose of religion's good precepts is the enhancement of human morality and the well-being of society. Human beings do not exist for the sake of God and religious service, but rather religion and God function to encourage human welfare. Certainly, therefore, Jefferson was not opposed to religion. To the contrary, he was interested in articulating a principle by which true and significant religion could be recognized. And in his case, the criterion was a rational, utilitarian one—the usefulness of religion for the individual and society.

Second, Jefferson makes it clear that the only kind of religion that passes the test of social and moral utility is the religion of universal morality. True religion, in other words, is nothing but universal morality; it is "the response of healthy and reasonable men to needs determined by general interest and social utility."[20] Only those moral precepts in which *all* religions agree, says Jefferson, are necessary for society to observe. The "particular dogmas" upon which religions differ, specifically those that are not directly connected to morality, are of no concern to society as a whole. They are, in all probability, wrong, and in any case they are socially irrelevant. Moral, socially relevant religion is universal morality—nothing more, nothing less.

Third, Jefferson's confession in his letter to Fishback reveals how we are able to discern this true religion of socially useful universal morality. The creator has impressed universal moral precepts on the human conscience in such an indelible way that not even the variety of opinions that arise in people's minds can alter these moral convictions. As we pointed out earlier, Jefferson recognized a variety of "opinions," "beliefs," and "ideas" among people. The independence that he granted to conscience or the moral sense was due to his belief that morality is and would remain universal, unvarying even amidst the variety of brain structures and opinions. Moreover, the common universal moral precepts, rather than peculiar and diverse opinions, bear testimony to what is the rational and natural order.

David Little summarizes the three points above in a succinct fashion when he says:

> As in everything else, the sure standard of the moral sense is the only norm for evaluating what is useful and what is beside the point in all religious traditions. By that standard, naturally, the only aspect of religion worth salvaging is the common moral core. The leftover dogmas and superstitions may safely be humored by an enlightenment society until they blow away in the wind, with the rest of the theories.[21]

It is a fair question how Jefferson's view of true religion squares with the religious "facts" of his day and with the views of other people. In other words, was there universal agreement among the Americans of Jefferson's day on a core of moral principles? What about those religious groups that did take their "dogmas" seriously? Were they willing to grant that their own "particular dogmas" were secondary to universal morality or perhaps even wrong? And if not, how are we to judge between Jefferson's religion (which then was not universal) and the religions of those groups that were not followers of Jeffersonian rationalism?

In the light of these questions, it becomes clear that Jefferson's letter of 1809 is really a statement of hope, faith, and what ought to be—it was a new ecumenical ideal. Jefferson recognized that the variety of human opinions would probably continue to frustrate any ultimate agreement on many issues. He fondly hoped that some human faculty other than the brain (namely, the moral sense) would bear testimony to what was morally universal, rational, and natural for religious belief. But even in respect to the moral precepts of humanity, Jefferson could really only say, as he admitted elsewhere, that "What all agree in, is probably right. What no two agree in, most probably wrong."[22]

But what precisely do all agree in? And do all agree that only what is universally agreed among them *ought* to be believed? And what about those doctrines that more than two agree in but which are not believed universally? Jews and Christians, for example, do not both believe in the Trinity, though both believe in God. Most Christians were quite unwilling in Jefferson's day, as now, to give up their faith in the "peculiar dogma" of the Trinity. Jefferson, of course, thought that just such a doctrine ought to be dismissed, and he had relinquished it. But this only demonstrates that Jefferson's own idea of the true religion was not universal, even though it was one that he thought ought to be universalized.[23]

Healey indicates that Jefferson's religion was based on what we might call a "common core" of religious belief, "a group of tenets on which all sects could be expected to agree." This core did not include "creed or dogma," says Healey, "but it did most certainly embrace the field of morality and also the rational or philosophic proofs of the existence of God."[24] What we have here, however, is nothing more than Jefferson's confession of the Stoically rooted Enlightenment faith—a faith in universal, natural, moral religion, which he insists should be the only true religion.[25] In fact, however, not everyone in America and Europe, much less in the rest of the world, was an Enlightenment deist.[26]

Furthermore, many, if not most, Christians did not agree with Jefferson that religion serves chiefly a utilitarian function for personal and social welfare. Nor would most religious groups of Jefferson's day have agreed that only the universal moral elements in all religions constitute the true religion. And clearly not everyone in Jefferson's day was willing to admit that a universal moral conscience exists apart from the diversity of minds, opinions, and special revelations.

But perhaps what is even more significant, Jefferson's religion was not a moral system exclusively; it included some important "particular dogmas" not directly related to morality. Consider, for example, Jefferson's conviction that the true religion of morality is a rational and natural religion independent of any special revelation. Surely this conviction is much more than a precept of the moral sense. Jefferson here articulates an argument, in fact a belief, that true religion cannot have any supernatural revelation as its source. Nature, reason, and conscience are sufficient for moral religion.[27] But not everyone agreed with Jefferson. Almost all the Christian churches stood on the firm conviction that apart from the special revelation of Christ and the scriptures true religion cannot exist.

What can we say then to Jefferson? Is the affirmation or denial of special revelation merely a moral precept of social utility, or is it a "dogma" over which people are divided, thus making it impossible for any universal religion to exist? Is the conviction about the validity of special revelation a conviction of the moral conscience only, or also of reason? Jefferson's rejection of special revelation was not, in fact, a universally accepted core precept, nor did it enjoy the simple and universal moral assent of all. The naturalistic rejection of revelation is, however, an integral part of Jefferson's whole philosophy, which cannot stand if peculiar and special revelations are admitted as possible. Jefferson, therefore, is not simply reporting the facts of reality when he writes about the only true and universal religion. To the contrary, he is involved in urging upon others (evangelistically proclaiming to them) a specific religious commitment and faith that entails conversion and the rejection of other religious faiths.

And what happens if other religious groups refuse to accept Jefferson's gospel? The logical conclusion is that they will have to be excommunicated, at least in principle, from the universal community of moral humanity, from the only true religion. In fact Jefferson is explicit in this regard with respect to Calvin and his followers. Calvin and the Calvinists, says Jefferson, are not participants in the true religion; they must be viewed as atheists. In a letter to John Adams in 1823, Jefferson explained:

> I can never join Calvin in addressing *his* God. He was indeed an atheist, which I can never be; or rather his religion was daemonism. If ever man worshiped a false God, he did. The Being described in his five points, is not the God whom you and I acknowledge and adore, the Creator and benevolent Governor of the world; but a daemon of malignant spirit. It would be more pardonable to believe in no God at all, than to blaspheme Him by the atrocious attributes of Calvin. Indeed, I think that every Christian sect gives a great handle to atheism by their general dogma, that, without a revelation, there would not be sufficient proof of the being of a God.[28]

Jefferson does not engage in any examination of the biblical evidence that Calvin used, in order to try to show that the biblical texts were illegitimate or that Calvin had misinterpreted the material. Jefferson does not engage in philosophic or scientific argument to show why the biblical (and other) materials used by Calvin ought to be rejected as evidence. No, he simply puts Calvin's idea of God alongside his own rational, moral idea and concludes with utmost sectarian dogmatism that Calvin's God must go. Nor does Jefferson's attack stop at Calvin. All Christian sects tend to insist upon revelation to some extent. They go beyond what is available to the common moral sense of everyone and thus simply give encouragement to atheists.

The meaning of religion for Jefferson is clear. He was indeed a religious believer, neither nonreligious nor irreligious. But his religion was a very definite, particular religion—the religion of Enlightenment rationalism that entailed the fundamental principles of (1) social/moral utility as its purpose, (2) universal morality as its chief content, (3) the "moral sense" as its infallible receptor, and (4) antirevelational rationalism as its discriminating judge of truth.[29] Dogmas other than the above Jefferson identifies as the products of the singular, novel, individual, and sometimes fraudulent "opinions" of people who do not limit themselves to the universal testimony of moral conscience but dogmatically build up "creeds" and "doctrines" on the basis of their own private ideas of "revelations" that are not rational or natural. From Jefferson's standpoint it is necessary to acknowledge the existence of churches and sects that are constituted upon such foundations, just as one has to acknowledge the existence of a variety of opinions among people as a consequence of the peculiar structure of each person's mind. But the beliefs of such sects and churches and individuals cannot, from Jefferson's point of view, be admitted as valid for the moral and religious foundations of society in the universal community of humanity.

The fact that the naturalistic religion of Enlightenment rationalism was not universal in Jefferson's day did not diminish his conviction that it ought to become universal. To the extent he believed his to be the only true religion, Jefferson was simply advancing, as an evangelist, a particular religion rooted in the Enlightenment ideal of a universal, rational humanity. Moreover, he advanced this religion over against the Christian religion, which had become thoroughly fragmented among competing groups of Protestants and Catholics that excluded one another and still excluded Jews. Jefferson hoped that his religion would bring *all* people together in a moral community on the basis of what was common among them.

The clear implication is that Jefferson's religion could become universal (and not exclusive) only if other claims to "true religion" were gradually dropped. Short of that, however, Jefferson's religion could function as the universal common denominator in the public realm if all other religious groups admitted to its authority while remaining satisfied to hold on to their own peculiar dogmas in a limited, private, nonuniversal realm. If other religions would fade away entirely after their members were converted to the Jeffersonian religion, then clearly Jefferson's hope would be fulfilled. But Jefferson's hope would be realized almost as fully if other religions were to admit that it was *not* necessary for them to dominate and guide the universal order of humanity in an institutional and structural way, and that they were willing to live as peculiar "sects" among other peculiar "sects" in an equal fashion, each recognizing in Jefferson's common rational morality the framework which could integrate them all in a universal order. Each religious group would then be free to hold its private dogmas without coercive support or impairment, while Jeffersonians would be free to organize the universal order on a common, rational, moral basis in the hope that gradually the peculiar "opinions" of the sects would wither away under exposure to the light of reason.[30]

The word *religion,* then, has two references or meanings in Jefferson's thinking. It can identify the true faith of rational, natural morality which is the universal truth. Or *religion* can be used with reference to the groups and sects of Christians, Jews, and others that hold on to their own differing dogmas and creeds. Obviously, in the first sense religion has very positive connotations for Jefferson, while in the second sense the word has distinctly negative connotations.[31]

One might imagine that Jefferson and his fellow rationalists had quite a difficult time convincing Christians of this distinction in the meaning of religion. However, such was not the case.[32] In the first place the Christian churches and groups thought of themselves as *religious* groups. They held their religion as their most important identifying characteristic. In their usage, *religion* was the term that referred to their special creedal, ecclesiastical, and personal commitments. And they were aware of the fact that a number of different religious "sects," "churches," and groups existed.

By contrast, Jefferson's natural, rational, universal morality had no ecclesiastical identification and usually did not even go by the name *religion*. It was, of course, as we have seen, a "natural religion," but Jefferson made very little of the word *religion* to identify it. The key identifying adjectives for his faith are "moral," "rational," "natural," and so forth. Thus Jefferson's natural religion was regarded not so much as a competing religion but as a philosophy for universal, moral order among all people, while the word *religion* continued to refer to the various religious groups other than the Enlightenment rationalists.

Second, most of the Christian groups saw their special religious doctrines and practices as wholly individual matters, involving their relationship to God, their personal relationships locally and in the home, and the condition of their souls. It was not at all strange for them to expect that in the larger realm of social and political order some general, universal moral principles ought to hold. The public political arena was viewed by many Christians as a primarily "secular" (this-worldly, *not* religious), rational, and natural arena. Thus Jefferson's principles for a universal morality could be accepted for that realm as long as they were perceived as part of a rational philosophy rather than as part of a new religion.

Jefferson, on the other hand, was concerned precisely with the public, political realm. The complex world of ecclesiastical and personal piety was of little interest to him. He was more than willing to have his religion accepted as a public moral philosophy since that is exactly what it was. Due to their own perspective, therefore, the churches and sects clearly did not understand that Jefferson's moral philosophy was a religion. While the religious groups held on to their different religious perspectives and allowed Jefferson's moral philosophy to fill the public void, Jefferson's religion was able thereby to become the public philosophy of the new nation.

Thus, the Christian groups reaffirmed their dualistic position in the world, accepting both their own particular religious perspective for private life as well as the common, public philosophy of Jefferson for their public, secular lives. Jefferson, however, stood fast with his integral, monistic view of life, discounting as useless and insignificant the "private" beliefs and "opinions" of the sects. The Christians held on to both religion *and* philosophy, religion *and* politics; Jefferson held a single philosophy of personal life and politics as an integral religious totality.

Finally, we should note that many Christian groups in early America were aware of the fact that their doctrinal and moral differences did and could continue to cause political conflict and turmoil when incorporated into the foundation of political order and civil rights. By the early part of the nineteenth century most religious groups in the United States, including the previously established churches, had been driven to the realization that another, more universal basis for religious freedom in the political order was needed than the one provided by the privileged establishment of one church. As long as they continued to identify "religion" with their diverse ecclesiastical groups, they could accept Jefferson's moral philosophy as a purely secular political instrument for public peace. The religious groups, not Jefferson, contributed the interpretative framework of a sacred (religious) and secular (not religious) duality in which the principles of nonecclesiastical, political life were seen as neutral, rational, and nonreligious. Jefferson, however, understood the principles of universal social and political life not as secular and neutral but as common, universal, moral, rational, and true; they were, very simply, the only principles which belonged to the true religion—the natural religion of universal, public morality.

"The Republican Vision of Thomas Jefferson," Notes

1. Robert Healey, *Jefferson on Religion and Public Education* (New Haven, Conn.: Yale University Press, 1962), p. 17. See also Daniel Boorstin, *The Lost World of Thomas Jefferson* (Boston: Beacon Press, 1966 [1948]), pp. 27-56.

2. Peter Gay, *The Enlightenment: An Interpretation* (New York: Vintage Books, 1966), p. 55.

3. Thomas Jefferson to Peter Carr, 10 August 1787, in James B. Conant, *Thomas Jefferson and the Development of American Public Education* (Los Angeles: University of California Press, 1970), p. 102. The letter can also be found in some standard collections of Jefferson's writings, e.g., Julian P. Boyd, ed., *The Papers of Thomas Jefferson*, XII (Princeton, N.J.: Princeton University Press, 1955), p. 16; and Saul K. Padover, ed., *The Complete Jefferson* (New York: Duell, Sloan, and Pearce, 1943), pp. 1059-1060.

4. Thomas Jefferson to John Adams, 11 January 1817, in H. A. Washington, ed., *The Writings of Thomas Jefferson* (Washington, D.C.: Taylor and Maury, 1854), VII, 56.

5. Healey, *Jefferson*, p. 41.

6. Note the thorough description and analysis of this anthropology in Eric Voegelin, *From Enlightenment to Revolution*, ed. John H. Hallowell (Durham, N.C.: Duke University Press, 1975), pp. 35-73. Some earlier interpretations of Jefferson, especially those of Daniel Boorstin *(The Lost World of Thomas Jefferson)* and Carl Becker *(The Declaration of Independence* [New York: Alfred Knopf, 1966]), emphasized Jefferson's roots in the philosophy of John Locke. Garry Wills *(Inventing America: Jefferson's Declaration of Independence* [New York: Vintage Books,

1978]) has challenged those interpretations by pointing to the distinctive character of Scottish Common Sense moral philosophy which is more likely to have been the primary influence on Jefferson. Our interpretation demonstrates the validity of much of Wills's reinterpretation while refusing to admit too great a difference between Locke and the Scottish realists when it comes to social and political philosophy. For further background see John C. Vanderstelt, *Philosophy and Scripture* (Marlton, N.J.: Mack Publishing Co., 1978), pp. 9-74; and Ernst Cassirer, *The Philosophy of the Enlightenment* (Boston: Beacon Press, 1951), ch. 3, "Psychology and Epistemology."

7. Healey, *Jefferson,* pp. 40-41.

8. Thomas Jefferson, *Notes on the State of Virginia* (New York: Harper & Row, 1964), p. 152.

9. Jefferson to Carr, 10 August 1787, in Conant, *Thomas Jefferson,* p. 101.

10. Becker, *Declaration of Independence,* p. 39.

11. See Healey, *Jefferson,* p. 174.

12. John Dewey, *Freedom and Culture* (New York: Putnam, 1939), pp. 155-156.

13. Elwyn A. Smith, *Religious Liberty in the United States* (Philadelphia: Fortress Press, 1972), p. 37.

14. Thomas Jefferson to Thomas Law, 13 June 1814, in Adrienne Koch and William Peden, eds., *The Life and Selected Writings of Thomas Jefferson* (New York: Modern Library, 1944), p. 636. See Wills, *Inventing America,* pp. 198-206.

15. Becker, *Declaration of Independence,* pp. 74ff.

16. Becker, *Declaration of Independence,* p. 57. One of the best studies of the background and development of natural law in connection with its modern influence is Leo Strauss, *Natural Right and History* (Chicago: University of Chicago Press, 1953), esp. pp. 81-251. On Locke see also Basil Willey, *The Seventeenth Century Background* (Garden City, N.Y.: Doubleday Anchor Books, 1953), pp. 263-292; and C. B. Macpherson, *The Political Theory of Possessive Individualism: Hobbes to Locke* (New York: Oxford University Press, 1962), pp. 194-262.

17. Wills, *Inventing America,* p. 175.

18. Becker, *Declaration of Independence,* p. 40. See also Becker's *The Heavenly City of the Eighteenth-Century Philosophers* (New Haven, Conn.: Yale University Press, 1932), esp. pp. 33-70. Cf. Edward S. Corwin, *The "Higher Law" Background of American Constitutional Law* (Ithaca: Cornell University Press, 1929), p. 59: "Between a universe 'lapt in law' and the human mind all barriers were cast down. Inscrutable deity became scrutable nature. On this basis arose English deism, which, it has been wittily remarked, 'deified Nature and denatured God.' "

19. Thomas Jefferson to James Fishback, 27 September 1809, in Saul K. Padover ed., *Democracy by Thomas Jefferson* (New York: Appleton-Century, 1939), pp. 177-178.

20. Healy, *Jefferson,* p. 160.

21. David Little, "The Origins of Perplexity: Civil Religion and Moral Belief in the Thought of Thomas Jefferson," in Russel E. Richey and Donald G. Jones, eds., *American Civil Religion* (New York: Harper & Row, 1974), p. 200.

22. Jefferson to Adams, 11 January 1817, in Washington, *Writings,* VII, 55.

23. Cf. Little, "Origins of Perplexity," p. 194: "There is no doubt that Jefferson took his own Unitarian position as normative, and, therefore, as superior to all com-

petitors. He fully expected, he said, 'that the present generation will see Unitarianism become the general religion of the United States.' He expected this inevitable upsurge of right religion because, as Americans became liberated from the foolish distractions of theological controversy and, accordingly, more eligible for guidance by sense perceptions, competing religious views would wither away."

24. Healey, *Jefferson,* p. 98. Note Jefferson's letters, cited above, to Thomas Law, 13 June 1814, and to James Fishback, 27 September 1809.

25. For background and further discussion of this argument, see Ernst Cassirer, *The Myth of the State* (New Haven, Conn.: Yale University Press, 1946), pp. 169-170; Healey, *Jefferson,* p. 115; and Cassirer, *The Philosophy of the Enlightenment,* ch. 4, "Religion," pp. 134-196.

26. For a brief survey of the actual state of affairs, see Cushing Strout, *The New Heavens and New Earth: Political Religion in America* (New York: Harper & Row, 1974), pp. 50-100.

27. According to Little, Jefferson "was certain that all conventional theological disputes, particularly those making appeals to revelation, were nothing but the 'charlatanry of the mind.' " ("Origins of Perplexity," p. 194). On this subject of revelation and miracles, see especially Jefferson's *The Morals and Life of Jesus of Nazareth,* in Andrew A. Lipscomb and Albert F. Bergh, eds., *Writings of Thomas Jefferson,* XX (Washington, D.C.: The Thomas Jefferson Memorial Association, 1903).

28. Koch and Peden, *Life and Selected Writings,* pp. 705-706.

29. Benjamin Franklin's confession of faith, as another example from this period, fits this same pattern. See Strout, *New Heavens,* p. 80.

30. Cf. Little, "Origins of Perplexity," p. 195: ". . . Jefferson did favor tolerating religious views other than his own, but only because he believed these views were quite irrelevant to the conduct of political affairs, and they would eventually wither away, anyway. But more important, he certainly regarded his religion as the obvious (and inevitable) substitute for all traditional versions of Christianity and by implication, for all other religions."

31. See Thomas Jefferson to Thomas Cooper, 2 November 1822, where he explains his desire to have different religious sects represented at the University of Virginia, with each maintaining its independence, to allow them all to mix with the mass of students and thus to "soften their asperities, liberalize and neutralize their prejudices, and make the general religion a religion of peace, reason, and morality," in Washington, ed., *Writings* VII, p. 267.

32. See Mark A. Noll, "Christianity and Humanistic Values in Eighteenth-Century America: A Bicentennial Review," *Christian Scholar's Review* 6 (1976):114-126; and Nathan O. Hatch, *The Sacred Cause of Liberty: Republican Thought and the Millennium in Revolutionary New England* (New Haven, Conn.: Yale University Press, 1977).

Study Questions

Were the Founders Christian?

1. Bellah describes a coming together of the Puritan covenant pattern with the classical republican pattern. Would you describe the mixture as Christian or not? Why?

2. What are the two major principles of revolutionary America's social consensus Bellah claims emerged from the Puritan-classical synthesis? Are they the same as the "fundamental principles of the Christian world view" Whitehead discusses in chapter 1? How are they the same? How are they different?

3. According to Bellah, what is the key difference between the "civil" (Calvinist, classical) and "utilitarian" (liberal) views of the public order?

4. In what ways do Bellah and Gill agree that the Declaration of Independence reflects Christian ideas? How do their arguments differ? From what you have read, do you believe the Declaration is a Christian document? Why?

5. Do you agree with Gill that even though the founders' generation was "Christian" in its values and ethics, deism held the reins in shaping the religious ideology that influenced the founding of America?

6. In what ways do Skillen and Gill agree or disagree about the "Christian" character of the founders' public philosophy? Do you believe it was Christian? In what ways?

7. Skillen argues that Jefferson's rationalist philosophy was actually his religion. Do you agree?

8.   Is Skillen correct in asserting that the church in America has adopted Jefferson's Enlightenment understanding of religion?

9.   In your view is Skillen correct in arguing that the restriction of Christianity's cultural influence to morals and ethics is the result of the dominance of rationalism, not Christianity, in our society?

Part III

Is American Civil Religion Christian?

To this point the readings have primarily focused our attention on the relationship of the Christian faith to the assumptions, values, and ethics of the broad public consensus of early America. In this section we shift our discussion from the moral and ethical character to the legal and institutional expressions of that early consensus. The readings that follow uncover the extent to which America's public and legal structures express a civil religion that is Christian.

The first two chapters of this section broadly trace the origins and development of America's civil religion. Rockne McCarthy's essay covers developments prior to the revolutionary period, and John Whitehead's covers those since. Both pieces discuss the benefit for society of a broad religious consensus. McCarthy is skeptical while Whitehead's evaluation depends on the degree to which the consensus is Christian. The next article, by Phillip Hammond, covers the same historical ground but focuses on the role of legal institutions in the evolution of America's civil religious consensus. McCarthy's final contribution summarizes the ideology of American civil religion and analyzes further its institutional impact.

Religious Freedom

In the section's first chapter McCarthy defines civil religion as "the public legal establishment of a religiously-rooted world-and-life view." Civil religion finds expression in the way people structure their public institutions, not simply in the religious responses of individuals and communities (as Bellah emphasizes). This point is similar to Whitehead's contention in chapter 1 that the world view (religious beliefs) of a society has consequences for the way the society is ordered. By showing how civil religion is reflected in the very shape of government, McCarthy wonders whether any state ever can avoid the imposition of some kind of "religious beliefs" upon its citizens. In raising this issue he touches perhaps the most significant (certainly the most cumbersome) problem addressed by these readings. The issue is religious freedom. How can a people of differing religious perspectives and incompatible world views practice the free exercise of such religious diversity and still sustain a single national community?

The question of religious freedom fundamentally underlies much of the frequently acrimonious debate over the "American" way of relating religion and politics. If Bellah were correct in chapter 3, those who tend toward the liberal philosophical tradition see religious freedom more in terms of the separation of church and state. They are fearful that groups such as the Moral Majority (which advocate a return to "biblical" foundations) want to use government to impose their religious beliefs or morality on everyone else. Those who tend toward the classical republican tradition see religious freedom more as an expression of our common way of life. They are fearful that groups such as the American Civil Liberties Union are already using the power of government to disrupt the widely accepted practices of our republic's common life by threatening the free exercise of religious convictions in public.

Both sides justify their positions as being consistent with American civil religion (that is, with The American Way). Both sides are convinced that their position can form the basis of freedom within national unity. Maybe Bellah is right. Maybe both sides *are* within the American tradition. One emphasizes the liberal pattern, and the other emphasizes the classical republican one. If so, then both really are faithfully "American," with their struggle being an expression of what Bellah describes as the inherent incompatability within America's civil religion. The legal and institutional implications of this underlying incompatibility are addressed in the following chapters.

Religious Domination

McCarthy begins by tracing the historical role institutions and structures have played in the fostering of civil religion. He explains how in the Middle Ages "the importance of . . . maintaining the integral unity of Christendom" meant that churches, schools, and other societal institutions "provided instruction within the framework of the assumptions and values of a Christian society." After the unity of the Middle Ages was shattered by the Renaissance and Reformation, this same principle for maintaining peace and unity was taken over by the new emerging states so that education was "carefully directed by the public authorities as a means of propagating and enforcing a peculiar way of life among the people." McCarthy argues that this was as true for the "civic" humanist Italian city-states as it was for the "theocratic" states of Calvinist Geneva and Catholic Spain.

Even though a variety of confessional groups emerged with the breakdown of medieval unity, McCarthy shows how "the new political structure of any given area still did little to protect the civil rights of religiously dissenting individuals, groups, and institutions." McCarthy emphasizes that it was this same understanding of "political structure" that was transmitted to North America. The colonists "attempted to keep the new political communities" in America "glued together by means of an enforced confessional homogeneity." He concludes by implying that such is still the case in America where an "educational establishment" has replaced an established church as the promulgating institution of America's civil religion.

In the next chapter Whitehead continues the story of the unfolding of America's religious consensus. His attitude toward it, however, is markedly different from McCarthy's. Although not advocating a "political structure" that would "propagate and enforce a peculiar way of life among the people," he clearly endorses the "Christian content" of the early American "system," and criticizes the fact that the content is no longer Christian.

Shortly after the Constitution was written, Whitehead explains, Christianity began to withdraw from the public arena into a "privatized" piety. Pietism inevitably resulted "in the church adopting a religious form of Platonism" which "created an unbiblical dichotomy between the spiritual and temporal worlds." This development was disastrous for Christianity and for America. Whitehead argues that Christianity "inevitably declines if it devotes itself solely to the inward life," and with such a decline, American public life became "increasingly open to domination by those with non-Christian views."

Following the civil war, Darwinism emerged to fill "the spiritual and philosophical vacuum created by the Christian retreat from society." Shortly thereafter humanism freely moved "into all areas of life . . . as a dominant thought form and force in American society." According to Whitehead, it was Christianity's failure to maintain its influence in American society that permitted the rise of secular humanism.

Whitehead defines humanism as "the fundamental idea that men and women can begin from themselves without reference to the Bible and, by reasoning outward, derive standards to judge all matters." Cut loose from the anchor of biblical absolutes, secular humanism sets up "a new system of arbitrary absolutes, a philosophical relativism that changes with opinion but that demands absolute submission to its arbitrary will of the moment." The only solution, he argues, is to return America to her "Christian foundation." Christians must strive against "autonomous, secular humanism" because it is "a religious ideology" that is unalterably opposed "to any other religious system."

Religious Pluralism

Whitehead's plea, of course, underscores the question which is of major importance to this section of readings. How can divergent, religiously held world views be accommodated within a single national structure? Whitehead's conclusion reflects a belief that they cannot (or at least should not) be accommodated. He seems to indicate that there can be but one "religious" tradition as the basis for an undergirding national consensus. If it is not biblical, it will become pagan. Therefore, talk of "religious pluralism" in this context, Whitehead argues elsewhere, is likely to be a ploy of liberal humanists to frustrate the efforts of Christians to return America to her biblical base.

In contrast, McCarthy argues that belief in religious unity (or consensus) as a prerequisite for national community is an unfortunate tenet of civil religion inherited from the Middle Ages. He argues later in chapter 10 that it has been used to justify unfair discrimination against those who have religious perspectives different from the dominant one (whether biblical or pagan). Therefore on *biblical grounds,* he argues it ought to be scrapped for a perspective that recognizes religious pluralism as a basis of national consensus.

Whether civil religion's thrust toward religious unity is an inevitability to be captured (Whitehead) or a tendency to be broken (McCarthy), it seems clear that the history of America's civil religion is the story of differing religious perspectives mixing and vying for cultural predominance. In the midst of such ambiguity, how has the changing shape of America's civil religion been clarified? Who has been "the keeper of the flame" for American civil religion? Phillip Hammond argues in the next chapter that it has been the law. Hammond, like Bellah, believes the churches have provided the moral and ethical symbolism of American civil religion. But it is the courts which have instructed citizens in civil religion itself. Using Emile Durkheim's conception of religion, Hammond shows how America's legal institutions are agencies for articulating and elaborating our civil religion, just as the public schools are agencies for socializing us into civil religion.

Understanding religion to be "the imagery (myth, theology, and so forth) by which people make sense of their lives—their 'moral architecture,' " Hammond explains that religious pluralism refers to a situation where one "meaning system" confronts another. Such was the case in colonial America, for example, where theists confronted rationalists, Puritans confronted deists, and Protestants confronted Catholics. He explores how America was led to represent her identity through a "uniting religion" which emerged out of diverse religious communities. Here "religion" means the expression of the integral unity of a community. So a unifying "civil religion" emerged to express, at the level of the national community, that which all the divergent religious communities within the nation held in common.

In this way religious pluralism in America meant that the churches "in some sense" became "less religious" since they no longer enjoyed "a monopoly in articulating the ideology by which ultimate meaning" was understood by the nation. As the churches became less religious "in this special sense," the law became more religious. In short, Hammond argues, "the history of the [U.S. Supreme] Court can be interpreted as a halting, hesitant, but 'inevitable' effort to perform for American society the religious task of providing a common moral understanding."

It should be noted that Hammond does not view the law's assumption of this religious obligation as a result of the recent rise of secular humanism. Rather, he traces its roots back to the impact of Puritanism on the common law and to the religious pluralism of early America. Puritanism legitimized religious pluralism by ending church monopolies. Thus Puritanism "left legal systems, especially the common law tradition, the task of formulating a new religion, so to speak."

Of course, much of Puritanism's theological conceptions were expressed in common law principles. But because of religious pluralism (or what he also calls "ethical diversity") among the churches, laws came not only to inform citizens what to do and what not to do, but also came "to assess the *morality* of what they did." The emerging common law began to develop a unifying "religious and moralistic character." He approvingly quotes G. L. Haskins as saying that "the common law was the 'cornerstone,' the Bible merely the 'touchstone,' of early Massachusetts." It was not that the Bible did not provide much of the religious symbol and myth for colonial American society. It did. But the institutions that shaped and promulgated America's civil religion were legal, not ecclesiastical. "The culture may yet have been Puritan at its roots, but the courts replaced the churches as the vehicle for expressing the moral standards of that culture."

The Meaning of Religion

Hammond finishes his essay by briefly describing how the court's understanding of "religion" has changed over the last century. Where once "religion" was equated with "Christianity" (however general and vague), Hammond points out that now the courts have come to the conclusion that "religion" for legal purposes means simply "conscience." "Having tried for a century to regard it on its own terms—as sacred, special, and compelling—courts realize the attempt is futile." It is futile, explains Hammond, because efforts to allow free exercise of religion, *because it is religion,* conflict with religion's "disestablishment." Therefore, the courts have been forced to articulate a "higher obligation" from the vantage point of a new common or civil religion that is not representative of any one "religious tradition."

Hammond points out that the court's attempt to articulate this higher obligation has forced the creation of a new rhetoric found in common law and developed in legal institutions. In this new rhetoric, procedure takes precedence over substantive precepts. (This movement from precept to procedure is precisely what Whitehead criticizes as a move from the "Christian content" of early American jurisprudence to the contemporary "arbitrary disposal of a judge.") Thus, concludes Hammond, because of religious pluralism the rhetoric of procedure becomes the new common or civil religion.

We should note several things at this point. First, Hammond understands "religion" to mean such things as ethics and morality, theological beliefs (myths), and denominational practices (traditions). Second, he sees colonial Puritanism as the source of civil religion's biblical "symbols" as well as its court-defined "content." Third, he adheres to the assumption that civil religion must be a "unifying religion" of "common moral understanding." It is on these points that Hammond's discussion with our other authors is most fruitful.

Hammond equates "religious pluralism" with "ethical diversity." He understands "religious traditions" to be expressions of theological beliefs (myths) outside of which courts may stand to articulate common, civil religion. He sees civil religion as giving expression to "the moral standards" of a community. Reflecting back on the argument in chapter 6, we recall that Skillen seems to suggest that Hammond is practicing a form of rationalism when he limits "religion" to ethics and moral standards, or "religious traditions" to theology. And, we recall, Skillen sees rationalism to be just as much a religion as Christianity. So Hammond's belief that the courts operate from a vantage point outside any one "religious tradition" is itself an expression of one kind of (i.e., rationalist) religious tradition. What Skillen implies, of course, is that when the courts attempt to formulate a "common religion," they are in fact favoring the promulgation and enforcement of their own religion over against other religions. In short, they are establishing religion.

Hammond's analysis of the impact of Puritanism on common law and on civil religion contrasts with Whitehead's assumption about the biblical base of early America. Whitehead argues that the Puritans' theism and belief in absolutes are quite different from the secularism and relativism of today. But Hammond's argument is principally a structural one, not a theological or ideological one. He agrees with Whitehead that biblical symbolism shaped the belief system of our early civil religion. He agrees that the reduction of the meaning of religion from "Christianity" to "conscience" has been a relatively recent development in the courts. But, he argues, since Puritanism provided the rationale for ending church monopolies on articulating the basis for the social order, another societal structure (i.e., the court) was forced to play that role.

Is it possible that in the very earliest days of the republic, Christianity sowed the seeds for the kind of judicial assumption of power that we see today? Skillen and McCarthy imply that at least two conditions would have had to have been present for this to be true. First, Christians would have had to believe that "religion" dealt only with churches and private beliefs and not with the shaping of a public philosophy. If such had been the case, breaking the monopolies of churches on articulating the social order would have been easily accepted. Second, Christians would have had to agree that a non-religious universal public philosophy common to all was both possible and necessary. If this had been the case, granting legal institutions the responsibility for articulating the common, unifying philosophy (civil religion) would have seemed perfectly appropriate. Skillen and McCarthy argue that both conditions were present.

It is interesting that both Hammond and Whitehead appear to hold the assumption that civil religion, whether understood as "common moral understanding" (Hammond) or as "fundamental principles of moral judgment" (Whitehead), serves as a unifying religion that provides purpose and meaning to the national community. In this they are at odds with Skillen and McCarthy who argue that religion involves more than morality. Therefore, in defense of religious freedom, Skillen and McCarthy say they must reject the assumption that civil religious unity is either proper or necessary. McCarthy expands upon his reasoning in the last chapter of this section.

Pluralism and Civil Religion

In chapter 10 McCarthy claims that the "very nature" of civil religion entails "the establishment" of an "nonpluralistic public legal order." He may be overstating his case here. At the end of his article McCarthy advocates a "political perspective that gives rise to a public legal order" which allows pluralism. It may be difficult to distinguish between a "civil religion" that "structures" a political order and a "political perspective" that "gives rise" to one. But be that as it may, McCarthy offers a challenging argument that explains how America's civil religion has operated ideologically to exclude from full public participation those whose outlooks differ from the "established" consensus.

McCarthy explains that the "theology" of America's civil religion consists of individualism and liberalism (he uses these terms interchangeably). The individualist liberal tradition, he argues, has dominated American political thought and the structuring of America's public order as few ideologies ever have done in any nation. Since this ideology represents a political perspective "based on certain fundamental religious assumptions about man and society," he argues that it is *"every bit as religious* as earlier established religions." McCarthy claims the religious *assumptions* underlying the dominant ideology in public life justify the assertion of a civil religion in America. This is parallel to, but distinct from Bellah's earlier claim that the use of religious *symbolism* in public life justifies the assertion.

McCarthy continues by discussing how civil theology has affected America's understanding of herself as a people and shaped her civil institutions (including political parties and public schools). McCarthy's main concern is the destructive results of civil religion on societal structures, such as families, schools, churches, and even the government. The "established" character of civil religion's theology does not permit true pluralism and has meant the distortion of governmental responsibility and the infringement of government (particularly through the courts) on other societal structures.

Civil religion, McCarthy holds, results in the "undermining not only of the structural identity and task of the state but also of many other societal institutions necessary for a meaningful life in modern society." What is needed, McCarthy concludes, is a new perspective that will break civil religion's "religious unity" assumption—the assumption that for social order there must be consensus on "fundamental religious assumptions." Because of the gospel, McCarthy claims Christians ought to work to break hegemonic civil religion by actively working "for the civil rights of all individuals, groups, and institutions in American society."

It is instructive at this point to compare McCarthy's point of view with Whitehead's. Both McCarthy and Whitehead fear and abhor statism (the expansion of governmental power beyond its rightful sphere). Whitehead would strengthen the federalism of the Constitution and thus limit the national government's power. McCarthy would promote a "structural" pluralism that would limit governmental power at all levels by recognizing the authority and rights of non-governmental institutions (such as families, churches, schools, etc.).

Both criticize and object to the privatization of religion (the dualism that limits religion to some "sacred" side of life associated only with private belief and spiritual discipline). Whitehead objects to it because he wishes to re-"establish" Christianity in public, to reassert biblical symbolism and ethos in public life. McCarthy objects because privatization leads to the public dominance of secularism, and secularism and Christianity (both being equally religious) ought to be treated equally in public.

Both are upset with the legal developments that have secularized the schools. Whitehead argues (based on America's religious heritage) that the courts should allow at least a generalized theism to remain in the schools. McCarthy argues that the courts should not favor secularism over religion in the schools (as if secularism were religiously neutral), but should treat both equally. Both acknowledge that American political activity and laws used to flow from the Judeo-Christian ethic. Whitehead urges Christians to work to re-establish this traditional "Christian" consensus of the nation. McCarthy urges Christians to work for "a truly pluralistic public legal order."

7. Civil Religion and the Foundations of the Republic

Rockne M. McCarthy

The nature of "civil religion" has been much discussed and debated in recent years.[1] For the purposes of this chapter we will consider civil religion from the point of view of the structure of the state and the responsibility of government rather than from the position of the religiously responsive individual or community. From the viewpoint of the political structure, a civil religion is the public legal establishment of a religiously rooted world and life view. Since modern states are made up of individuals, groups, and institutions of different basic commitments, the political establishment of one religion inevitably restricts the civil rights of those individuals, groups, and institutions that do not hold the established view, thus excluding them from full participation in the public legal community.

Given our understanding of civil religion, the questions with which we will be concerned in the following chapters include the following: Is a state free of religious impositions upon its citizens simply by virtue of the fact that it has no established church? Can a state avoid altogether the imposition of "beliefs" upon its citizens? Can it maintain a neutral distance from all religious matters? If a state remains free of entanglement with churches, synagogues, and other similar institutions, does it still run the danger of entanglement with religion by other means and through other kinds of institutions? How do schools fit into the picture framed by the First Amendment's stipulations regarding the relationship between government and religion?

While it is certainly true that major economic and social changes accompanied the formation of modern states, so did profound religious change. Indeed, the political struggles over religion were so basic and serious that they frequently outweighed social and economic issues in the minds of the factions that were attempting to create and control the new states. Moreover, while a twentieth-century American may have the impression that our country's political-religious struggles were all settled long ago, it is our contention that American federal and state constitutions have framed a civil-religious structure that perpetuates such struggles with respect to politics, religion, and education.

Apart from any questions concerning the personal piety and religious habits of individuals in the United States, the very political structure of the republic poses unsettled problems and dilemmas for contemporary America. In order to demonstrate this point we must begin with a brief exploration of some European roots of the American colonial experience.

The High Middle Ages

In what we now call the High Middle Ages of European civilization the church was more than a private association with limited ceremonial and educational functions. As one of the few differentiated institutions of medieval society it actually served as the chief integrator of cultural life. Joseph R. Strayer points out that economic life, Gothic art, chivalric poetry, scholastic philosophy, and the university system of education were all part of an organic, integrated, homogeneous culture.[2] The civilization of the twelfth century, he says, "was remarkably self-sufficient and self-consistent; it had a flavor, a texture, almost a personality, of its own."[3] The integral identity of this culture was due in large part to the shaping power of the Roman Catholic Church, a church which also functioned as the primary force in what we now call the state or the political community.

Strayer's comment about scholastic philosophy and the university system as central to the social structure of the High Middle Ages points to the role that education plays in promoting societal cohesion, identity, and unity. Education in both its formal and informal expressions is one of the means by which groups share together, defend, and propagate their deepest convictions about the meaning of life. In a rural, homogeneous community the family and extended kinships may be largely responsible for transferring these convictions and perspectives. In that situation it is often impossible to discover where the family leaves off and the larger community begins; education, transferring the wisdom and values of the community as a whole, remains within the family. In differentiated societies, however, formal education becomes more independent, so that the process of instructing the community as a whole is increasingly vested in schools and universities rather than in the family.

In the European High Middle Ages the importance of formal institutions of education for maintaining the integral unity of Christendom was well understood. In the cathedral and parish churches, guild schools, monasteries, and universities, the aim was to provide instruction within the framework of the assumptions and values of a Christian society. The medieval triad of *regnum, sacerdotium,* and *studium* expressed well the ideal of one commonwealth, one church, and a common academic study of the moral and natural law which undergirded the unity of culture and faith.[4]

Although medieval writers distinguished *regnum* (political authority) and *sacerdotium* (religious authority), the state and the church could not be divided. Medieval theory insisted there was only one society, the church, under one king, Christ. And although medieval writers distinguished between *studium* (education) and *sacerdotium,* students in medieval schools were in one sense all clergy, and the curriculum was essentially clerical.[5] In the Middle Ages the liberal arts, the *trivium* and the *quadrivium,* were pursued in the interest of the church, for the whole society, to the glory of God.

Renaissance and Reformation

The Renaissance and Protestant Reformation challenged and then broke the organic unity of the medieval world. The "conflict of spirits" that emerged was not confined to pamphlets nor contained within ecclesiastical and university debates. The question of political power could not be avoided. When the bloodletting of the Thirty Years' War ended in 1648 with the Peace of Westphalia, Europe was clearly divided religiously and politically with the consequences that each major confessional group was granted its own territorial arena within which it could become or remain dominant. Lutheranism took over much of Germany and the Scandinavian countries; Anglicanism eventually came out on top in England; Calvinism came to rule in Geneva, Scotland, and the Netherlands; Catholicism retained its hold in much of Central Europe and in Spain; and civic humanism grew to preeminence in certain Italian city-states. In all these different religiously and politically defined territories it was still assumed that education could not be a matter of indifference but should be carefully directed by the public authorities as a means of propagating and enforcing a particular way of life among a people.

The recovery of classical antiquity during the Renaissance meant that the ancient Greek view of education came to new life. Education was one of the special concerns of the Greek city-state or *polis*. Though the law appears to have been less rigorous in Athens than in Sparta, where the father could have nothing to do with the formal education of his son, Athenian children were, nevertheless, instructed by masters appointed by the political authorities. Plato made quite clear the motive for this: "Parents ought not to be free to send or not to send their children to the masters whom the city has chosen, for the children belong less to their parents than to the city."[6]

During the Renaissance many of the ideals of the ancient Greek polis reemerged to influence the Italian city-states. Guided by many of the same concerns that the ancient Greeks held, Renaissance scholars saw the need for public support of education. Vittorino da Feltre, considered by some the most important and successful schoolmaster of the Renaissance, argued that the state had a special interest in education. According to Vittorino, "The education of children is a matter of more than private interest; it concerns the State, which indeed regards the right training of the young, as, in certain aspects, within its proper sphere."[7] Although not all scholars agreed with Vittorino, it was clear that during this period nonecclesiastical control and support of education were on the increase.[8] Renaissance scholars and princes no less than the Greeks and medieval clerics recognized the importance of education in defining and holding together a people.

The leaders of the Protestant Reformation also recognized the important role education plays as a means of social integration. In Germany, for example, the Reformation undercut the power of the Catholic Church and swept away the existing ecclesiastical controls over the schools. To meet this new situation Martin Luther appealed to the temporal authorities, the mayors and councilmen of Germany, to increase their support for and control over education.[9] In the wake of the Lutheran Reformation the bitter conflict between the Catholic Church and the secular authorities over the control of education came to an end. City officials assumed full power over the schools, and princes established schools and universities throughout their principalities.[10]

Luther dealt with education in tracts and sermons and letters. His most important work on education, "Letter to the Mayors and Aldermen of all the Cities of Germany in Behalf of Christian Schools," was written in 1524.[11] The letter was the beginning of Luther's efforts to place education under the control of the temporal authorities. In Luther's mind compulsory education was a necessary part of the church-state establishment. The state, church, and school were all to play a crucial role in the articulation and support of a Christian society.

John Calvin was able to realize his ideal for education more easily than Luther. While Luther had to deal with large numbers of separate states and independent cities, Calvin had the advantage of being able to focus his attention on a single city-state. At Geneva Calvin fashioned a community in which education played an extremely important role in defining the city as a whole.[12] Calvin's understanding of the relation of state, church, and school was to influence, among others, the New England Puritans.

The competing world views that were represented in the different political-religious territories of Reformation Europe ushered in and guided the development of new political structures—the modern states. For decades each confessional group clung to the established principle of religious uniformity enforced by the power of the sword. "One faith, one territory" continued to be the accepted pattern of sixteenth- and seventeenth-century life. Although the medieval ecclesiastical unity had broken down and a variety of confessional groups had emerged, the new political structure of any given area still did little to protect the civil rights of religiously dissenting individuals, groups, and institutions. Within each territory political authorities supported a civil-religious order which in turn defined the cultural unity of the people.

The only major challenge to this political tradition came from the Anabaptist groups that emerged in the course of the Reformation. Desiring freedom to be left alone to follow their own understanding of primitive Christianity, they formed voluntary associations and rejected the attempts of political authorities to enforce religious uniformity. Viewing all civil authority as outside the perfection of Christ, Anabaptist groups rejected any political participation. The various European political authorities judged such a position to be subversive of the political order, and the Anabaptists were threatened and persecuted from all sides.

The Anabaptists were a people without political power or influence; they controlled no state in which to establish and maintain their own schools. They did not look to compulsory political authority to guarantee instruction in their way of life. That they survived prolonged persecution is a testimony to the effectiveness of their ability to sustain and transmit within their group their unique values and perspective on life without political support. They were, however, an exception to the rule of a people using the power of the sword to enforce religious and educational uniformity.

Early American Foundations

The settlement of the "new world" took place at a time when people still believed that every territory commanded a common faith. Among other things, America provided an opportunity for differing confessional groups to build social and political communities consistent with their world views. As Sidney Mead explains, the original intention of the colonists was to perpetuate the pattern of religious uniformity in the different settlements.[13] Thus the same civil-religious pattern exhibited in Europe was initially transplanted in the new world.

In the Puritan colonies of New England the faith of the "saints" guided their errand into the wilderness and provided the basis for the Bible commonwealth. In the Massachusetts Bay Colony the Puritans planted the seeds of a new civil-religious order. Even the Separatists at Plymouth put forth their beliefs as the basis of the public legal order of their colony.[14] In the South, and particularly in Virginia, the older Anglican religion was officially (if not fully in practice) established as the basis for the society which emerged under the first chapter of Virginia in 1606 and the Royal Colony in 1624. Likewise, in the earliest settlements in the "middle colonies," from the Dutch Reformed settlements on the Hudson to the Swedish communities along the Delaware, an individual's political standing was based in part upon his or her acceptance of the orthodox religious beliefs of the community. In each of the original settlements dissenting individuals, groups, or institutions were excluded from full participation in the political community.

The European understanding of education as a means of social integration was also imported by the first settlers that came to America.[15] In each settlement the colonists formed communities and developed educational practices according to their special visions of the pious life and of the good society.[16] Before long, two patterns became discernible in colonial America with respect to the proper role of political authorities in education. One position was that the government had a legitimate responsibility to encourage, support, and direct education. This arrangement was only possible, however, in religiously homogeneous settlements or in a political setting in which one group controlled the government and could use the power of the state to impose its world view through education on all students. In this framework a civil religious order came to expression in established schools as well as in an established church.

Other groups, however, took the position that the government should play only an indirect role, if any at all, in education. In a few of the colonies, especially those that demonstrated greater religious diversity, education was the responsibility of more than one group, none of which had sufficient political power to impose its view of life on all schools by political means. Thus the conviction grew, more as a result of historical circumstances than as a matter of principle, that government should not control education or perhaps even support schools at all.

Puritan New England was an example of the first type of educational pattern. In the Puritan settlements the central concern for establishing a Christian commonwealth was clearly reflected in the way government took an active role in supporting education. In 1642 the Massachusetts General Court enacted the first of a series of laws designed to encourage education. Municipal officials in every settlement were required to insure the children's "ability to read and understand the principles of religion and the capitall laws of the country."[17] It was not long before every family and town was required to provide a minimum of education for every child.[18] From its inception Massachusetts Bay was a commonwealth with an educational spirit, a true *paideia;* education played a central role in the Puritan vision of culture building.[19]

The role of the family was still primary in the early education of Puritan children. Although the early laws which established schools specified the need for literacy and job training, they did not require compulsory schooling outside the family. The family fulfilling its obligations to its children remained the center of the educational process. The state became involved in primary education only because parents began to neglect their duty to teach their children to read, to catechize them, and to train them for useful employment. Thus, the first schools were organized because the saints feared "the great neglect of many parents and masters in training up their children in learning and labor, and other implyments which may be proffitable to the common wealth."[20]

In the Puritan covenantal community, citizenship was limited to the elect, to full church members. Recognition of an individual's civil rights (voting, holding public office, and so on) was contingent upon that person's membership in the covenant of grace and the church covenant. Those individuals who were not of the elect but who nevertheless resided in the commonwealth were referred to as the "inhabitants." Inhabitants were required by law to pay taxes, attend the Puritan church, and obey the civil laws instituted by the elect, but they were excluded from the privileges of active citizenship. Only the elect were citizens. Since all education had to conform to the standards of the Puritan religion, the inhabitants were thus required to provide financial support not only for a church but also for schools that did not necessarily reflect or express their own views of life. The realities of Puritan civil religion were thus restrictive for all those that stood outside of the Puritan mainstream.

By the end of the seventeenth century the homogeneous religious character of Massachusetts Bay had disappeared. The saints had lost their full political control. But even before the demise of the Puritan experiment, the efforts of the General Court to raise the standards and tighten the enforcement of laws pertaining to public education were meeting with resistance.[21] Bailyn indicates that the Puritan ideal of an equal minimum of education for everyone "could not be maintained beyond the early period of religious enthusiasm and past the boundaries of the original clustering settlements."[22] The increasing size, diversity, and scattering of the population, the political instability occasioned by the colonial wars, and the continual shortage of public funds meant that support for education of the Puritan variety was limited indeed.[23] The waves of revivalism throughout the eighteenth century produced many schools, colleges, and academies, but they were the products of denominational interest and competition. Thus, the development of a statewide system of common schools would have to await the emergence of new ideas, new leadership, and new social conditions in the early nineteenth century.[24]

The second form of educational arrangement, in which the state played a very limited role in education, was the characteristic pattern in the middle and southern colonies. The failure to achieve the same level of educational establishment as in Massachusetts Bay was largely the result of the diversified religious character of these colonies rather than an indication of a lack of Quaker, Lutheran, Catholic, Dutch Reformed, or Anglican concern for education.

In Pennsylvania, for example, the Quakers found themselves in a curious predicament. On the one hand they were the proprietary party in the colony and were committed to Quaker education as an expression of true piety. On the other hand, they were heirs of the Protestant movements that championed religious freedom. The dilemma was resolved only by the exigencies of history.

Despite William Penn's original plan that the "Governor and Provincial Council shall erect and order all public schools," a common system of education could not be implemented in a colony that was so religiously pluralistic.[25] J. P. Wickersham has demonstrated that there is little evidence of public support for education in the records of the proprietors, the governors, the Provincial Council, or the General Assembly from Penn's time up to the outbreak of the Revolutionary War.[26] Penn himself seems to have decided, however reluctantly, to abandon his original idea concerning the relationship of state and schools in the face of the diverse religious opinions throughout the colony. In the last "Charter of Privileges," which was granted by Penn in 1701 and which continued in force until the adoption of the constitution of 1776, there was no mention of education. Wickersham concludes that without doubt Penn "intended to make education universal through the Province by public authority," but Pennsylvania "was so distracted by clashing principles, intestine feuds and warring factions" that the original plan was impossible to carry out.[27]

Pennsylvania did not follow the Puritan example of using the power of the state to attempt to propagate one particular world view through the schools. According to Lawrence Cremin, it was in the Pennsylvania experience that for "the first time in earnest . . . Americans had to contend with the dilemmas of public education in a pluralistic society."[28] Although the situation evolved more as a matter of historical circumstances than as a consequence of a conviction about what ought to be the proper relationship between the state and the schools in a pluralistic society, education in colonial Pennsylvania remained the responsibility of families and of the different religious communities.[29]

A similar relationship between government and schools characterized much of the South. In the case of Virginia, for example, the early government attempts to support education met with failure. The reason for the failure was not that the original colony was merely a commercial enterprise backed by the Virginia Company of London. Perry Miller reminds us of the extent to which a religious motive was behind the establishment of the colony by pointing out that within Virginia originally "the government was formed by a conscious and powerful intention to merge the Society with the purposes of God."[30] The Anglicans of Virginia were no less concerned than the Quakers of Pennsylvania or the Puritans of Massachusetts that their society, including education, should reflect the values of a particular way of life. Indeed, from the beginning of the Virginia colony in 1607, repeated attempts were made to educate both young Indians and the children of the settlers.[31] But neither the original efforts of James I to erect in Virginia "some churches and schools for the education of the children of those [Indian] barbarians" nor the first plans of the Virginia Company to build a public free school "for the education of children and grounding of them in the principles of religion, civility of life and humane learning" were successful.[32]

Those early attempts by the governing authorities in Virginia to support education were followed by other equally unsuccessful attempts. The continued failures can be traced, in part, to two causes. First, Virginia became the home of different ethnic and religious groups, as did Pennsylvania. In addition to the Anglicans there were Huguenots, German Protestants, Presbyterians, Quakers, Catholics, and others that settled in Virginia. To impose a uniform system of public education on such a diverse population could present enormous problems. A second cause for the failure was Virginia's plantation economy. Because the population was spread out on plantations and farms, it was extremely difficult to impose any type of uniformity. To a large extent the diverse population and the plantation system shaped the direction of Virginia's educational system and kept it from developing along the lines of that in Puritan New England.

In time what emerged in Virginia was state-supported education only for some poor and orphaned children. In the same year as the famous Massachusetts statute of 1642, Anglican Virginia ordered its county officials to "take up" children of disabled parents "to maintaine and educate them."[33] Those families who could pay sent their children to private tutors or private schools, while poor children had to do without schooling if they were not among the fortunate few to receive free public education. For the great majority of children whose parents did not provide educational opportunities there was no alternative. This remained the case in much of the South well into the nineteenth century.

The political structures of colonial America contained, for the most part, the essential characteristics of the European civil-religious establishments that took shape following the religious wars of the Reformation period. The old world had been left behind, but the colonists made their own attempts to keep the new political communities glued together by means of an enforced confessional homogeneity. Established churches were one of the means many of the colonies used to accomplish this goal. But closely associated with both church and state in the effort to nurture social homogeneity were the schools.

Schools have been and remain fundamentally important institutions for the identity and continuity of a people, whether that people understands itself as a "religious, covenant people" or as an "independent political people." Colonial America displayed a variety of means of providing for education. But the question that grew in importance during the eighteenth century, the period when established churches were slowly losing both their political control and their special privileges within the colonies, concerned the responsibility of the government for schools. If a uniform ecclesiastical confession could no longer provide the social glue for a political community, then how could that society be held together as a moral and human community? Would it be necessary for the states to set up schools to instruct everyone in the common way of good republican citizenship? If so, would there be any difference between a civil-religious order that came to expression in a church establishment and a civil-religious order that manifested itself in an educational establishment?

"Civil Religion and the Foundations of the Republic," Notes

1. Donald R. Cutler, ed., *The Religious Situation: 1968* (Boston: Beacon Press, 1968) and Russell E. Richey and Donald G. Jones, eds., *American Civil Religion* (New York: Harper & Row, 1974) are collections of essays that demonstrate the nature and extent of the debate about civil religion.

2. Joseph R. Strayer, *Western Europe in the Middle Ages* (New York: Appleton-Century-Crofts, 1950), p. 8.

3. Strayer, *Western Europe*, p. 8. See the excellent book by Walter Ullmann, *Medieval Political Thought* (Baltimore: Penguin, 1965).

4. Sir Ernest Baker, *Church, State and Education* (Ann Arbor, Mich.: University of Michigan Press, 1957), p. *i*.

5. Baker, *Church, State and Education*, p. 58.

6. Plato, *Laws*, VII, quoted in Fustelde Coulanges, *The Ancient City: A Study on the Religion, Laws and Institutions of Greece and Rome* (Garden City, N.Y.: Doubleday, 1956), p. 221.

7. William Harrison Woodward, *Vittorino de Feltre and Other Humanist Educators* (Cambridge: The University Press, 1905), p. 100.

8. Nonecclesiastical control and support of education were on the increase in part because Italian towns throughout the Middle Ages had kept control of their ancient municipal academies. The Italian towns also provided the freedom for lay teachers, like Vittorino, to conduct their own schools. It is reported that in the second half of the thirteenth century as many as eighty secular teachers were working in Milan, and in Florence the numbers were so large the teachers formed one of the largest guilds.

See Frederick Eby and Charles Flinn Arrowood, *The History and Philosophy of Education Ancient and Modern* (New York: Prentice-Hall, 1946), p. 819.

9. Frederick Eby, *Early Protestant Educators: The Educational Writings of Martin Luther, John Calvin, and Other Leaders of Protestant Thought* (New York: McGraw-Hill, 1931), p. 5.

10. Eby, *Early Protestant Educators,* p. 6.

11. For the full text of this letter as well as other of Luther's works on education, see F. V. N. Painter, *Luther on Education* (St. Louis: Concordia, 1928).

12. Eby, *Early Protestant Educators,* p. 7. For a fuller discussion of the role of the schools in Calvin's Geneva, consult W. Fred Graham, *The Constructive Revolutionary: John Calvin and His Socio-Economic Impact* (Richmond, Va.: John Knox, 1971), pp. 145-151.

13. Sidney Mead, *The Lively Experiment: The Shaping of Christianity in America* (New York: Harper & Row, 1963), pp. 17, 20.

14. In reference to Plymouth Colony, Mead points out that as the colony "prospered it made support of the church compulsory, demanded that voters be certified as 'orthodox in the fundamentals of religion' and passed laws against Quakers and other heretics" (Mead, *The Lively Experiment,* p. 17).

15. Lawrence A. Cremin makes clear that "the idea that schooling ought to be generally available for the advancement of piety, civility, and learning was accepted throughout the colonies: in New England, that acceptance was manifested by the actual existence of a substantial number of schools; in Virginia and Maryland, where scattered settlements rendered this less feasible, that acceptance was manifested by a continuing concern that more schools be brought into being. . . . Whenever it took root, schooling was viewed as a device for promoting uniformity, and controlling elements of society" (*American Education: The Colonial Experience, 1607-1783* [New York: Harper & Row, 1970], p. 192). Cremin's work is an excellent discussion of the complex history of education in colonial America.

16. For a discussion of the assumptions, traditions, and institutions of late sixteenth- and seventeenth-century English education, see Bailyn, *Education,* pp. 15-29.

17. Act of 1642. The Massachusetts Educational Laws of 1642, 1647, and 1648 are reprinted in David B. Tyack, ed., *Turning Points in American Educational History* (Lexington, Mass.: Xerox College Publishing, 1967), pp. 14-17.

18. The Education Law of 1647 stipulated that every township of fifty householders should provide a teacher "whose wages shall be paid either by the parents or masters of such children, or by the inhabitants in general" and "that where any towne shall increase to the number of 100 families or householders, they shall set up a grammar schoole, the master thereof being able to instruct youth so farr as they may be fitted for the university" (Tyack, *Turning Points,* p. 16). The following year the Massachusetts General Court passed another act setting forth specific penalties for neglect of the two previous laws.

19. Although the Puritans had organized their schools to preserve and propagate their way of life, it soon became obvious that those efforts were being frustrated by the secularizing forces of the seventeenth century. Will Herberg has pointed out that "nothing is more striking than the fact that, whereas the purpose of Puritan education was Christian, its philosophy and psychology were humanistic, harking back to Athens rather than to Jerusalem." Herberg, "Religion and Education in America," in James Ward Smith and A. Leland Jamison, eds., *Religious Perspectives in American Culture,* vol. 2 of Religion in American Life (Princeton: Princeton Uni-

versity Press, 1961), p. 15. For a discussion of the role of the Great Awakening and subsequent revival movements in the secularization of education, see pp. 12-18. On the meaning and significance of *"paideia"* and of the Greek roots of educational ideas and ideals, see Werner Jaeger, *Paideia: The Ideal of Greek Culture,* 3 vols. (New York: Oxford University Press, 1943-1945).

20. Law of 1642, in Tyack, *Turning Points,* p. 14.

21. Cremin, *American Education,* pp. 181-192, 520-526.

22. Bailyn, *Education,* p. 81. While support for education continued in Boston and other coastal communities, the neglect elsewhere "was so great that in 1718 the General Court condemned those 'many towns that not only are obliged by law, but are very able to support a grammar school, yet choose rather to incurr and pay the fine or penalty than maintain a grammar school,' and raised the fine for negligence to the considerable sum of £30" (Bailyn, *Education,* p. 82).

23. For a discussion of the problems of financing public education see Bailyn, *Education,* pp. 41-45, 108-112. For example: "Everywhere—in the middle colonies and in the South as well as in New England—the support for schools and even colleges came not from the automatic yield from secure investments but from repeated acts of current donation, whether in the form of taxes, or of individual, family, or community gifts. The autonomy that comes from an independent, reliable, self-perpetuating income was everywhere lacking. The economic basis of self-direction in education failed to develop" (Bailyn, *Education,* p. 44).

24. The assumption, as set forth by such nineteenth-century educational historians as Ellwood Cubberly, that the roots of modern public education are to be found in Puritan New England has been forever laid to rest by such contemporary historians as Tyack and Bailyn. Tyack points out that ". . . the Puritans' achievement in education is inseparable from their religious world view and from the trials they encountered in establishing a city upon a hill; it is misleading to read present views of public education into the Puritan experiment. The founding of public education as it is known today would stem from a new world view and new trials in the ninteenth century" (Tyack, *Turning Points,* p. 5). For Bailyn's similar comments see *Education,* pp. 3-16. See also Lawrence Cremin, *The Wonderful World of Ellwood Patterson Cubberly: An Essay on the Historiography of American Education* (New York: Teachers College Press, 1965).

25. Penn's statement is found in "The Preface to Penn's Frame of Government" written in England early in 1682. Extracts are printed in J. P. Wickersham, *A History of Education in Pennsylvania* (New York: Arno Press, 1969 [1886]), pp. 32-33. See also Thomas Woody, *Early Quaker Education in Pennsylvania* (New York: Arno Press, 1969 [1920].

26. Wickersham, *History of Education in Pennsylvania,* p. 52.

27. Wickersham, *History of Education in Pennsylvania,* pp. 53-54.

28. Cremin, *American Education,* p. 306.

29. A statistical summary of the kinds of schools and number of schoolmasters in Philadelphia between 1689 and 1783 can be found in Cremin, *American Education,* pp. 538-539.

30. Perry Miller, *Errand into the Wilderness* (New York: Harper & Row, 1955), p. 126.

31. Sadie Bell, *The Church, the State, and Education in Virginia* (New York: Arno Press, 1969 [1930]), pp. 21-23.

32. Quoted in Cremin, *American Education,* pp. 12-13.

33. Quoted in Bailyn, *Education,* p. 26.

8. From a Christian America to . . . ?

John W. Whitehead

The framers of our nation understood the need for Christian content in the system they were developing. The knowledge of God as revealed in the Bible was widely diffused in colonial America, although the America of the eighteenth and early nineteenth centuries was not Christian in the sense that great multitudes had a personal relationship with Christ. But it was Christian to the extent that the American citizenry thought and acted from a biblical (or Judeo-Christian) base. This fact has been noted by many historians, among them C. Gregg Singer in his *A Theological Interpretation of American History:*

> A Christian world and life view furnished the basis for this early political thought which guided the American people for nearly two centuries and whose crowning lay in the writing of the Constitution of 1787. This Christian theism had so permeated the colonial mind that it continued to guide even those who had come to regard the Gospel with indifference or even hostility. The currents of this orthodoxy were too strong to be easily set aside by those who in their own thinking had come to a different conception of religion and hence of government also.[1]

Alexis de Tocqueville, the French historian who wrote one of the definitive works on early America, *Democracy in America,* remarked:

> America is still the place where the Christian religion has kept the greatest real power over men's souls; and nothing better demonstrates how useful and natural it is to man, since the country where it now has the widest sway is both the most enlightened and the freest. . . .[2]

A dominant aspect of the Christian influence on early nineteenth-century America was the interest and energy it displayed toward the external world and society. This was a result of the application of the cultural mandate. But the gradual dominance of the pietist movement in Christianity changed all this. Philip Jacob Spener and his successor August Hermann Francke, turned Protestant Christianity inward; Christians began to abandon the cultural mandate to pursue the development of their interior spiritual life.

Although it began as a renewal movement, Pietism ultimately tended to degenerate into mere personal religiosity without much direct influence on society and culture. Religion became "privatized" and ceased to affect public life. The foundation laid by the colonists and the founding fathers was so strong that Christianity continued to pervade society for decades after Pietism. But eventually such influence began to wear off as the new generations of Christians turned inward and ceased any attempts to shape their society.

Although Christianity cannot survive if it neglects personal commitment and the spiritual life of the individual, it also inevitably declines if it devotes itself solely to the inward life. To be effective, Christianity must be both. The inward redemption must flow outward and affect the temporal world.

In *Redeemer Nation,* Ernest Tuveson, Professor of English at the University of California at Berkeley, notes that the dominant influence of early American Christianity began with the idea that God was "redeeming both individual souls and society in parallel course."[3] The religious revivals that dominated the early nineteenth century, as Harvard historian Perry Miller points out in *The Life of the Mind in America,* were not aimed merely at saving souls but also at redeeming the physical aspects of the community.[4] Simply put, colonial Christianity saw God as working in the whole culture, not merely in the hearts of men.

This attitude led to the abolition of the slave trade in Great Britain and effectively began the train of events that saw slavery abolished in the United States. William Wilberforce and others in England spent a lifetime fighting evils such as slavery because of their Christian faith and their determination to apply that faith's principles to the external world. In America Christian groups such as the Quakers fought slavery, applying their Christianity.

Even the early pietists were active social reformers. Unfortunately, the later wave of the pietistic movement looked inward. Their focus was, and still is, on the areas of life that were believed to be spiritual as opposed to the secular or worldly, including both politics and the arts. This view eventually led to a reduction of the Christian influence on the external world, leaving the field increasingly open to domination by those with non-Christian views.

Pietism, especially in its present form, stresses only the personal "salvation" experience. Bible study becomes simplistic, and any form of intellectualism is considered unspiritual. Pietism inevitably resulted in the church adopting a religious form of Platonism, the belief that the spiritual world is somehow superior to and above the physical-temporal world. It created an unbiblical dichotomy between the spiritual and temporal worlds.

The Civil War and Its Aftermath

Another force that diminished the influence of Christianity was the American Civil War (1861-1865), which played havoc with virtually every aspect of society. The social and spiritual upheaval it brought paved the way for the humanistic movement, which resulted from the introduction of Charles Darwin's theory of evolution by natural selection. Darwin himself never fully abandoned the conviction that there is a God. But by making man the product of "natural selection" rather than God's direct handiwork, he helped to rob man of a sense of responsibility to his Creator and of all obligation to heed the Creator's laws. Darwin himself remained a bourgeois, Victorian Englishman of traditional behavior and morality, but he effectively undermined traditional morality for the next generation.

Darwin's book, *The Origin of Species by Means of Natural Selection or the Preservation of Favoured Races in the Struggle for Life,* was published on November 24, 1859. All 1,250 copies were sold on the day of publication. Darwin set forth the concept that all biological life evolved from simpler forms by a process called "the survival of the fittest." Darwin's idea was popularized by Thomas Huxley. Herbert Spencer, who actually coined the phrase "survival of the fittest," extended the theory of biological evolution to all areas of life, including ethics.

In addition to removing the origin of man from God's direct supervision, Darwinism further undermined any normative, divine order to nature because now nature itself was evolving. The best is yet to come, so we cannot discern right principles of conduct from the natural order as it now exists.

George Bernard Shaw said that "the world jumped at Darwin."[5] In a sense, the world was waiting for a world view with scientific prestige to render the Bible obsolete, because the church, now so involved in Pietism, was not answering society's basic questions about the world and its meaning.

With the spiritual and philosophical vacuum created by the Christian retreat from society, humanistic thought (which had its roots in earlier eras, the late Renaissance, and the eighteenth-century Enlightenment) moved unopposed into all areas of life and became entrenched as a dominant thought form and force in American society. This led to the Victorian era of unadulterated, capitalistic rule at its best and worst, capitalism that knew how to develop the country both economically and scientifically but without compassion. It was, as historian Amaury de Reincourt noted in *The Coming Caesars,* a "merciless . . . age when social Darwinism ruled supreme. . . . With Roman-like ruthlessness, these Spencerian apostles confused mechanical expansion with historical progress and the very success of industrialization contributed to ensnare them in their own intellectual traps."[6]

As a consequence, J. D. Rockefeller could justify his industrial monopoly without restraint: "The growth of a large business is merely a survival of the fittest."[7] Likewise, Andrew Carnegie could expound on his conversion to Darwinism: "Light came as in a flood and all was clear. Not only had I got rid of theology and the supernatural, but I found the truth of evolution."[8]

Without the Judeo-Christian base, people were manipulated by the humanistic industrializers in what became, and still is, a pagan form of the biblical cultural mandate.

What, Then, Is Humanism?

The concept of humanism is somewhat elusive, particularly since some of its earlier forms were neutral or even positive. If one thinks of humanism as emphasizing the dignity of man, Christianity is in a sense humanistic, for it teaches that man is made in the image and likeness of God.

But humanism can quickly negate the Christian belief in man's fallen state and his need for God's revelation in the Bible. Erasmus of Rotterdam, the leading classical scholar of the early sixteenth century, supported some of the Reformation's cries against the Catholic church on the ground that Catholicism was no longer true to the text of the Bible. But he came to oppose Martin Luther and the Protestant Reformation because he vehemently objected to Luther's understanding of the Fall of man and its consequences. Even the relatively mild "Christian" humanism of Erasmus and others objects to any emphasis on man's fallen condition and his resulting depravity. Christian humanism all too often turns into a belief that man can arrive at ultimately valid and important truths on his own without recourse to God's revelation in the Bible, which is open rebellion against God and his sovereignty.

The term *humanist* was originally applied to those scholars who revived the study of "humane" as opposed to "sacred" literature—that is the works of pagan antiquity. Beginning with the reasonable suggestion that pagan literature was of some value, humanism, under the influence of Aquinas, went on to place it on the same level as scripture and then to ultimately rank it as superior. Humanism often begins with what appears to be an innocuous, altogether reasonable interest in the classics of antiquity, but it almost invariably ends in the deification of man and rejection of God. The Italian Renaissance rediscovered the beauty of Greek and Roman antiquity. For a time the Catholic Church sensed the Renaissance's doubtful and even dangerous characteristics and resisted the movement. Ultimately, Roman Catholics very largely compromised with humanism, leaving the criticism of humanism to the Protestants of the Reformation.

But modern humanism has lost even a tenuous connection with God by denying that there is any order to nature, and insisting that man is totally autonomous. Because of its connection with classical literature and art, early humanism often appeared much more urbane and sophisticated than biblical Protestantism. Today's humanism, however, has lost much appreciation for classical culture and is scarcely more appreciative of the *Laws* of the philosopher Plato than the law of God as revealed in scripture. The humanism that we encounter today is almost exclusively opposed to Christianity and indifferent to the pagan classics. But this sometimes escapes detection because there have been Christians in the past who were favorable to the older humanism.

For our present purposes, humanism can be defined as the fundamental idea that men and women can begin from themselves without reference to the Bible and, by reasoning outward, derive the standards to judge all matters. For such people, there is no absolute or fixed standard of behavior. They are quite literally autonomous (from the Greek *autos,* self, and *nomos,* law), a law unto themselves. There are no rights given by God. There are no standards that cannot be eroded or replaced by what seems necessary, expedient, or even fashionable at the time. Man is his own authority, "his own god in his own universe."

Historian Ralph Henry Gabriel has explained the connection between the humanism that appeared subsequent to the Civil War and the effects of Darwinian thought on Judeo-Christian theism:

> The appearances of an aggressive humanism, a new religion of humanity, immediately after the end of the Civil War is one of the more significant events in the history of American democratic thought. The objective of the religion of humanity was to secure and to protect a larger human freedom and to make men understand that liberty implies responsibility. Like Morgan, the post-Appomattox humanists turned to science. When the anxieties of war relaxed, there was a sudden impact of Darwinism upon Christian orthodoxy. Auguste Comte, who died in 1857, gave the world a positivist philosophy which affirmed that the theological stage in the progress of humankind had ended as had also the succeeding stage of rationalistic philosophies. Mankind, thought Comte, had entered, in the nineteenth century, the age of science; in this new intellectual world man was destined to become the master of his own destiny. Comtean positivism affected American thought at the moment

when Darwinism was challenging the old religious doctrines of the nature of man.[9]

During the nineteenth century humanists were thrusting their ideas into education, science, and the arts. Revivalistic piety, however, with its emphasis on the inner self, virtually abandoned these areas.

Unfortunately, the church has been all too willing to use the categories of "secular" and "religious" when no such distinction exists in reality. All things have been created by God. Thus, all things have their origin in God and should be under Christ's lordship. The pietist renunciation thus raises a core issue: the *lordship of Christ*.

To the true Christian, Christ cannot be Savior and not Lord. Christ is Lord over *all* areas of life—not merely the spiritual. Indeed, it is incorrect to make a fundamental distinction between spiritual and secular. Christ is Lord of the intellectual life, the business life, the political life.

If Christ is not Lord over the arts and science, then man is. This is humanism in practice. It was difficult for the church to dispute humanistic ideology because the church itself was practicing humanism by separating the spiritual from the totality of life and reality.

The Tension

We are all captives, to a greater or lesser extent, of the age in which we live. In our case we are locked into an age where humanism has come to full flower and is now confronting Christianity with a fierceness as never before.

Autonomous, secular humanism has replaced Christianity as the consensus of the West. This has had devastating effects, especially in the way man views himself. Now man has become only one part of the larger cosmic machine, some sort of dot in an improbably futuristic never-never land as posed in Carl Sagan's *Cosmos*. Perhaps man is interesting as a piece of evolving machinery, but certainly man is nothing that can command any final dignity, love, or respect.

Humanism, contrary to popular belief, is not a tolerant system. It preaches against religious "dogmatism," but imposes its own. Professor Harvey Cox of the Harvard Divinity School has noted in his work *The Secular City* that humanism, or secularism as he calls it, is an "ideology, a new closed world view which functions very much like a new religion. . . . It is a closed ism."[10]

Humanism is not only indifferent to alternative religious systems, but as a religious ideology it is opposed to any other religious system. Moreover, Cox believes that secularism is a menace to freedom because it "seeks to impose its ideology through the organs of the State."[11] The humanistic consensus is interested in eliminating Christianity, because individual Christians have an absolute standard by which to judge the system. Despots know very well the consequence of ideas.

The church's response has been inadequate, as Professor Berman has noted: "The significant factor in this regard . . . has been the very gradual reduction of the traditional religions to the level of a personal, private matter, without public influence on legal development, while other belief systems—new secular religions ('ideologies,' 'isms')—have been raised to the level of passionate faiths for which people collectively are willing not only to die but also . . . to live new lives."[12] As a result, Christianity has lost much of its public character as well as its political strength. Says Berman:

> For the most part, people go to church as individuals, or as individual families, to gain spiritual nourishment to sustain them in activities and relationships that take place elsewhere. . . . We are thus confronted with the combination of a "religionless Christianity" and what may be called a "Christianity-less religion."[13]

This problem has been multiplied by the fact that the Christian community, by and large, seems intent on only emphasizing such spiritual quests as personal evangelism. Although personal evangelism is an important aspect of Christianity, it cannot be the only aspect of the faith. The modern church seems to have—to mix metaphors—won some souls but lost the battle for society.

There have, of course, been exceptions to this rule of passivity. Francis Schaeffer's activity against abortion-on-demand is a good example. However, as Harold O. J. Brown states in the *Na-*

tional Review: "It is certainly significant, and in some ways unfortunate, that the symbolic leaders of middle-of-the-road evangelicalism have not seen fit to identify with the concerns of Schaeffer. . . ."[14]

The failure of Christianity to influence society has resulted in an America that is saturated with a new system of arbitrary absolutes, a philosophical relativism that changes with opinion but that demands absolute submission to its arbitrary will of the moment.

A Speaking Church

The solution to the humanistic crisis in values is a return to the Christian foundation that was reestablished and strengthened in the Reformation. It is a return to truth not simply for truth's sake but because the truths of the Creator work in the real world God has created—a world conceived to produce beauty, humanity, compassion, and dignity in his creation.

The silent church can no longer hide under the cloak of noninvolvement, as though it were neutral. Noninvolvement is choice. It is choosing to allow humanism to proceed unrestrained. Noninvolvement is, therefore, negative involvement. If the church continues its silence, the only option will be to capitulate and be dominated by a humanistic culture that will not tolerate Christianity. As this humanistic culture crumbles, we will no doubt see a continued return to the cruelty that characterized past pagan civilizations. In the end, we will come to be at the arbitrary disposal of a judge, a court, or even a führer, preferring arbitrary laws to no law at all.

"From a Christian America to . . . ?" Notes

1. C. Gregg Singer, *A Theological Interpretation of American History* (Nutley, N.J.: Craig Press, 1969), p. 284.

2. Alexis de Tocqueville, *Democracy in America* (New York: Schocken Books, 1961), p. 291. Moreover, Tocqueville noted: "Unbelievers in Europe attack Christians more as political than as religious enemies; they hate the faith as the opinion of a party much more than as a mistaken belief, and they reject the clergy less because they are the representatives of God than because they are friends of authority." (Tocqueville, *Democracy in America,* p. 300).

3. Ernest Lee Tuveson, *Redeemer Nation: The Idea of America's Millennial Role* (Chicago: University of Chicago Press, 1968), p. 12.

4. Perry Miller, *The Life of the Mind in America* (London: Victor Gallancz, 1966), p. 10ff.

5. Douglas Dewar and H. S. Shelton, *Is Evolution Proved?* (London: Hollis & Carter, 1947), p. 4.

6. Amaury de Reincourt, *The Coming Caesars* (New York: Coward—McCann, 1957), p. 179.

7. Herbert Agar, *The Price of Union* (Boston: Houghton Mifflin, 1950), p. 552.

8. Agar, *Price of Union,* p. 552.

9. Ralph Henry Gabriel, *The Course of American Democratic Thought,* 2d ed. (New York: John Wiley and Sons, 1956), p. 183.

10. Harvey Cox, *The Secular City* (New York: Macmillan, 1965), p. 18.

11. Cox, *Secular City,* p. 18.

12. Harold Berman, *Interaction of Law and Society* (New York: Abingdon Press, 1974), pp. 67-68.

13. Berman, *Interaction of Law and Society,* p. 72.

14. Harold O. J. Brown, "The Road to Theocracy?" *National Review,* 31 October 1980, p. 1329.

9. Pluralism and Law in the Formation of American Civil Religion

Phillip E. Hammond

While Rousseau is generally credited with coining the term "civil religion," analysis of civil religion in sociology has been influenced more by Emile Durkheim. Durkheim was, of course, an intellectual heir to Rousseau, but nevertheless a gap of great proportions separates them: For Rousseau civil religion is a sensible thing for leaders to create and encourage; for Durkheim it is an emergent property of social life itself.

On this rather simple difference hangs a conceptual issue obscuring almost all contemporary analyses of modern-day civil religion. Those influenced by Rousseau often begin with a bias *against* civil religion on the grounds that it is or easily can be an idolatrous fraud perpetrated on naive believers. Those influenced by Durkheim, by contrast, often begin with a bias *in favor* of civil religion on the grounds it is inevitable in any case and may—in its finest forms at least—be the transcendental expression of the profoundest values of a people.

Each of these points of view is therefore likely to have a blind spot, an aspect of civil religion left unquestioned and thus never made problematic in theory. For those largely in the Rousseau camp this blind spot is their difficulty in taking seriously the claims of a civil religion. Durkheim's followers, on the other hand, give little thought to the question of *how* a civil religion comes to be. This chapter addresses the latter question by looking at the role played by religious pluralism and law in the formation of America's civil religion.

Durkheim's Conception of Religion

Generally speaking, Durkheim's civil religion theory has been understood to mean that, to the degree a collection of people *is* a society, it will exhibit a common ("civil") religion. A corrupt, though understandable, interpretation of this theory holds that religion therefore unites a people or integrates the society. Such an interpretation is plausible, of course, if one reads literally Durkheim's definition of religion (what "unites into one single moral community"). Other statements in *Elementary Forms* are just as conducive to that interpretation (for example, *"Rites are means by which* the social group reaffirms itself periodically").[1]

But it is the fact of unity more than the fact of religion with which Durkheim begins. Religion is more the *expression* of an integrated society than it is the *source* of a society's integration. "Men who feel themselves united, partially by bonds of blood, but still more by a community of interest and tradition, assemble and become conscious of their moral unity," Durkheim goes on. "They are led to represent this unity."[2] Here is the key passage. It is in this kind of reasoning that Durkheim connects religion and integration—not that religion produces the cohesive society but rather that the phenomenon of cohesion has a religious quality.

This argument is not at all unknown. In 1937 Talcott Parsons observed that the real significance of Durkheim's work on primitive religion lay in his recognition not that "religion is a social phenomenon" but that "society is a religious phenomenon."[3] In other words, the very existence of society—the fact of stable social interaction itself—implies religion. The question is whether and how it is expressed.

Durkheim, of course, found religion expressed in the totemistic practices of the Arunta. The persuasiveness of his argument lies in the rather direct link between the *experiences* of unity allegedly felt by the Arunta and their ritualistic *expressions* of that unity. But Durkheim did not mean his theory to rest on the directness of this link. ("We cannot repeat too frequently that the importance which we attach to totemism is absolutely independent of whether it was universal or not."[4]) Had Durkheim lived longer, he very likely would have pursued the religious significance of societal integration in a modern context. When he asked rhetorically, "What essential difference is there between an assembly of Christians celebrating the principal dates of the life of Christ . . . and a reunion of citizens commemorating . . . some great event in the national life?" he was certainly hinting at this issue.[5] But it was only a hint. Was he noting that Christianity is no longer the language by which unity is expressed? Did he believe he could identify the "religions" that do express for modern societies what totemism expressed for the Arunta? Would he agree that these are "civil" religions?

Answers to these questions are not easy to come by. The analysis of modern civil religion gives evidence of one rather direct application of Durkheim's thesis—expecting in any society a reasonably close analogue to totemism. This work in civil religion, however, fails to deal with the "linkage" that totemism so conveniently provided. Why should a people, *dis*united by denominationalism, multiple ethnic traditions, class differences, and such be led to represent their unity anyway? Around what are they unified? Arguing they are unified by a civil religion may be a difficult task, but it is made easier if a plausible cause can be made for why a civil religion might develop in the first place.

This chapter therefore attempts to outline two related issues: (1) How has a single, uniting religion emerged out of the variety of Christian (and non-Christian) groups in American society? (2) Is this religion simply "there," to be expressed by those Americans who choose to do so, or are there structural settings (analogous to the "effervescent" phases in Durkheim's Arunta) where its enunciation is, so to speak, fostered, even compelled?

The common interpretation of Durkheim's thesis—that a society is integrated to the degree it possesses a common religion—is therefore given two twists in what follows: First, the major terms in the thesis are revised and taken to mean that to the degree a society is integrated the expression of its integration will occur in ways that can be called religious. And second, because conflict obviously endangers societal integration, wherever resolution of conflict occurs is a likely scene for the expression of this religion. In the religiously plural society, churches cannot resolve conflicts, at least between parties from different churches. But legal institutions *are* called upon to do so. Without claiming that legal institutions—and they alone—are responsible for American civil religion, I argue only that law has played a critical role in that civil religion's development.

In developing this argument I shall (1) take a close look at the notion of religious pluralism, finding it to mean much more than mere multiplicity of groups defined by ecclesiastical characteristics; (2) look at the historical form taken by pluralism in American society as a set of pressures to which responses were required; and (3) identify the "religiousness" of the response made by legal institutions. In so doing I am attempting to apply Durkheim's thesis to religiously plural societies and thereby show how a civil religion can develop.

Religious Pluralism

The term "pluralism" is widely used today by social scientists. At a minimal level it refers simply to heterogeneity. In the hands of political scientists, anthropologists, and political sociologists, for example, arguments occur over whether pluralism impedes or secures democratic government. Theorists also differ in their understanding of how pluralism works—whether it provides multiple channels to power holders or supplies group anchorage for would-be alienated individuals. And there is the intricate argument that pluralism permits multiple but contradictory group memberships, thus making political conflict erupt more often within an individual or a group than between contending political factions.

For all the specifications of "pluralism," however, the concept as used in political analysis almost always refers to heterogeneity of *groups*. And since modern societies commonly contain several religious groups, the notion of religious pluralism has been seen as analogous to or even synonymous with racial or ethnic pluralism.

There is, of course, nothing incorrect in this usage. Methodists *are* a different group from Presbyterians, just as Catholics are different from Protestants or Christians from Jews. Still, the incompleteness of this notion of religious pluralism is apparent if instead of denominational differences one looks at historicocultural differences: the Judeo-Christian versus the Islamic tradition, a Western versus an Oriental religious outlook, a mystical versus an ascetic perspective. What can religious pluralism mean if reference is not to denominational or group heterogeneity but to a multiplicity of nonempirical belief systems? Understood this second way, religious pluralism builds on the classical understanding of religion in sociology and therefore requires fuller discussion.

Is American Civil Religion Christian?
Pluralism and Law in the Formation of American Civil Religion

Whether formulated by Durkheim (a system of beliefs and practices related to sacred things), by Webster (that which finally makes events meaningful), or by Tillich (whatever is of ultimate concern), religion in its "classical" sense refers not so much to labels on a church building as to the imagery (myth, theology, and so forth) by which people make sense of their lives—their "moral architecture," if you will.[6] That human beings differ in their sensitivity to and success in this matter of "establishing meaning" there can be no doubt. Moreover, people certainly differ in the degree to which they regard historic, institutionalized formulations as personally satisfactory. Thus some are churchgoers and some are not; some would change the prevailing theology or ritual and others would not. Societies might be said to differ in whether they offer only one or more than one system for bestowing ultimate meaning.

Teggart asserted social change results from "the collision of groups from widely different habitats and hence of different idea-systems."[7] And if Teggart assumed human history records few stable "pluralistic" situations (that is, single habitats with multiple idea systems), he was very likely correct. The word "religion" in its plural form does not even enter the language of the West until the mid seventeenth century and does not become common until the eighteenth. Closely related words—piety, obedience, reverence, and worship—never do develop plural forms.[8]

Religious pluralism (in the sense "religion" is used here) is not equivalent, then, to a choice between Rotary and Kiwanis, the Cubs or the White Sox, the Methodists or the Presbyterians. Rather, as Teggart notes, the consequence for the individual of confronting competing idea systems is liberation from "traditional group constraints" and "enhanced autonomy."[9] Correlatively, Smith observes the word "religions" (plural form) comes into use only as one "contemplates from the outside, and abstracts, depersonalizes, and reifies the various systems of other people of which one does not oneself see the meaning or appreciate the point, let alone accept the validity."[10] In other words, though religious pluralism can mean the existence simply of religious differences, it can also refer to a situation qualitatively different from other pluralisms: When one meaning system confronts another meaning system, the very meaning of "meaning system" changes.

In the Western world this change is most readily seen in the separation of church from state—the explicit differentiation at the structural level of religion and polity. But as MacIntyre, referring to British society, contends, "It is not the case that men first stopped believing in God and in the authority of the Church, and then subsequently started behaving differently. It seems clear that men first of all lost any over-all social agreement as to the right ways to live together."[11] The accuracy of this time sequence determines the viability of the notion of religious pluralism being presented here: If the separation of church and state is regarded as only a political event, then churches are seen as voluntary associations, and pluralism indicates merely the presence of multiple religious groupings. Alternatively, if the separation of church and state arises from a situation of competing meaning systems (that is, is essentially a political response to a *religious* state of affairs), then the existence of multiple churches indicates something far more profound than simply a choice of religious groups. Needless to say, this latter interpretation of religious pluralism is the one used here.

My previous comments are no mere attempt to legislate the use of terms in sociological discourse. They mean to suggest that viewed in a certain way the concept of religious pluralism can have new theoretical importance.

John Courtney Murray, in discussing the "civilization of pluralist society," uses the notion of religious pluralism in both senses outlined.[12] First, religious pluralism implies different people's different histories—here Murray essentially is merely re-labeling those differences. Second, because discussion of concrete affairs goes on in abstract terms—in "realms of some theoretical generality"—pluralism implies the existence of different sets of terms, different realms. Discourse, Murray says, thus becomes "incommensurable" and confused. Compare MacIntyre's analysis: "If I tell you that 'You ought to do this,' . . . I present you with a claim which by the very use of these words implies a greater authority behind it than the expression of my feelings. . . . I claim, that is, that I could point to a criterion . . . you too ought to recognize. . . . It is obvious that this activity of appealing to impersonal and independent criteria only makes sense within a community of discourse in which such criteria are established, are shared."[13] Kingsley Davis says it more succinctly yet: "As between two different groups holding an entirely different set of common-ultimate ends, there is no recourse."[14]

Religious pluralism need not imply *entirely* different sets of "common-ultimate ends," of "impersonal and independent criteria," or of "moral architectures." But it may be argued that *some* level of sharedness must exist for institutions to exist, and religious pluralism would appear to reduce that sharedness.

But does it? Once a society permits multiple meaning systems to exist side by side, does it cease to *be* a society? Doubtless that can happen, but it is more normal for a society to work toward a new, more generalized, common meaning system. It is easier to form a social contract than for all to go to war against all. Still, as is now recognized, "mere" social agreement, a rationally derived document, is insufficient. Commitment to its rightness is also required. Every contract has its noncontractual element, Durkheim said; every legal order possesses its charismatic quality, Weber noted. And that noncontractual element, that charismatic quality, that commitment is articulated finally in terms that are (by definition) "religious." In a single society, then, can more than one set of religious terms exist? And if they coexist, can they continue to function as they are thought to function in a society with a religious monopoly?

Obviously, individuals do not generally confront each other's "moral architectures" in any direct fashion. Such situations do arise, of course, but manifestations of moral commitments more often occur as *institutional* conflicts and conflict resolution. The city government decides between road improvement and welfare payments. The corporation chooses to reward longevity or quality of service. The church elects to immerse or sprinkle. The citizenry is ordered to stop plowing and go to war. In all such instances (assuming the absence of sheer coercion) persons feel—or can come to feel—an *obligation* to justify their behavior. But this is not because of any prerecognized specific norm; there is no detailed prescription for every conceivable act. Rather, the obligation is in "realms of some theoretical generality," to use Murray's phrase. It is, as Talcott Parsons notes, a "generalized obligation" that is morally binding. A person or an institution demonstrates integrity not only by choosing right from wrong in a concrete situation but by maintaining a "commitment to the pattern over a wide range of different actual and political decisions, in differing situations, with differing consequences and levels of predictability of such consequences."[15]

Such commitment in any but the simplest, thoroughly ascribed society must be to a "generalized symbolic medium," not to specific norms.[16] Given the integrative potential of such a generalized symbolic medium—of action, policy to policy, person to person—the question can be raised whether in a single society more than one such medium can exist. Or if "pluralism" exists, can any one medium command the same commitment it might in a monopolistic situation?

The relation between a "generalized symbolic medium of values" and what I earlier referred to as "moral architecture" or "set of religious terms" is quite clear and has long been recognized. The "primary moral leadership in many societies," Parsons writes, "has been grounded in religious bodies, especially their professional elements such as priesthoods."[17]

Religious pluralism, as just interpreted, clearly has had enormous impact on those institutions regarded as religious before pluralization: churches, clergy, theology, and so forth. In some sense they become "less" religious if they no longer enjoy a monopoly in articulating the ideology by which ultimate meaning is bestowed. Reduction in ecclesiastical power, the transformation of ritual into a "leisure" time activity, and the "privatizing" in general of theology into pastoral counseling or religious "preference" all reflect this altered status.

If churches become less religious in some ways, some other places in the social structure may become *more* religious. If pressures are great in a society for a single generalized symbolic medium, a single reality-defining agency, and churches no longer are the targets of those pressures, the pressures will be exerted elsewhere. It is my contention that in America *legal* institutions feel those pressures greatly, that portrayal of the sacred or articulation of the charismatic tends to be expected of them. In this special sense the law has become more "religious." The pages that follow show how a "common American religion" emerged from religious pluralism and illustrate how current legal institutions express that common religion. In these efforts the Durkheimian blind spot is overcome; I will be investigating just how a civil religion—in this case America's—came to be.

Religion and Law

The impact of Puritanism on the common law is now widely acknowledged.[18] David Little has traced the close connections between Puritan theology and early seventeenth-century common law.[19] Considering the volatility of the seventeenth century, it is hardly surprising that religious and legal reformation possessed common elements. But tracing out those elements in detail is, as Little shows, an exceedingly difficult task. For example, the codifying common lawyer, Sir Edward Coke, remained a loyal Anglican all his life, paying no special attention to Puritan theological debates going on at the time. And yet in the jurisdictional struggle between church courts and common law courts Coke not only claimed the latter's superiority but justified the claim by reference to common law tradition.[20] In so doing he effectively sided with Puritanism in its struggle against Anglican traditionalism.

Pound's assertion of Puritanism's "impact" is not well documented. It does little more than show how "individualism" in the common law had analogues in Puritanism, but as Pound himself makes clear, this individualism in the common law has many other roots. Moreover, Puritanism may have contributed (or did contribute) as much to a renewed interest in "collectivism" in the law, considering the stress it placed on the covenant, on the "contractualism" it posited between man and God or man and man. David Little claims "explicit Puritan influence on the particulars of common law was nil." Nevertheless, he continues, "It is my contention that the concurrence of important tensions and changes in legal and religious outlook toward the end of the sixteenth and at the beginning of the seventeenth centuries is more than coincidence. In this I believe I am not far from Pound's interest . . . [in his effort] to understand how a system of law comes to embody and perpetuate a general way of looking at social life—a special system of values."[21]

The argument by which Little so carefully weaves together these two entities—Puritanism and common law—does not follow

Pound, then, in method. He does not see a *direct* impact of one on the other. Instead Little argues the common law was in a fluid state at the time, seeking principles of legal interpretation for frequent new activites and conflicts. Where might such principles be found? More accurately, perhaps, how might they be articulated? Little's answer is twofold: First, the religious revolution of the seventeenth century—a revolution that defined new "order" in the church, in the parish, in the "priesthood of all believers," and in social life generally—provided an ideologically parallel case. Second, Puritan theological conceptions found outlet in the common law's articulation of its principles. "Obviously, the crown and the courts could not work together indefinitely so long as each was making the kind of claims to authority it was. A solution had to be found, but it would have to come from sources other than the old English order [that is, the "ancient realm or the Anglican tradition"]. . . . The deep-seated tensions of early seventeenth-century English society had to be solved by some rather novel rearrangements of political and legal insitutions."[22] In other words, Puritanism was an "ordering" ideology *available* to a common law seeking theoretical foundation.

What is underplayed in this approach, however, is the additional role Puritan theology played in *legitimizing* religious pluralism. Calvinism, Anabaptism, and subsequent "Protestantisms" contributed a new interpretation of order; but *they also provided a theological rationale for ending church monopolies on articulating that order,* thus pressuring legal institutions into the attempt themselves. As one historian of nationalism puts it: "The Protestant Revolution, by disrupting the Catholic Church and subjecting the Christian community to national variations of form and substance, dissolved much of the intellectual and moral cement which had long held European peoples together. At the same time it gave religious sanction to the notion, already latent, that each people, and each alone, possessed a pure faith and a divine mission."[23]

Puritanism, then, did more than offer an alternative articulation of social values for seventeenth-century England even as it did more than provide parallel support to common lawyers in their fight against traditionalism. In addition, though not all at once, of course, Puritanism forced onto society's agenda the item of pluralism, the question of "religious liberty," the separation of church and state, the matter of "intellectual and moral cement." In so doing it left legal systems, especially the common law tradition, the task of formulating a new religion, so to speak. This process is most clearly evidenced in the activity surrounding the U.S. Supreme Court, to which I turn presently. First, however, I must take two intermediate steps.

The first concerns the doctrine of religious liberty. I have just argued that Protestantism provided a theological rationale for ending church monopoly. Any doctrine of religious liberty will lead to the separation of civil authority from matters of faith, hence possibly to pluralism. But inasmuch as Zwingli's Zurich, Calvin's Geneva, or Puritan New England are ordinarily seen as having been religiously *in*tolerant, the task of tracing the establishment of religious liberty is a critical one.

The first *idea* of religious freedom is, of course, lost to history, but it may be accurate to suggest 1523 as a significant date in the *social structuring* of the idea in the West. In October of that year Conrad Grebel and others (who "became" the Anabaptist movement) challenged Zwingli's use of civil power to enforce religious conformity. Bender highlights it thus: "Here is where the first break in the Reformation occurred that led inevitably to the founding of Anabaptism. In 1523-25, at Zurich, are the crossroads from which two roads lead down through history: the road of the free church of committed Christians separated from the state with full religious liberty, and the road of the state church, territorially fixed, depending on state support, and forcibly suppressing all divergence, the road of intolerance and persecution."[24]

The "logic" of religious toleration was established, then, even though occasions of reneging were obviously frequent. Thus Geneva must be considered a theocracy by all accounts, but Calvinism's English counterparts, the Presbyterians, really had no rebuttal for their "leftist Puritan" challenger, Henry Robinson. A real commitment to the doctrine of predestination, he said, precluded religious persecution. Those not elected by God could not possibly be saved; "uniformity of profession" cannot be confused with "certainty of grace."[25] A doctrine of religious liberty and therefore of pluralism was clearly implied here, even if its widespread institutionalization was a long time in coming.

Soon after Henry Robinson came another Robinson—this one the Reverend John—who also symbolizes the Protestant theology of pluralism. As spiritual leader of what became the Mayflower Pilgrims (though he remained in Leyden, never coming to Massachusetts), John Robinson is remembered today as the author of the phrase, "The Lord hath more truth and light yet to break forth." One does not have to believe the Massachusetts colonists *wanted* to be religiously tolerant; it is enough merely to acknowledge that a theology allowing religious liberty (or legitimating pluralism) was being clearly enunciated, however long before it became practical reality.

The second step concerns law and authority in colonial America. Not surprisingly, without many of the traditional encumbrances the emerging American society was freer than old societies to manifest religious pluralism and its consequences. This is especially apparent in the Supreme Court's articulation of the newly emerging "common" religion. As will presently be shown, the history of the Court can be interpreted as a halting, hesitant, but "inevitable" effort to perform for American society the religious task of providing a common moral understanding. Before I deal with that dependent variable, however, I must take a second intermediate step, this time into colonial history.

American colonial life has been highly romanticized. With respect to the subject at hand, should one remember witch hunts or Roger Williams? Was Massachusetts Bay a theocracy or the fount of town meeting democracy? Historians' judgments on these questions vary, but it seems important to my thesis to maintain that the pressures of pluralism and their impact on legal institutions did not wait for the revolution and constitutionmaking. Is there evidence in colonial America, then, that these pressures were felt from the beginning?

C. K. Shipton points out "there never was an established church in Massachusetts, there was no agreed-upon body of dogma, and serious moral deviation was punished by the state, not the church. . . . Many of the normal functions of the established churches in Europe were here transferred to the state." Towns maintained a minister at public expense, it is true, but all inhabitants, including vocal Quakers, Baptists, and Presbyterians, partici- pated in his selection, "with the result that the minister's theologi- cal difficulties were usually with the civil body rather than with the church."[26] Meanwhile the civil body—township or colony—was able to escape the "chaotic confusion of laws" in England by ad- ministering them "in one tribunal," according to Howe. "Ecclesiastical, maritime, statutory, and equitable" laws were sub- sumed under the common law, which Bay colonists recognized "as a set of unchanging principles of public law, principles which our usage would describe as 'constitutional.' "[27] G. L. Haskins goes further; the common law was the "cornerstone," the Bible merely the "touchstone," of early Massachusetts.[28]

It may have been an intensely moralistic atmosphere, there- fore, but churches had no monopoly in defining what was moral. Anticipating the distinction between "professed doctrines of reli- gious belief" and "actions" as it arose in *Reynolds* v. *United States* (98 US 145 [1879])—a case resulting in the prohibition of plural marriage—a number of persons came to see that religious "liberty" could become behavioral license unless the obligations between people were subject to the jurisdiction of a secular tribunal. By mid eighteenth century in New Haven, William Livingstone rephrased a "Puritan principle" to read "The civil Power hath no jurisdiction over the Sentiments or Opinions of the subject, till such Opinions break out into Actions prejudicial to the Community, and then it is not the Opinion but the Action that is the Object of our Punish- ment."[29]

Shipton suggests this principle of freedom of thought, often believed to be state policy first in Virginia, whence it entered the U.S. Constitution as a "natural right," may have been bor- rowed from Puritan New England. If the revivalistic Great Awak- ening (1730-1745) was a last ditch effort to reinstate the "old order" against the onslaught of the coming denominational pluralism, it would be accurate to say the cause was hopeless. The Puritan "old order" itself quite clearly contained the ideas that had already destroyed its ordering capability.

But "ordering" could not be avoided. "Natural rights mean simply interests which we think ought to be secured," but it is clear that legal institutions increasingly had the task not only of securing those rights but of defining them as well.[30] Laws, that is to say, not only would inform citizens what to do and what not to do but would have to serve as well to assess the *morality* of what they did. The common law as influenced by Puritanism in England, then, was transferred to America, but in the transfer its moral-architectural ("religious") features stand out because the pressures of pluralism also stand out. To a degree hitherto unknown in the West, people were free to adopt any religion. The consequence, however, was that the simultaneously emerging common law was forced to take up the slack, giving it, as Pekelis insists, a "religious and moralistic character."[31] That is to say, the pressures for a single moral architecture (single "reality-defining" agency, single "generalized symbolic medium") were felt in common law institutions. American society well illustrates the effect of those pressures.

The Religious Character of Legal Institutions

The institutions of the common law seem to have had their "religious" flavor for a long time. The law for Edward Coke, writes David Little, "is more than the measure of reason. It is . . . the measure and source of virtue as well."[32] Just as Puritanism had the effect of making every issue a moral question, so also, as Pound noted, did every moral question become a legal question.[33] The notion of "contempt of court," as found in English and American law, illustrates the point well:

> The Anglo-American idea . . . means that the party who does not abide by certain specific decrees emanating from a judicial body is a contumacious person and may, as a rule, be held in contempt of court, . . . fined and jailed. . . . Now, this very concept of contempt simply does not belong to the world of ideas of a Latin lawyer. It just does not occur to him that the refusal of the defendant . . . may, as soon as a judicial order is issued, become a matter to a certain extent personal to the court, and that the court may feel hurt, insulted, "contemned."[34]

Where the law is highly codified, where, so to speak, the law is asked to specify duties—the situation more nearly found in "civil law" or Latin cultures—the courts can act more administratively, less "judgmentally." But where the task of justifying, articulating, or "interpreting" the law is asked of the courts—where "aspirations" as well as "duties" are at issue—courts must take on a "religious" character.[35] Only in a sense, Pekelis reminds us, does the United States have a written constitution. "The great clauses of the Constitution, just as the more important provisions of our fundamental statutes, contain no more than an appeal to the decency and wisdom of those with whom the responsibility for their enforcement rests."[36] Whether courts are thought to "interpret" or to "make" the law, the fact remains that common law courts find and give *reasons* for their decisions. And in the act of reasoning they do more than cite statutes; they also develop the single symbolic moral universe—the moral architecture. The common law, then, has a "collective" character as pronounced as the individualism more often viewed as its distinctive feature. Any *concerted* effort, even to promote individual interests, will yield a collective enterprise. But if religious liberty is among the promoted interests, the concerted effort takes on an interpretative task *on behalf of* the collective.

> We must say that the aspects of legal life in England and America . . . do not substantiate the contention of the individualistic character of the common-law technique. On the contrary, the strength of the enforcement devices, the clerical and moralistic character of the legal approach at large, the duty of disclosure, the close control exercised by the community upon the individual and upon the law, if compared with the analogous legal institions of the Latin countries, seem to disclose rather a more collectivistic than a more individualistic character of the common-law system. . . . It seems to us that what is generally considered as and taken for the individualistic aspect of American life is simply the existence and coexistence of the plurality of communities and—let's not be afraid of this quantitative element—of an extremely great number of communities of various types.[37]

Though this chapter's central notion, religious pluralism, is rendered by Pekelis simply as "communities of various types," the elements of the argument are all these by implication: (1) Plurality of the religious systems requires redefinition of order but does not escape the need for order. (2) Legal institutions therefore are called upon not only to secure order but to give it a uniformly acceptable meaning as well. (3) The result is a set of legal institutions with a decided religiomoral character. The historical context of these forces in the West has led the common law to become their medium, the legal philosophy of the Enlightenment their symbols, and the U.S. judicial system most concretely their vehicle of expression.

No clearer illustration can be found than Nelson's analysis of the legal situation in Massachusetts during the years just before and after the revolution. In prerevolutionary times, he notes, juries reached verdicts and applied the law consistently "largely because men selected to juries shared a . . . set of ethical values and assumptions."[38] By the 1760s, however, this ethical unity no longer obtained because Puritan theology itself contained the seeds of pluralism; the Great Awakening was but the early eighteenth-century flowering of those seeds, leading to religious diversity in New England. The result was that as soon as "jurors could no longer agree whether a community gained or lost when, for instance, a millpond flooded a meadow, jury verdicts indeed became 'fluctuating estimates' that were 'utterly indefinite and uncertain,' and *it became essential to transfer to the judiciary the power of finding law*" (italics added).[39] Moreover:

> By the beginning of the nineteenth century . . . judges were abandoning the notion that they should adhere rigidly to precedent. . . . [The difference] was less in what the courts did than in their understanding of what they properly could do. . . . As long as juries had found the law . . . adherence to precedent had imposed little burden on the legal system. . . . But once the law-finding power passed to judges, who began to exercise it by rendering written opinions that remained available for all to read, precedent threatened to impose a straightjacket on future legal development and to bar all future legal change.[40]

One can inquire whether other institutions also served to express those moral standards. Thus, "Congress quickly assumed a theological function and began interpreting events in religious terms and exhorting other patriots on doctrine and morality. . . . But as the early years faded and the years of war began to pass, Congress made progressively fewer pronouncements which required any reference to the foundation of things in God and busied itself more and more with mundane affairs such as the disposition and pay of the Continental Army."[41]

More important, however—and more in keeping with the Durkheimian spirit of this chapter—one can ask if any agency in American society has been *required* to express those moral standards. I assert here that such a "theological function" was unavoidably thrust upon the judicial system. Ethical diversity then, or what I have called religious pluralism, had the effect of putting onto the judicial agenda the task of declaring, indeed promulgating, the moral standards for the community at large. The culture may yet have been Puritan at its roots, but the courts replaced the churches as the vehicle for expressing the moral standards of that culture.

Religion in the Legal System: A Disappearing Rhetoric

Little documentation is needed for the claim of an expanding judiciary in American history. "Actually, between 1820 and 1890 the judges were already taking the initiative in lawmaking. Far anticipating the leadership of the executive or administrative arms, the courts built up the common law in the United States—a body of judge-made doctrine to govern people's public and private affairs."[42]

The present thesis, however, contains a critical corollary less widely acknowledged: With this expansion the judiciary adopted the task of articulating the collective's moral architecture. Federal judges, as Albanese puts it, "rode circuit with the gospel of the civil religion and preached sermons in which the Constitution, its virtue and its promise, figured prominently."[43] Of course, many have spoken of "the nine high priests in their black robes" and of the sacredness imputed to the Constitution and other artifacts of the legal order. But in keeping with Eugene V. Rostow's characterization of the contemporary Supreme Court as a "vital national seminar," it is worth noting that the original charge to the Court was only that it render an aye or a nay.[44] It quickly began handing down written opinions also, however, and under Marshall began the practice of trying for a single majority opinion, which gave "judicial pronouncements a forceful unity they had formerly lacked."[45]

With the expansion of judicial explanation came the difficult problem of knowing what religious rhetoric, if any, was allowed in the explanation. I have already referred to the *Reynolds* v. *United States* case (1879) wherein Mormon polygamy was outlawed. "Can a man excuse his practices . . . because of his religious belief?" asked Mr. Chief Justice Waite. "To permit this would be to make the professed doctrines of religious belief superior to the law of the land. . . ." Were "religious" exceptions to be made, the opinion held, "then those who do *not* make polygamy a part of their religious belief *may be found guilty* and punished" (98 US 145 [1879], italics added).

Here in a single decision is exemplified the paradox confronting American courts because they are in a religiously plural society—a paradox that hands to them the erstwhile religious task of articulating a moral architecture. On the one hand citizens cannot use religious beliefs to justify any and all actions. On the other hand truly religious belief, it is thought, *ought* to be manifest in action; else why assume in finding Reynolds innocent society might find nonpolygamists guilty? Protestantism enhanced the development of the concept of religious liberty and thus religious pluralism. But this in turn led, as Pound and others saw, to making everything a moral question yet also a legal question. Courts, then, could not resolve legal questions without resorting to moral answers. But the rhetoric and imagery available for expressing these moral answers could not be drawn from the language of orthodox religion as the implications of religious pluralism became clearer. Instead the rhetoric—if it was to have *general* meaning—had to be drawn from another sphere, but from a sphere no less religious in its functioning.

Thus says Bickel:

> The function of the Justices . . . is to immerse themselves in the tradition of our society and of kindred societies that have gone before, in history and in the sediment of history which is law, and . . . in the thought and the vision of the philosophers and the poets. The Justices will

then be fit to extract 'fundamental presuppositions' from their deepest selves, but in fact from the evolving morality of our tradition. . . . The search for the deepest controlling sources, for the precise 'how' and the final 'whence' of the judgment . . . may, after all, end in the attempt to express the inexpressible. This is not to say that the duty to judge the judgment might as well be abandoned. The inexpressible can be recognized, even though one is unable to parse it.[46]

It would be difficult to find a better description of "religion" as it is outlined in classical sociology.

This change in rhetoric that the courts have felt obliged to use is readily illustrated in so-called church-state cases.

1. *Church of the Holy Trinity* v. *United States,* 143 US 226 (1892). Events in our national life, wrote Mr. Justice Brewer, "affirm and reaffirm that this is a religious nation." Moreover, in holding that a statute prohibiting aliens from being imported for labor was not intended to prevent a church from hiring a foreign Christian minister, the Court quoted approvingly from two previous judicial opinions showing "we are a Christian people, and the morality of the country is deeply ingrafted upon Christianity" and "the Christian religion is a part of the common law of Pennsylvania."

2. *United States* v. *Macintosh,* 283 US 605 (1931). Forty years later the Court was faced with the question of whether citizenship could be denied a person because he held reservations about taking arms in defense of his country. It is evident, said Mr. Justice Sutherland, "that he means to make his own interpretation of the will of God the decisive test which shall include the government. . . . We are a Christian people, according to one another the equal right of religious freedom, and acknowledging with reverence the duty of obedience to the will of God. But, also, we are a nation with the duty to survive." Citizenship was denied.

3. *Zorach* v. *Clauson,* 343 US 306 (1952). Two decades later in its decision that released-time religious instruction is permitted provided it occurs off public school grounds the Court asserted—in Mr. Justice Douglas's words—that "We are a religious people whose institutions presuppose a Supreme Being." This

statement, as well as the result, drew the dissent of Mr. Justice Black, who claimed, "Before today, our judicial opinions have refrained from drawing invidious distinctions between those who believe in no religion and those who do believe."

4. *United States* v. *Seeger,* 380 US 163 (1965). Here, in another conscientious objection case, the Court decided "belief in relation to a Supreme Being," thus exemption, is to be determined by "whether a given belief that is sincere and meaningful occupies a place in the life of its possessor parallel to that filled by the orthodox belief in God of one who clearly qualifies for the exemption." More than monotheistic beliefs qualify—Mr. Justice Clark noting the "vast panoply of beliefs" prevalent. Seeger's beliefs qualified, therefore, and he was exempted. In a concurring opinion, Douglas went further in acknowledging how pluralism forces rhetorical change. Hawaii, he noted, at the time the Selective Service law was passed (1940), probably had more Buddhists than members of any other "faith," and how could a concept like Supreme Being be helpful in determining a Buddhist's eligibility for exemption? This from the Justice who thirteen years earlier had written that American institutions "presuppose" a Supreme Being.

5. *Welsh* v. *United States,* 398 US 333 (1970). The result in *Welsh* was identical with that in *Seeger,* the Court finding the facts to be the same so that the legal application was the same. The opinion, by Mr. Justice Black, contained an even more expanded notion of religion, however. Exemption from Selective Service is to be allowed on "registrant's moral, ethical, or religious beliefs about what is right and wrong," provided "those beliefs be held with the strength of traditional religious convictions." Moreover, inasmuch as the government had argued that Welsh's beliefs were less religious than Seeger's, the Court responded this "places undue emphasis on the registrant's interpretation of his own beliefs. The Court's statement in *Seeger* that a registrant's characterization of his own belief as 'religious' should carry great weight . . . does not imply that his declaration that his views are nonreligious should be treated similarly . . . very few registrants are fully aware of the broad scope of the word 'religious' [as interpreted by law since *Seeger*]."

It is instructive to see what developed in the course of a century. In *Reynolds* the Court recognized that "religion" is not defined in the Constitution but agreed that even if the state had no power over opinion, it was free to regulate actions. And polygamy, it said, has always been "odious" to Western nations, leading as it does to "stationary despotism." Therefore though there is no implication that Mormon *opinion* is punishable by law, Mormon *action* clearly is. A few years later the Court can speak of the "Christianity" of the nation, of its people, and of its morality, which therefore permits a church (though not a secular employer) to import alien labor. Though a *church* is entitled to special exemption from a law for religious reasons, an *individual* is not. Even if "We are a Christian people," and even if Macintosh is a professor in a Christian seminary, the government's interest in self-preservation is greater than a person's right to religious free exercise.

In *Zorach* v. *Clausen* the remark that "We are a religious people" might be seen as gratuitous—this is the only case here involving the establishment rather than the free exercise clause—except that what is allowed by the court is a *religious* program. Black, in dissent, wonders about the rights of *irreligious* people; are they protected by the First Amendment mention of "religion"? They might be, it would appear from the *Seeger* and *Welsh* cases, since what is "religion" gets even broader interpretation, to the point in *Welsh* where Black says the law may have to regard as religious something persons themselves claim is nonreligious.

At this point it would seem the definition of religion is so broad as to be meaningless in deciding cases, at least free exercise cases. From a time when the rhetoric used to justify a decision could be presumptively Christian, there comes the time when it cannot even be presumptively religious. *Seeger* and *Welsh* set out a distinction—any sincere and meaningful belief occupies a place parallel to that of orthodox belief. As Harlan argued in his concurring opinion in *Welsh,* however:

> My own conclusion . . . is that the Free Exercise Clause does not require a State to conform a neutral secular program to the dictates of religious conscience of any group. . . . [A] state could constitutionally create exceptions to its program to accommodate religious scruples. That suggestion must, however, be qualified by the

observation that any such exception in order to satisfy the Establishment Clause of the First Amendment, would have to be sufficiently broad to be religiously neutral. . . . This would require creating an exception for anyone who, as a matter of conscience, could not comply with the statute.

"Religion" for legal purposes becomes simply "conscience," and Congress, if it is to grant conscientious exemptions, "cannot draw the line between theistic or nontheistic beliefs on the one hand and secular beliefs on the other." For all intents, assuming the eventual "triumph" of Harlan's position or something like it, the law simply dispenses with the notion of religion as commonly understood. Having tried for a century to regard it on its own terms—as sacred, special, and compelling—courts realize the attempt is futile. All efforts to allow "free exercise" of religion *because it is religion* conflict with the requirement of "no establishment" or special treatment. Religious pluralism requires articulation of "highest obligation" not in orthodox religious language but otherwise. What form does this take?

Religion in the Legal System: An Emerging Civil Religious Rhetoric

If the analysis here is correct, a new rhetoric is still in developing stages. Were this new civil religion—this new moral architecture—fully mature, it would be part of the common culture, but instead considerable doubt is expressed over the shape, authenticity, even the existence of an American civil religion. I do not postulate a fully mature civil religion here, however. Instead I argued commitment to religious liberty (pluralism) makes impossible the use of rhetoric of any *one* religious tradition; so pressures are great to create a new rhetoric, that is, find a new religion. In the American case this new rhetoric is found in the common law and develops in legal institutions. Procedure takes precedence over substantive precepts and standards, not because *procedures* are uniquely required in plural societies—*all* societies require procedures—but because the *rhetoric* of procedure is required to justify outcomes between parties whose erstwhile religions are different.[47] The rhetoric of procedure thus becomes the new common or civil religion.

It is in this context that the jurisprudence of Lon Fuller can best be understood. When he remarks on the impossibility of distinguishing the law that *is* from the law that *ought* to be or when he discusses the imperceptible line between the "morality of duty" and the "morality of aspiration," he is insisting the law itself has concretely the task of portraying the ideal, whether it wants to or not.[48] And though Fuller has not included this point in his argument, I argued here that the "law" takes on this task to the degree that "religion" is denied it as a result of pluralism. Thus the "internal morality" of the law informs and guides a judge even though the "external morality" (interests) of contending parties must remain of no concern to him.[49] Fuller finds a "natural law" rubric congenial for analyzing this process, a fact that bespeaks even more the degree of transcendency that the law takes on.

Conclusion

Legal institutions do not take on this transcendent or civil religious task single-handedly, of course. Public schools certainly play a critical role in socializing youngsters into the "transcendence" of the law. As Kohlberg has framed the issue:

> It has been argued . . . that the Supreme Court's Schempp decision [prohibiting school sponsorship of prayer and Bible reading] calls for the restraint of public school efforts at moral education since such education is equivalent to the state propagation of religion conceived as any articulated value system. The problems as to the legitimacy of moral education in the public schools disappear, however, if the proper content of moral education is recognized to be the values of justice which themselves prohibit the imposition of beliefs of one group upon another. . . . [This] does not mean that the schools are not to be "value-oriented." . . . The public school is as much committed to the maintenance of justice as is the court.[50]

One can, however, usefully distinguish agencies for socialization into the civil religion from agencies for articulating or elaborating it. Public schools are the new "Sunday schools," it might be said, whereas courts are the new pulpits.

"Pluralism and Law in the Formation of American Civil Religion," Notes

1. Emile Durkheim, *Elementary Forms of Religious Life,* trans. Joseph Swain (New York: Collier, 1961 [originally published in French in 1912]), pp. 62, 432.

2. Durkheim, *Elementary Forms,* p. 432.

3. Talcott Parsons, *Structure of Social Action* (New York: McGraw-Hill, 1937), p. 427.

4. Durkheim, *Elementary Forms,* p. 114.

5. Durkheim, *Elementary Forms,* p. 475.

6. P. L. Berger and Thomas Luckmann, "Secularization and Pluralism," *Yearbook for the Sociology of Religion* 2 (1966), pp. 73-85, refer to "sacred comprehensive meanings for everyday life."

7. Frederick J. Teggart, *The Processes of History* (New Haven, Conn.: Yale University Press, 1918), p. 118.

8. Wilfred Cantwell Smith, *The Meaning and End of Religion* (New York: Macmillan, 1963), p. 43.

9. Teggart, *The Processes,* p. 118.

10. Smith, *The Meaning,* p. 43.

11. Alasdair MacIntyre, *Secularization and Moral Change* (London: Oxford University Press, 1967), p. 54.

12. John Courtney Murray, *We Hold These Truths* (Garden City, N.Y.: Doubleday, 1964), p. 27.

13. MacIntyre, *Secularization,* p. 52.

14. Kingsley Davis, *Human Society* (New York: Macmillan, 1950), p. 143.

15. Talcott Parsons, *Politics and Social Structure* (New York: Free Press, 1969), p. 445.

16. Parsons, *Politics,* p. 455.

17. Parsons, *Politics,* p. 455.

18. Roscoe Pound, "Law in Books and Law in Action," *American Law Review* 44 (1910), pp. 12-34, and *The Spirit of the Common Law* (Francetown, N.H.: Marshall Jones, 1921).

19. David Little, *Religion, Order and Law* (New York: Harper & Row, 1969).

20. Little, *Religion,* p. 185.

21. Little, *Religion,* pp. 239 and 240.

22, Little, *Religion,* p. 225.

23. C. J. H. Hayes, *Nationalism: A Religion* (New York: Macmillan, 1960), p. 36.

24. Harold S. Bender, *The Anabaptists and Religious Liberty in the Sixteenth Century* (Philadelphia: Fortress Press, 1953), p. 8.

25. Little, *Religion,* pp. 255-256.

26. C. K. Shipton, "The Locus of Authority in Colonial Massachusetts," in G. A. Billias, ed., *Law and Authority in Colonial America* (Barre, Mass.: Barre Publishers, 1965), pp. 137 and 138.

27. Mark De W. Howe, "The Sources and Nature of Law in Colonial Massachusetts," in Billias, *Law and Authority,* pp. 14-15.

28. G. L. Haskins, *Law and Authority in Early Massachusetts* (Hamden, Conn.: Archon Books, 1968), esp. ch. 10.

29. Shipton, "The Locus," p. 143.

30. Pound, *The Spirit,* p. 92.

31. Alexander Pekelis, *Law and Social Action* (Ithaca, N.Y.: Cornell University Press, 1950), p. 56.

32. Little, *Religion,* p. 177.

33. Pound, *The Spirit,* p. 43.

34. Pekelis, *Law,* pp. 45-46.

35. Lon Fuller, *The Morality of Law* (New Haven, Conn.: Yale University Press, 1964).

36. Pekelis, *Law,* p. 4.

37. Pekelis, *Law,* pp. 66-67.

38. William E. Nelson, *Americanization of the Common Law: The Impact of Legal Change on Massachusetts Society, 1760-1830* (Cambridge, Mass.: Harvard University Press, 1975), pp. 165-166.

39. Nelson, *Americanization,* p. 166.

40. Nelson, *Americanization,* p. 171.

41. Catherine Albanese, *Sons of the Fathers* (Philadelphia: Temple, 1976), p. 194.

42. J. Willard Hurst, *The Growth of American Law* (Boston: Little Brown, 1950), p. 85.

43. Albanese, *Sons,* p. 218.

44. Eugene V. Rostow, "The Democratic Character of Judicial Review," *Harvard Law Review* 66 (1952), p. 208.

45. Robert McClosky, *The American Supreme Court* (Chicago: University of Chicago Press, 1960), p. 40

46. Alexander Bickel, *The Least Dangerous Branch* (Indianapolis: Bobbs-Merrill, 1962), pp. 236-238.

47. Talcott Parsons, *Societies: Evolutionary and Comparative Perspectives* (Englewood Cliffs, N.J.: Prentice-Hall, 1966), p. 27.

48. Lon Fuller, *The Law in Quest of Itself* (Boston: Beacon Press, 1966), and *The Morality.*

49. Fuller, *The Morality,* pp. 131-132.

50. Lawrence Kohlberg, "Education for Justice: A Modern Statement of the Platonic View," in J. M. Gustafson et al., eds., *Moral Education* (Cambridge, Mass.: Harvard University Press, 1970), pp. 67-68.

10. American Civil Religion

Rockne M. McCarthy

History attests to the fact that in pluralistic societies political authority and power have rarely been used in a just manner. This is particularly true with respect to individuals, groups, and institutions which represent a view of life not shared by those in positions of government responsibility. The unjust use of political authority and power is often directly related to the presence of a civil religion in society. Indeed, the very nature of a civil religion entails the establishment of a nonpluralistic public legal order in society.

In order to demonstrate the existence of a civil religion in the United States, the nonpluralistic structure of the public legal order must be exposed. Moreover, the relationship between an established civil religion and the discrimination experienced by individuals, groups, and institutions in American society must be unveiled. Such a task might well appear dubious to many Americans, since most believe that the very strength and uniqueness of their country lies in its pluralism. To assume the pluralistic character of the American public legal order, however, would be a mistake.

Early Development

The separation of church and state is one of the basic assumptions of American thought and society. Many interpret this principle to mean a complete and permanent separation of the spheres of religious activity and civil authority. This interpretation grew out of philosophical and historical developments preceding the founding of American political order.

In the Middle Ages, the Church provided both spiritual and political unity for Europe. During this period the church-state establishment promoted orthodoxy and sought conformity in ways that were oppressive to those suspected of heresy. With the Renaissance and Reformation came the breakdown of religious and political unity in Europe, but, although more churches and states came into existence, individuals scarcely gained in freedom. The various states adopted official religions, and deviation from the creed of the established church often meant persecution.

Among the ideas spawned by the eighteenth-century Enlightenment and the age of republican revolutions was the notion that the only way to achieve social peace was to subdue the passions engendered by sectarian conflict. Many political philosophers argued that this could be accomplished by separating the private life of the spirit from the public life of the state. To do so meant nothing less than redefining the nature of religion by limiting religion to theological and ecclesiastical matters and viewing the rest of life as the domain of nonsectarian activity. The hope was that political stability could be achieved on the basis of a supposedly nonsectarian political order.

Apologists for the political tradition of the Enlightenment have argued that liberal-democratic states have provided social stability along with freedom for individuals and groups to practice their private religious beliefs. One of the claims of this essay, however, is that what occurred in the supposedly nonsectarian political sphere of life was the establishment of a nonpluralistic public legal order based upon an individualist social philosophy. In the vacuum left by the disestablishment of churches, a political ideology *every bit as religious* as earlier established religions gave rise to a nonpluralistic political order. The political thinking of the American founding fathers developed in the context of an Enlightenment tradition which assumed a dualistic view of life and religion.

Historical as well as philosophical considerations were involved in the emergence of an American civil religion. Having long been a haven for various groups of dissenters, the new country faced the problem of extensive religious diversity among its inhabitants. The colonies shared a general cultural heritage from the Old World, but any attempt to establish one particular church at the national level would have subverted the hope for political union. The colonies have been united against England largely on the basis of political and economic issues, and in these areas it was possible in time to arrive at majority opinions. The absence of a denominational majority was an important historical factor which coincided conveniently with the new philosophical assumption that the state represented a rational, nonsectarian agreement among citizens to govern themselves.

We must emphasize again, however, that nonsectarian does not mean nonreligious. As Conrad Cherry remarks, discussing the separation of church and state in America:

> The disestablishment of the church hardly meant that the American political sphere was denied a religious dimension. In fact, that dimension so permeates the political, educational and social life of America that it constitutes a civil religion that cannot be identified with Protestantism, Catholicism, or Judaism as such. Americans may be participants in *both* the religious dimension of their civil life *and* one of the traditional Western religions.[1]

While it is true that the federal government did not establish a national church, a nonecclesiastical public faith did come to structure the public legal order of the Republic in a nonpluralistic way. Yet Enlightenment political assumptions, thought by some to be "self evident" nonsectarian truths, are judged by others to be nothing more than sectarian claims concerning human nature and the political order.

Several of the prominent characteristics of the civil religion which developed in America can be discussed under the headings of Civil Theology, Civil Peoplehood, and Civil Institutions.

Civil Theology

At the heart of a civil religion is a civil theology. The Enlightenment produced a liberal (individualist) tradition in which the rights of sovereign individuals are absolutized. This atomistic view of the sovereign individual became the central dogma of the American civil theology and a master assumption of American political thought.[2] Proclaimed to the world at the very birth of the Republic in the Declaration of Independence, the notion of the sovereignty of the individual served as the basic political assumption underlying the Constitution. The Declaration presented the individual as a being who was by nature free, independent, and autonomous. Human beings governed themselves by rationally discovering the "Laws of Nature and Nature's God"[3] and freely contracting together to abide by those laws. The consent of the people thus became the only *legitimate* source of political authority and power. Making the "People" the creators of the state, concludes R. R. Palmer, made possible a revolutionary concept of government in America.[4]

The belief in the sovereignty of the people was set forth in the Preamble to the United States Constitution. The statement that "We the people . . . do ordain and establish" expresses clearly the idea of the people as the *constituent* authority. Through their reason the people discerned the "will of the majority" and formed their government. The process of majoritarian rule, which emerged directly from the doctrine of popular sovereignty, continued in the elected and appointed governing bodies. In America all political authority and power flowed from the people and came to expression through the will of the majority. Alexander Hamilton, for instance, articulates this faith of the people in the people in *The Federalist Papers:* "The fabric of American empire ought to rest on the solid basis of THE CONSENT OF THE PEOPLE. The streams of national power ought to flow immediately from that pure, original fountain of all legitimate authority."[5]

John Locke is recognized as the philosophical founder of the American liberal tradition. In his view of social reality, individuals are sovereign, and therefore inherently free of every associational relationship. From such a perspective, all social entities are mere abstractions. Every institution, including the state, is an artificial creation of sovereign individuals and represents the sum total of the individuals who voluntarily compose the institution. Thus, only individuals have rights because only individuals are "real," that is, possess ontological status.[6]

This Lockean view of social reality is not, however, accepted by everyone as a self-evident truth. It represents one of several political perspectives of the social order, all of which are based on certain fundamental religious assumptions about man and society.[7] Nevertheless, an individualist view has so shaped American political thought and judicial reasoning that the public legal order of the Republic has never been pluralistic. For this reason, one may legitimately speak of the establishment of a civil religion in America.

Evidence that an individualist perspective has given rise to a nonpluralistic public legal order in the Republic is not hard to uncover. An investigation, for instance, of the Supreme Court's interpretation of the Constitution regarding such matters as the nature of religion and the rights of associations demonstrates a persistent legal bias on the part of the Court against the recognition of the rights of institutions *as* institutions. Although it is true that associations such as business corporations have been acknowledged to have rights, those rights are recognized either on the basis of the right of *individuals* to associate or on the assumption that institutions are artificial *persons*. Both arguments reflect an individualist and, therefore, a nonpluralistic view because the many institutions that make up a society—business corporations, families, churches, schools, and even the state itself—are not recognized as having civil rights and liberties based upon their *own* structural identity and task in society.

The Court's individualist perspective with respect to the state is evident, for example, in the 1793 case of *Chisholm* v. *Georgia*. In this historic decision the Justices warned against the danger of state absolutism. But in their argument rejecting state sovereignty the Court assumed that a state was merely an "artificial person" which owed its very existence to the will of individuals. The Court thus let it be known that only individuals are sovereign, and that any other view represented an "unnatural and inverted order of things." The Court continued:

> Sentiments and expressions of this inaccurate kind (implying the sovereignty of the state) prevail in our common, even in our convivial language. Is a toast asked? "The United States" instead of the "People of the United States," is the toast given (sic). This is not politically correct. The toast is meant to present to view the first great object in the union: It presents only the second: It presents only the artificial person, instead of the natural persons, who spoke it into existence.[8]

The Court's view reflects a national acceptance of an Enlightenment liberal view of the public legal order. As Louis Hartz has argued, the Lockean creed became "enshrined in the Constitution" of the United States.[9] This American commitment to the doctrines of individual sovereignty and majoritarian rule impressed Alexis de Tocqueville on his visit to America during the 1830s:

The people reign in the American political world as the Deity does in the universe. They are the cause and the aim of all things; everything comes from them, and everything is absorbed by them.[10]

At the heart of America's civil religion, therefore, is a civil theology. The Enlightenment produced an individualist liberal tradition which came to dominate American thought and to structure the public legal order as few ideologies anywhere have done. The commitment of Americans to this tradition made the Declaration of Independence and the Constitution the most sacred documents of the American civil religion.

Civil Peoplehood

People who share basic convictions about themselves and the world often manifest their sense of common cause and identity in what might be called a "civil peoplehood." For some time scholars have written about Americans' understanding of themselves as a chosen people, as a peoplehood.[11] The roots of this belief lie deep in the American past. The New England Puritans, for example, appropriating the covenantal language of the Old Testament, believed that they were God's chosen people, the elect who were creating a new Israel in the New World. Full participation in the Puritan peoplehood hinged upon the elect's membership in the covenant of grace, the church, and the political covenants.[12] Although the Puritan distinction between the elect and nonelect gradually disappeared with the secularization of American society, the concept of a covenanted peoplehood remained a key element of the national consciousness. By the end of the eighteenth century the Puritan covenants were replaced by the founding Republican documents: the Declaration of Independence and the Constitution. These new inviolable covenants not only bound the Republic together, but also identified a new republican peoplehood by establishing the grounds for citizenship.

The very meaning of the term "citizen" was unique in the American context. As R. R. Palmer has pointed out, the modern concept of "citizen" first appeared in the Massachusetts Constitution of 1780.[13] From there it found its way into the Federal Constitution of 1789. John Adams wrote in the Massachusetts preamble: "The body politic is formed by a voluntary association of individuals. It is a social compact, by which the whole people covenants with each citizen and each citizen with the whole people that all shall be governed by certain laws for the common good."[14] Palmer observes:

> The thought here, and the use of the word "covenant," go back to the Mayflower compact. But whence comes the "social" in social compact? And whence comes the word "citizen"? There were no "citizens" under the British Constitution, except in the sense of freemen of the few towns known as cities. In the English language the word "citizen" in its modern sense is an Americanism, dating from the American Revolution.[15]

Adams' terminology, as Palmer remarks, may reflect the influence of Rousseau.[16] The fact that Rousseau's idea of the "citizen" was closely tied to his concept of "civil religion" may provide a clue to understanding the moral-religious meaning of citizenship in the American experience.

In the minds of many Americans and even to some extent in the thinking of the Supreme Court until the adoption of the Fourteenth Amendment, citizenship meant more than being born in the United States or possessing a valid certificate of naturalization. René Williamson suggests that we have "inherited from the Greeks and the French Revolution the feeling that citizenship ought to have something to do with shared ideals and that participation without such sharing is ethically reprehensible and politically unwise." He continues:

> We give vent to this feeling when we say of someone: "He is legally an American citizen, but he is not really an American." We feel an American monarchist would be a caricature of a citizen and that an American Nazi or Communist is not truly a citizen either, the law to the contrary notwithstanding. What we mean when we react in this manner is that citizenship is more than a legal bond and that such people do not and cannot share with us what we consider to be the presuppositions of

citizenship. Citizenship means membership in a community, and how can there be community without a common loyalty to shared ideas? This feeling has found its way into our naturalization laws which prescribe not only a willingness to defend the United States but also an understanding of and affection for the Constitution.[17]

If the meaning of "citizen" is ambiguous in the American experience, the meaning of the American Revolution is not. Most Americans at the time interpreted the Revolution as proving conclusively that they and the American Republic (one and the same) were the primary agents of God's meaningful activity in history. Believing themselves to be (pre-)destined by a benevolent deity (whether the biblical God of the Christians or the God of nature of the rationalists) to be freed from England, they also felt called to spread the gospel of republicanism to all people. As early as 1765, John Adams wrote in his diary that, "I always consider the settlement of America with reverence and wonder, as the opening of a grand scene and design in Providence for the illumination of the ignorant, and the emancipation of the slavish part of mankind all over the earth."[18] Such a notion can be found in the sermons of clergymen as well as in the writing of Deists such as Adams and Jefferson.

This messianic vision was implicit in the Declaration of Independence, where, as Albert Weinberg points out, Jefferson was sufficiently confident of his intuition of divine purposes to present the case for American independence as "indubitable dogmas of truth and destiny."[19] Weinberg remarks that "The Americans . . . had faith not only in the justice but also the inevitability of independence. . . . Thus the first doctrine which reflected the nationalistic theology of 'manifest destiny' was that of God's decree of independence."[20] When the Constitution went to the states for debate and ratification, its defenders were quick to describe its significance in terms of American destiny. As Alexander Hamilton agreed:

> It has been frequently remarked that it seems to have been reserved to the people of this country, by their conduct and example, to decide the important question, whether societies of men are really capable or not of establishing good government from reflection and choice,

or whether they are forever destined to depend for their political consideration on accident and force. If there be any truth in the remark, the crisis at which we are arrived may with propriety be regarded as the era in which that decision is to be made; and a wrong election of the part we shall act may, in this view, deserve to be considered as *the general misfortune of mankind.*[21]

It is interesting to note that belief in the messianic mission of Americans and America has served as the apologetic for each of the alternative rationales for America's foreign policy.[22] The first of these, expressed as early as Washington's "Farewell Address," is the principle of "isolationist withdrawal, the conception of innocent nation, wicked world."[23] America was to be an example to the world as Hamilton had suggested, but only a moral example. To intervene actively in world affairs would be to expose the chosen people and the young Republic to the evil political forces of the Old World from which they had freed themselves. A second doctrine emerged as the American people and the Republic became stronger and more confident. If the lesson of republicanism could not always be taught by the power of moral example, it might be spread by the use of force—especially to peoples in regions adjacent to the United States.[24] This militaristic messianic mission came to full expression during the era of Manifest Destiny. Americans believed that they had a mandate to spread a republican faith and republican institutions to all of North America. It was the destiny (a secularized idea of Providence) of the American people and the Republic to invade and possess new lands and territories. The Mexican war (1846-48), for instance, was seen by many as a means of regenerating the Mexicans by spreading the "good news" of a republican way of life. The same justification had been used many times before to rationalize the taking of Indian lands and possessions.[25]

Born in the revolutionary struggle with England, the American peoplehood matured in the nineteenth and twentieth centuries to include more people. But participation in the peoplehood came at a high price. For many immigrants who came to America during this period, Americanization was more than a legal process. The loss of cultural and group identity was often the cost of being allowed to become members of the peoplehood. But what was the fate of those who resisted Americanization? A consideration of the civil institutions of the American civil religion will prepare us to take up this important question.

Civil Institutions

The American civil religion comprises not only a civil theology and peoplehood, but also key political, social, and economic institutions through which it is embodied, interpreted, and propagated. The limited scope of an essay will permit me to develop this observation only with respect to public schools and political parties.

Public schools have always been one of the key sanctuaries of civil religion in America. The linkage between civil religion and public education is quite evident, for example, in the republican vision of Thomas Jefferson. Jefferson believed in the certainty of moral conscience and human reason, and, like many other eighteenth-century Deists, he rejected the supernatural, choosing instead to interpret Christianity as a rational moral code. He edited the Gospels to produce his own Bible, cutting the genuine sayings of Christ from the spurious, "as easily distinguishable as diamonds in a dunghill."[26] His profound distaste for theology and the church (Anglicanism was the established faith in Virginia) led him to advocate not only the Virginia Bill for Establishing Religious Freedom, but to propose a system of public primary and secondary schools for Virginia and to found the University of Virginia as a supposedly nonsectarian alternative to Virginia's Anglican College of William and Mary.[27]

Nowhere is Jefferson's own sectarian faith more apparent than in his work as the founder of the University of Virginia. In the stipulations for curriculum he chose not to establish a chair of divinity. To do so, he believed, would be to violate the principle of the separation of church and state because the University was endowed by public monies and administered by civil authorities. (The supposedly nonsectarian obligation to develop moral character was placed in the hands of the professors of ethics.) And yet, when it came time to hire the faculty, he wrote to James Madison about the need to find an orthodox advocate of states-rights republicanism to teach law, and declared:

> It is in our seminary that the vestal flame is to be kept alive; from thence it is to spread anew over our own and the sister States. If we are true and vigilant in our trust, within a dozen or twenty years a majority of our own legislature will be from one school, and many disciples will have carried its doctrine home with them to their several states, and will have leavened the whole mass.[28]

As David B. Tyack comments, " 'Seminary,' 'vestal flame,' 'disciple,' 'doctrine,' 'leavened the whole mass'—What are these terms if not the vocabulary of the sectarian."[29]

Jefferson, it should be noted, prescribed the texts to be used at the University of Virginia. The seriousness with which he approached the task is indicative of the fact that a new field of sectarian battle had emerged: Theological bigotry was yielding to political intolerance. Jefferson exclaimed:

> There is one branch in which we are the best judges, in which heresies may be taught, of so interesting a character to our own State, and to the United States, as to make it a duty in us to lay down the principles which are to be taught. It is that of government. . . . It is our duty to guard against the dissemination of such (Federalist) principles among our youth, and the diffusion of that poison, by a previous prescription of the texts to be followed in their discourses.[30]

Jefferson's choice of texts was enough to make a Federalist Virginian such as Chief Justice John Marshall complain that he was being forced by the state to support the propagation of opinions which he disbelieved and abhorred.[31]

Religious heresies did not concern Jefferson; they were in the area of grace, the private sphere of conscience. Political heresies, however, were a different matter, for they involved the area of nature, the public sphere of the American civil religion. Far from being nonsectarian, Jefferson's educational ideas were intimately tied to his hope for redeeming society through republican values.

Jefferson's ideas are worthy of comment because they were shared by those who believed that education was not an extraneous issue but rather one interwoven with a republican faith commitment. Out of this civil "religious" belief the public school was born. During the revolutionary era a common argument arose that republican institutions must rest on "virtue," and thus a growing need was felt for a universal system of public schools to teach the virtues of republicanism. In the first half of the nineteenth century, under the leadership of Daniel Webster, Edward Everett, Horace Mann, and others, the common school movement developed in earnest.

The public school system is presently experiencing a crisis. Older ideas, such as the view of America as an ethnic "melting pot," no longer expresses a common consensus. Nevertheless, John F. Wilson's remark is historically valid: ". . . the public school system certainly must be viewed as a powerful engine for reinforcement of common religion. . . . School systems are in fact the American religious establishment through their state symbolism, civic ceremonial, inculcated values, exemplified virtues, and explicit curricula."[32] Elwyn A. Smith concludes similarly that "the American public school system is the nation's equivalent to the European established church."[33]

Another institutional expression of the American civil religion can be seen in the nature of political parties and the majoritarian electoral system which effectively limits politics to a two-party system in the United States. The emergence of political parties was not anticipated by the founding fathers for at least two reasons. In the first place, political parties were considered evil by almost every writer in the early eighteenth century. This dislike and distrust of parties was based upon the conviction that factionalism was inherently dangerous to political freedom and stable government. Second, it was hoped that a common agreement on basic republican principles would make political parties unnecessary. Cecelia M. Kenyon has pointed out that while "Americans have regarded themselves, and have been regarded, as an essentially pragmatic people, . . . the preference for republicanism which crystallized at the time of the Revolution has constituted an ideological, doctrinaire element in their political outlook which has rarely been questioned."[34] The political parties that developed almost immediately in the new Republic, as well as their heirs, have been essentially pragmatic in their outlook precisely because of the existence of an ideological attachment to Lockean assumptions which has united parties in a common political creed. Unlike the ideological debates of European politics, the major debates within American politics have been characterized almost exclusively by functional and pragmatic questions.

Acceptance of Kenyon's thesis need not make one oblivious to the political divisions that have occurred in the course of American political history. It has long been recognized that there have been several turning points in American politics. Most scholars agree, for instance, that the elections of Thomas Jefferson, Andrew Jackson, and Abraham Lincoln represented significant political realignments. And yet it is also evident that in each case the realignment involved positions *within* a Lockean paradigm. The divisions represented differences in the application of republican principles rather than a fundamental questioning of the principles themselves.

Even the election of Lincoln that led to polarization of American society and resulted in civil war represented not a clash between two fundamentally different political ideologies but rather a conflict over which side, North or South, represented the true "faith of the fathers." Hence Jefferson Davis could argue in his inaugural address that, in seceding from the Union, the Confederacy was acting on the American belief "that governments rest on the consent of the governed, and that it is the right of the people to alter or abolish them at will whenever they become destructive of the ends for which they were established."[35] Similarly, speaking with equal conviction at Independence Hall in 1861 on his journey to Washington to be inaugurated President, Lincoln could vow, "I have never had a feeling politically that did not spring from the sentiments embodied in the Declaration of Independence."[36] The American Civil War represented a division within the faithful (the civil peoplehood) over the true meaning of the faith (the civil theology).

While political parties develop as institutional expressions of a civil religion without any public legal mandate, a majoritarian, nonpluralistic electoral system was established by federal and state law. The single-member electoral district emerged out of a liberal ideology, and, like the majoritarian public school establishment, it serves as a powerful instrument to preserve the ideological consensus in American society. This is because the single-member district makes it almost impossible for parties which stand *outside* the ideological consensus to elect someone to office. Since voting for a third or fourth party essentially wastes one's vote, the basic incentive in a single-member district is to vote for one of the major candidates or parties that stand *within* the ideological consensus. Casting a vote for a candidate of a minor party may be symbolically important, but when only the candidate who wins a plurality of votes is elected to office there is little chance to have that vote translated into direct representation.

A direct relationship thus exists between the legal establishment of a majoritarian single-member electoral system and the maintenance of a liberal Lockean consensus in America. The failure of the American system to produce major political parties representing fundamentally different views of public justice, as well as the political and legal restrictions on the implementation of proportional representation, are directly linked to the role political parties and the electoral system play as institutional expressions of a civil religion in American society.[37]

Civil Religion, Civil Rights, and Christian Responsibility

One of the ironies of an Enlightenment ideology is that the concern to protect individual freedom from the authoritarian control of the state has led, in the case of America, to the undermining not only of the structural identity and task of the state but also of many other societal institutions necessary for a meaningful life in modern society. The refusal to recognize the rights of institutions as institutions is a form of discrimination which manifests the ontological assumptions of an individualist political ideology. Such discrimination leads on the policy level to a program of ignoring institutions, of conceding to them no claims of rights as institutions in cases involving their very identity.[38]

Moreover, the rights of individuals as well as of groups have not always fared well in the majoritarian, nonpluralistic public legal order ruled by the American civil religion. De Tocqueville was one of the earliest writers to warn against the dangers of a majoritarian liberal tradition. He pointed out, for example, that with respect to religious freedom Americans were in danger of losing their liberty to the authoritarian "voice of the people." Behind the veil of religious toleration, a "tyranny of the Majority" was developing in America. De Tocqueville concluded that faith in public opinion was becoming "a species of religion," and the majority "its ministering prophet."[39]

De Tocqueville observed that the majority not only made the laws in the Republic, but also had the ability to enforce majoritarian values. Though *laws* were supported by majority rule, the enforcement of majoritarian *values* was more subtle but no less real.

> The master no longer says, "You shall think as I do or you shall die"; but he says "you are free to think differently from me, and to retain your life, your property and all that you possess; but you are henceforth a stranger among your people. You may retain your civil rights, but they will be useless to you, for you will never be chosen by your fellow-citizens, if you solicit their votes; and they will affect to scorn you, if you ask for their esteem. You will remain among men, but you will be deprived of the rights of mankind. Your fellow creatures will shun you like an impure being; and even those who believe in your innocence will abandon you, lest they should be shunned in their turn. Go in peace! I have given you your life, but it is an existence worse than death."[40]

One who challenged the dogmas of the civil theology was not physically punished but was isolated and ignored by the majority. The person was labeled un-American and "excommunicated."

Given the development of a civil religion in America, one might ask why so few Christians have challenged the dogmas of the civil theology and separated themselves from the false demands of the civil peoplehood and civil institutions. Although the Christian community was heir to the biblical view that Christ is sovereign over *all of life,* many individuals and groups modified this confession by separating life into the realm of grace and the realm of nature, the "spiritual" and the "worldly." This dualism limits the Christian faith to the private aspect of one's life while consciously or unconsciously allowing one's public life to be directed by other norms. This form of religious individualism often took for granted or ignored public life outside the institutional church, and sought rather to build up religious cells of the "saved" within society. By concentrating so heavily on matters of the "soul," a distinctly Christian understanding of public justice and societal institutions did not develop.

Another factor which made it easy for Christians to accept a majoritarian, nonpluralistic public legal order was that they were the majority. Even if actions and laws were not distinctly Christian, it was obvious that many flowed from the Judeo-Christian ethic. If public schools, for example, were run by the state and inculcated republican values, as Horace Mann and others planned, they also reflected the basically Christian (largely Protestant) feelings of the majority. Roman Catholics and Jews attending these schools frequently felt uncomfortable. The Catholics, especially, began to organize their own schools for which they had to pay the cost while continuing to support public schools through their taxes. Setting up alternative schools was motivated by the Catholic conviction that the public school establishment represented a vehicle for imposing the sectarian beliefs of a Protestant majority upon a minority.

By the twentieth century Americans were becoming more secular in their beliefs. The secularization process was reflected in changing educational philosophies, curricula, textbooks, and personnel in the public schools. Protestant beliefs were being replaced by similar religious ones.

Now many Christians find themselves faced by the hard reality of the American civil religion: The majority rules, and they are no longer the majority. It is of course true that certain aspects of the civil religion are in crisis. The rejection of the melting-pot ideal, for instance, has strained the notion of a civil peoplehood. Civil institutions no longer command the loyalty they did in the past. Nevertheless, despite these developments, foundational dogmas of the civil religion remain largely unassailed. Basic tenets of the civil theology, such as the sovereignty of the people, are rarely questioned.

Hence the challenge and task facing Christians today is monumental. Christians must demonstrate how a political perspective conscious of its religious assumptions can break the bonds of a civil religion by structuring a truly pluralistic public legal order. Furthermore, Christians must actively work for the civil rights of all individuals, groups, and institutions in American society. The field of education is just one area in which an individualist, liberal ideology has structured a nonpluralistic public legal order which is fundamentally unjust.[41]

The first Amendment to the Constitution prohibits Congress from making any law respecting an establishment of religion. The Supreme Court has ruled in the famous 1963 decision outlawing oral prayer and Bible reading in the public schools that, with respect to religion, "the government is neutral, and while protecting all, it prefers none, and it disparages none. . . . In the relationship between man and religion, the state is firmly committed to a position of neutrality."[42] The Court's assertion that it has discovered a basis for its judicial reasoning which guarantees such neutrality rests on the assumption that the distinction between religious and nonreligious or secular activities can be determined. Yet one may justifiably argue that the Court has come to this conclusion because it has uncritically accepted an individualistic, liberal ideology which assumes, among other things, a secular/religious dichotomy. But such an assumption is self-evident only to those who stand within the liberal tradition. To those who do not, the religious/secular dichotomy is less of a neutral self-evident truth than it is a self-serving sectarian criterion used to secure, for example, public funds for some schools and to deny funds for others.

To the extent that the present system of public education is nonpluralistic, it fails to measure up to the standards of a truly democratic institution. More and more citizens and groups are coming to join in this criticism and to conclude that a system of state-supported and administered public education which is fundamentally rejected by individuals and groups who are, nevertheless, forced by law to support it financially without receiving proportional funding for alternative schools, is a violation of the rights of minorities by the majority. Christians who stand up for their civil rights must do so in the interest of the civil rights of all minorities, whether they be Jews, Black Muslims, Indians, or others whose beliefs necessitate a rejection of the educational context, outlook, purpose, and methods of the currently all-powerful, nonpluralistic, public school system.

What the Supreme Court and other government bodies have failed to realize in cases dealing with religion and the public schools is that the actions of individuals, groups, and institutions are inescapably guided by basic assumptions about human nature and society. Only after this has been realized can genuine neutrality arise which will give proportionally equal and just distribution of tax monies and services to all citizens, groups, and institutions which represent the many different ideological and religious perspectives and peoplehoods existing in our pluralistic society. The state must seek to do justice to the many diverse communities of belief as they concern themselves not only with their special ecclesiastical institutions but with such matters as education, industry, the arts, and the media.

One of the encouraging developments concerning issues of public justice is that individuals and groups from many different backgrounds and perspectives are more carefully questioning the norms of liberal majoritarian democracy. Evidence of this is a renewed interest in the normative character of societal pluralism. For example, *Consociational Democracy: Political Accommodation in Segmented Societies,* edited by Kenneth McRae, is a work that results from political studies of a number of smaller European democracies which reveal that an alternative exists to the commonly accepted classification of western-style democratic regimes.[43]

Discussions in the past have usually contrasted stable two-party systems based on alternating majority governments with more volatile multi-party systems based on fluctuating ministerial coalitions. It is now pointed out by a number of highly respected political scientists that the Netherlands, for example, is characterized by both a stable democratic government and substantial divisions in its social structure, divisions based on broad ideological or religious foundations. In such a "consolidational democracy" (characteristic also of Belgium, Austria, and Switzerland), political parties as well as other voluntary associations such as schools and labor unions are structured so as to acknowledge confessional differences.

This full recognition of the "spiritual families" (Catholic, Calvinist, or the secular religions of liberalism, socialism, or communism) means that no artificial dichotomy is recognized between the religious and nonreligious individual, between religious and secular institutions, or between sacred and profane culture. Full societal pluralism of consociational democracy is to be contrasted with Anglo-American democratic societies which, operating out of a dualistic view of life, encourage pluralism (the freedom of sectarian groups) in the *private* spheres of life (in church, home, etc.) while failing to encourage or fully recognize pluralism in the *public* life of the political community. American pluralism is thus a *limited* pluralism; it does not extend fully into the public legal order.

Clearly, what is needed in order to provide justice for all is a political perspective that gives rise to a public legal order that is more rather than less responsive to the diversified confessional life of modern society. The desire for full public recognition of the legitimate differences among peoples is being voiced at the grass roots of society. Out of the melting-pot myth is emerging a new ethno-religious consciousness from white ethnic groups, such as the Polish, Italians, Portuguese, Hispanics, as well as the Black, Chinese, and Indians. Their concern is the same: for equal protection and benefits under the law. Many groups are now demanding full public recognition of their life views in such things as the distribution of federal funds, their own schools, proportional representation in local government and media. Only time will tell if the rise in consciousness of different ethno-religious "peoplehoods" can serve as a foundation for fuller expression of societal pluralism. A political system such as a consociational democracy would, it seems, be more amenable to providing justice for the pluralism of "peoplehoods" in America than is the present liberal majoritarian system.

In summary, I have argued that a civil religion, with a civil theology, peoplehood, and institutions, has dominated American thought and structured an essentially nonpluralistic public legal order for American society.[44] The fact that the present political structure does not measure up to the norms of a truly pluralistic order is indicated by the discontent voiced by individuals, groups, and institutions demanding a fuller recognition of their civil rights. One can expect that the presence and the consequences of a civil religion will become even more apparent in the future. When this occurs there may be an increased willingness to explore how a pluralistic public legal order breaks the bonds of civil religion and allows all citizens, groups, and institutions to fulfill their unique identities and tasks in a free society under law.

"American Civil Religion," Notes

1. Conrad Cherry, *God's New Israel: Religious Interpretations of American Destiny* (Englewood Cliffs, N.J.: Prentice-Hall, 1971), p. 10.

2. The eminent historian Louis Hartz discusses the notion of atomistic social freedom as a basic assumption of American political thought in his book, *The Liberal Tradition in America* (New York: Harcourt Brace Jovanovich, 1955), p. 62. In the present essay the terms "liberal" and "individualist" are used interchangeably. As Hartz points out, the very nature of the liberal tradition is that it is individualistic and antistatist. The liberal tradition is to be contrasted to the European conservative tradition which is hierarchically oriented and statist. We have no American conservatives in the European sense, or almost none. In America "right wing" conservatism and "left wing" liberalism are two wings of the same liberal tradition.

3. The phrase in the Declaration of Independence, "The Laws of Nature and Nature's God," testifies to the belief that it was from nature that individuals discovered political truth. In this context, "Nature's God" was merely the necessary hypothesis that Jefferson and eighteenth-century Enlightenment thinkers used to demonstrate that reality was what human reason made it.

4. R. R. Palmer, *The Age of Democratic Revolution: A Political History of Europe and America, 1760-1800,* vol. 1: *The Challenge* (Princeton: Princeton University Press, 1969), p. 228.

5. Alexander Hamilton, "The Federalist No. 22," in *The Federalist Papers,* introduction by Clinton Rossiter (New York: The New American Library of World Literature, 1961), p. 152. Emphasis in the original.

6. For a more detailed discussion and analysis of an individualist view of society see Rockne McCarthy, "Liberal Democracy and the Rights of Institutions," *Pro Rege* (a faculty publication of Dordt College, Sioux Center, Iowa), vol VIII, no. 4 (June, 1980).

7. Universalism and Pluralism represent alternative views of social reality. See Rockne McCarthy, "Three Societal Models: A Theoretical and Historical Overview," *Pro Rege,* vol. IX, no. 4 (June, 1981).

8. *Chisholm* v. *Georgia,* 2 Dallas 419, 1L. Ed. 440 (1793).

9. Hartz, *The Liberal Tradition,* p. 9.

10. Alexis de Tocqueville, *Democracy in America,* ed. Richard D. Heffner (New York: The New American Library, 1956), p. 58.

11. Some of the recent systematic accounts are: Ernest Lee Tuveson, *Redeemer Nation: The Idea of America's Millennial Role* (Chicago: University of Chicago Press, 1968); Russell B. Nye, *This Almost Chosen People* (East Lansing: Michigan State University Press, 1966); and Richard W. Van Alstyne, *Genesis of American Nationalism* (Waltham, Mass.: Blaisdell Publishing Co., 1970). For many of the relevant documents as well as editorial insights see Conrad Cherry's *God's New Israel*. An older yet penetrating analysis can be found in H. Richard Neibuhr's *The Kingdom of God in America* (New York: Harper & Row, 1937).

12. For a detailed analysis see Perry Miller, *The New England Mind: The Seventeenth Century* (Boston: Beacon Press, 1961), pp. 365-462.

13. Palmer, *The Challenge,* p. 224.

14. Palmer, *The Challenge,* p. 223.

15. Palmer, *The Challenge,* p. 223-224.

16. Palmer, *The Challenge,* p. 224. Adams was familiar with Rousseau's *Social Contract,* and Book I, ch. VI may have provided a specific source for Adams's concept of "citizen."

17. René De Visme Williamson, *Independence and Involvement: A Christian Reorientation in Political Science* (Baton Rouge: Louisiana State University Press, 1964), p. 171.

18. John Adams, quoted in Tuveson, *Redeemer Nation,* p. 25.

19. Albert Katz Weinberg, *Manifest Destiny: A Study of Nationalist Expansionism in American History* (Gloucester, Mass.: Peter Smith, 1958), p. 16.

20. Weinberg, *Manifest Destiny,* pp. 16-17.

21. Alexander Hamilton, "The Federalist No. 1," p. 33. Emphasis mine.

22. Tuveson, *Redeemer Nation,* p. 213.

23. Tuveson, *Redeemer Nation,* p. 213.

24. Tuveson, *Redeemer Nation,* p. 213.

25. For a radical revisionist interpretation of the Atlantic Coast Indians' encounter with white settlers during the colonial period of United States history, see Francis Jennings, *The Invasion of America: Indians, Colonialism, and the Cant of Conquest* (New York: W. W. Norton & Co., 1976).

26. Quoted in David B. Tyack, ed., *Turning Points in American Educational History* (Waltham, Mass.: Blaisdell Publishing Co., 1967), p. 90.

27. For a full examination of Jefferson's religious perspective and its role in shaping a vision of public education in America, see Rockne McCarthy, James Skillen, and William Harper, *Disestablishment A Second Time: Genuine Pluralism for American Schools* (Washington, D.C.: The Christian University Press, 1982).

28. Thomas Jefferson, quoted in Tyack, *Turning Points,* p. 91.

29. Tyack, *Turning Points,* p. 91.

30. Jefferson, quoted in Tyack, *Turning Points,* p. 91.

31. Tyack, *Turning Points,* p. 91.

32. John F. Wilson, "The Status of 'Civil Religion' in America," in Elwyn A. Smith, ed., *The Religion of the Republic* (Philadelphia: Fortress Press, 1971), pp. 7, 8-9. For an analysis of the religious character of public education in America see Rousas J. Rushdoony, *The Messianic Character of American Education* (Nutley, N.J.: The

Craig Press, 1963). A convenient collection of documents can be found in Rush Welter, ed., *American Writings of Popular Education: The Nineteenth Century* (Indianapolis: The Bobbs Merrill Co., 1971).

33. Elwyn A. Smith, ed., *The Religion of the Republic*, p. viii. The same point was made much earlier by Sidney E. Mead, in "Thomas Jefferson's 'Fair Experiment'—Religious Freedom," p. 68. This is one of a collection of Mead's articles published together under the title, *The Lively Experiment: The Shaping of Christianity in America* (New York: Harper & Row, 1963).

34. Cecelia Kenyon, "Republicanism and Radicalism in the American Revolution: An Old-Fashioned Interpretation," in *The Reinterpretation of the American Revolution, 1763-1789,* ed. Jack P. Green (New York: Harper & Row, 1968), p. 305.

35. Jefferson Davis, quoted in Ralph Henry Gabriel, *The Course of American Democratic Thought,* 2d edition (New York: The Ronald Press, 1956), pp. 121-122.

36. Abraham Lincoln, speech, Philadelphia, February 22, 1861, in *Abraham Lincoln: Selected Speeches, Messages, and Letters* (New York: Holt, Rinehart, and Winston, 1957), pp. 136-137.

37. For a more detailed analysis of the differences between a proportional and majoritarian system of representation as well as the history of proportional representation in the United States, see Clarence Hoag and George Hallett, *Proportional Representation* (New York: The Macmillan Co., 1926); James Skillen, "Justice for Representation: A Proposal for Revitalizing Our System of Political Participation" (Washington, D.C.: Association for Public Justice, 1979).

38. Well-known sociologist Peter Berger and *Worldview* magazine editor Richard Neuhaus argue that freedom is weakened by public policies and court decisions which undercut the position of nonpolitical institutions in society. See *To Empower People: The Role of Mediating Structures in Public Policy* (Washington, D.C.: American Enterprise Institute for Public Policy Research, 1977). See also Rockne McCarthy, "Liberal Democracy and the Rights of Institutions."

39. Tocqueville, *Democracy in America,* p. 149.

40. Tocqueville, *Democracy in America,* p. 188. Tocqueville's reference is to an author, but it is clear that the example holds for anyone who challenges the will of the majority.

41. For a detailed look at the forces behind the rise of the American school system and a critical assessment of that system together with proposals for change, see Rockne McCarthy, et al., *Society, State, and Schools: A Case for Structural and Confessional Pluralism* (Grand Rapids: Eerdmans, 1981).

42. *School District of Abington TP., PA.* v. *Schempp,* 374 U.S. 203 (1963).

43. Kenneth D. McRae, ed., *Consociational Democracy: Political Accommodation in Segmented Societies* (Toronto: McClelland and Stewart, 1974). See also McRae's Presidential Address to the Canadian Political Science Association in 1979, "The Plural Society and the Western Political Tradition," *Canadian Journal of Political Science,* vol. XII, no. 4 (December 1979), pp. 675-688.

44. For different interpretations of the meaning of civil religion in America see Donald R. Cutler, ed., *The Religious Situation: 1968* (Boston: Beacon Press, 1968); and Russell E. Richey and Donald G. Jones, eds., *American Civil Religion* (New York: Harper & Row, 1974).

Study Questions

Is American Civil Religion Christian?

1.   Why does McCarthy argue that civil religion, by its very nature, means automatic discrimination against persons and groups with minority perspectives? Do you agree?

2.   According to Whitehead, how did Christianity lose its predominant influence in America? How was it the fault of Christians?

3.   After reading McCarthy and Whitehead, would you say that the Christian community in America is suffering the fate of a "minority perspective" in a nation with a civil religion that is now predominantly secular and humanistic? What reasons would you give in support of your answer?

4.   Would you say that Hammond supports the idea that our current civil religion is "secular"? Why?

5.   What is the crucial difference between Hammond's and Whitehead's reasons for our civil religion's "secularization" (the disappearance of traditional theism)?

6.   Hammond sees religion as a "meaning system" which provides a "moral architecture" for living. Whitehead sees Christianity as a "world view" which affirms certain "fundamental principles of moral judgment" for living. How would you say that these conceptions of religion are similar? How are they different?

7.   How is Hammond and Whitehead's view of religion different from McCarthy's view that religion entails "fundamental assumptions about man and society"? How does this difference relate to McCarthy's disagreement with them over the need for a single, unifying civil religion?

Part IV

Is There a Response That Is Christian?

Our readings have brought us to a significant divergence of opinion. The first side, articulated clearly by Whitehead, recognizes the fundamentally theistic character of America's traditional "Christian consensus" and urges its re-establishment in the nation. The other, represented by McCarthy's argument, questions how authentically "Christian" that early consensus was and points to a "disestablishment" of all "religious" perspectives so a "truly pluralistic" public order can develop. The volume's final two readings reflect these two divergent viewpoints by calling for two different kinds of practical Christian responses to the current political situation.

A Call to Reform America

The section begins with Whitehead's encouraging Christians to recognize the inevitable weakness of secular humanism and to remember that the Church has a cultural mandate "to be a dominant influence on the whole [of] culture." To be such an influence, Christians must reject today's concept of pluralism. Contrary to an earlier, more legitimate definition of pluralism, Whitehead charges that today's understanding means "that a Christian should not seek to force his or her religious beliefs on another." This notion of pluralism has led to a relativistic social consensus in which "nothing is right or wrong; it is only a matter of preference." This is contrary to the Bible and has kept the church from fulfilling its cultural mandate "to conquer alien belief systems and to convert the individuals holding them."

If America is to be "reformed in a Christian sense," it will need to be done at the grassroots. Whitehead sketches a strategy for a Christian reforming effort. Pastors must redefine "church activities in such a way to recapture the biblical emphasis that involvement in all areas of the culture is a necessary part of true spirituality." Christians must work to dismantle "piece by piece" the "giant federal machine." Christians must fight the humanistic influences rampant in the schools, media, and literature. Churches must begin to "flood the law schools with Christian law students who [will] eventually influence the legal and governmental system."

As an attorney, Whitehead is particularly concerned to stress the importance of law in our society. Christians must come to realize that "the entire American system is structured upon law." Thus, they must begin to study and understand the Christian foundation of law if they hope to reassert Christian influence. He is particularly outspoken on the role of the Christian who practices law. The Christian lawyer must see his practice not as a livelihood, but "as a vocation to take society by the horns and turn it around." Christians, he argues, need to be moving into the legal system, dedicated "to fighting the evil that now pervades the courts and the whole enterprise of law."

Whitehead concludes by summarizing the immediate objectives of Christian reforming action.

1) The federal government's power must be cut back "to its constitutional limit, returning much of the power of the federal bureaucracy to the state and local governments." To this end, Christians should work to get Congress to cut funds to federal agencies and to restrict the power and number of federal courts.

2) Where feasible, the Christian community should aggressively pursue legal action, taking the offense just as the ACLU has done in its efforts to push "their version of social change onto society through the courts."

3) Judeo-Christian theism must be reinstilled throughout the public education system, from elementary to university level. If it becomes clear that "there is little hope of revamping public education, . . . then Christians must remove their financial support from the system."

4) The church must begin to take seriously its duty to provide for the education and welfare of the people.

In the final analysis, the church must come to see that it is, by its very nature, a political institution. It is political, explains Whitehead, "from the standpoint that, as Christ's exclusive preserve, the state has no legitimate authority over it. The true church says 'hands off' to Caesar." Whitehead explains that this is a political statement because it delineates the authority of the state. But does the statement mean that the state is not part of Christ's exclusive preserve? Does it imply that Christ's authority over the state is diluted or shared in a way that is fundamentally different from his authority over the church? Or does it imply that Caesar, in some way, stands outside Christ's authority? The attitude that suggests human politics is less subject to Christ's lordship than is church activity is strongly criticized by Skillen in the final article.

The Politics of Grace

According to Skillen, "human politics is always God's business." The Lord, not "the will of the people," is king of politics. Of course, people do have political responsibilities, but Skillen explains, "the biblical perspective always places human political responsibility in the context of God's sovereignty and Christ's lordship." Skillen thus implies that government is just as much a part of Christ's preserve as is the church. Both employ human office and responsibility; both stand under the Lord's authority and judgment. Having established that human political responsibility is never a self-evident affair, Skillen argues that Christian politics ought then to reflect the character of God.

Skillen reminds us that our time, the time between Christ's first advent and his second coming, is "a time of great patience, long-suffering and grace on God's part." He argues that "God's gracious patience has considerable significance for politics"; namely, that we are to love our enemies, even our political ones.

Building directly on God's gracious patience and love, Skillen argues that Christian politics will manifest itself not in an attempt to control the state, nor in an attempt to flood political office with Christians so that the government may be used to promote Christian belief. Rather, Christian politics will mean that "Christians will work politically for the achievement of governmental policies that will protect, encourage, and open up life for every person and community of people, whatever their religious confession and view of life." Skillen agrees that this is a hard lesson for Christians to learn since throughout history governments have been used to enforce a single, dominant "religious" consensus. But to use government in this way, he argues, even in defense of Christian domination, is to violate God's intention for government. "It is not *Christian* justice for Christians to enjoy any political privilege at the expense of non-Christians."

In many ways Skillen's argument echoes McCarthy's criticism of civil religion's unity assumption. He shows how earlier political systems which enforced paganism (ancient Rome) and Christianity (medieval Europe) are comparable to modern liberal regimes which enforce supposedly "neutral" or "secular" civil religions. All equally violate the biblical norm of justice, according to Skillen, and must be rejected.

He warns Christians that "politics does not exist as a neutral enterprise" and that "religion cannot be kept out of the life of the state." But he is not here referring only to theological or moral beliefs, he is pointing to the "religious" impulse of civil religion to enforce a dominant perspective. He characterizes American civil religion as a "secularized Christianity" with just such an impulse. He summarizes by saying that if a Christian approach of patient, gracious justice does not rule human political life, "then some other religious dynamic will control it. If all people are not cared for in an evenhanded way in the public legal domain, then another religious impulse will lead to injustice and discrimination."

Like Whitehead, Skillen concludes his discussion by outlining a strategy for Christian action. But the contrast between the two plans for action is striking.

1) Christians must repent "that they have not always been ministers of God's gracious, patient justice to others."
2) Christians must recognize the "communal" responsibility they have for others and begin working together as a political community to take up the complex issues of our time "in the light of the Christian norm of patient, gracious, loving justice."
3) Christians must renew their way of "thinking and living in politics" so as to develop a common "Christian political mind" that can begin to grasp the principles of Christ's kingdom that hold for earthly politics.

We need to note the pattern of similarity and contrast in Whitehead's and Skillen's very different calls for Christian action.

Both Whitehead and Skillen agree that Christianity cannot be compromised with secular humanism in the Christian's approach to public life. But the focus of the struggle is understood differently.

For Whitehead Christianity in politics means striving to use public and legal structures to enhance or advance the biblical absolutes by which all moral judgments of life are measured. The fight with humanism is whether biblical absolutes or humanism's "new system of arbitrary absolutes" will govern in society. For Skillen, Christianity in politics means operating under the biblical norm of public justice so that public and legal structures are reformed to permit evenhanded treatment for the individuals, groups, and institutions (families, churches, and schools) of all religious communities. The fight with humanism is whether humanism's despotic impulse for a single, "universal" religion will govern in society.

Both Whitehead and Skillen believe that Christianity is not simply a privatized religion. Both affirm that the Christian community has a responsibility to influence society. Both strongly argue that Christians have an obligation to proclaim forcefully the biblical perspective before others, taking every thought captive to Christ and seeking the conversion of those holding alien belief systems. Whitehead believes it should be done, at least in part, through the force of law as Christians re-capture public and legal institutions. Skillen believes it should be done through a new commitment by Christians to a communal, political effort that seeks justice for all.

11. Plan for Action

John W. Whitehead

Prophets of doom surround us. Many believe that the current political and social order is crumbling. The humanistic foundation that undergirds the West cannot stand the tensions of contemporary society. Instead of making the Christian fret, this should cause him to rejoice. It means that Christians can do something to effect change. The Christian can speak with clarity in the midst of the chaos. And although things may grow worse—the collapse of the economy, threats of war, and such—the Christian must take Romans 8 seriously: "And we know that all things work together for good to them that love God, to them who are the called according to his purpose" (v. 28).

The Christian who sees no hope is not living consistently with the teachings of the Bible. We should view the world through the mind of Christ, because he is working for *all* things to come together for the good of the true church. It is the humanist who should have no hope. For him there is no God; only a cold grave awaits him.

We must, however, realize that things have steadily declined for the worse. It is difficult to find much truth on any subject in the media or even the law. Issues are not what they seem. The humanists have succeeded in rewriting and rewording most forms of communication—including the Bible. This is so people won't know what the truth is.

Such censorship was the focus of Ray Bradbury's novel, *Fahrenheit 451,* where a futuristic state burned all books in order to hide the truth from the people. As Bradbury wrote in an afterword to a later edition of the book: "Fire-Captain Beatty, in my novel *Fahrenheit 451,* described how the books were burned first by minorities, each ripping a page or a paragraph from this book, until the day came when the books were empty and the minds shut and the libraries closed forever." The Christian community, therefore, must realize that the humanists, like the firemen in Bradbury's tale, are slowly whittling away at the substance of truth in our world.

Recovering the Externality Idea

Philosophy is important. A person's philosophy dictates how he will act. If Christians continue to take the position that they are impotent in the face of the crises we face, then we will continue to have little effect on the culture.

Once, after I spoke on the obvious peril in the coming years, a lady told me that although the church may be persecuted, "Christians can go to the lions singing." Indeed, but we have a responsibility to try and stop the downward spiral before we get to the lions!

Often people come up and tell me they will be praying for me. I appreciate the power of prayer; I have seen its effectiveness in my own life. However, such a mentality can be a cop-out. It is easy to say, "I'll pray for you," and then go home and sink into an easy chair and watch television. If people who assume this position really mean it, they will act on their prayers. The apostle James tells us that faith is dead without works.

The church is holding "the truth in unrighteousness" when the church remains silent on the issues and fails to act as the Bible requires. Christians literally stagnate in churches that have no external political, legal, or moral impact upon the world. Truth cannot be bottled up and be effective.

The church must learn to externalize the principles of its faith as practiced by Christians during the Reformation and in early America. The truths of the Bible must flow from the mind into the world. A false pietism, a false "spirituality," and all the exclusively internal activities that so often make up the contemporary church neither bring revival nor reformation. The light must be taken from beneath the basket and placed on the hill.

Remembering the Cultural Mandate

The church has a mandate from the Creator to be a dominant influence on the whole culture, as I have mentioned before. In Matthew 5 Christ mandates or requires the church to be "salt" to the culture. "You are the salt of the earth; but if the salt has become tasteless, how will it be made salty again?" (v. 13, NAS). Salt not only preserves meats; salt makes one thirsty. If the church is fulfilling its proper role, the culture should be thirsty for the knowledge of biblical truth.

Salt, if placed on metal and dampened with water, will slowly eat through steel. The church, which holds truth, should be able to penetrate and defeat the arguments and actions of paganism. Any Christian who believes he cannot effectively answer the secularist's arguments either doesn't really know his Bible or has not taken the time to study how to apply what he believes.

There is a strong emphasis in some sections of the church today on personal evangelism. That is admirable, but it is only one part of being "salt" to the world. It cannot be the only emphasis. The church has to touch and influence the entire community. Christians are not simply witnessing machines. We are a *whole people,* and we live in a *whole world.* To give a large section of the world over to paganism without a fight is to cheat God.

As theologian J. Gresham Machen pointed out in 1912: "We may preach with all the fervour of a reformer and yet succeed only in winning a straggler here and there, if we permit the whole collective thought of the nation . . . to be controlled by ideas which, by the restless force of logic, prevent Christianity from being regarded as anything more than a harmless delusion."

Clearly, if Christ's mandate to be the salt is denied by the church (and it is a voluntary refusal to follow Christ's orders), then Christ sees the church as good for nothing but to be trampled under the feet of men. The consequence is persecution. It is a form of judgment, but it is also a way of forcing the church to respond to the cultural mandate.

But when the church refuses to act as salt, it also brings judgment upon the culture surrounding it. Not only must the church suffer but also the non-Christian culture. And when the final judgment comes, the blood of those who have never heard the consistent Christian message and die without Christ is on the hands of the church. It is a terrible burden to bear.

Pluralism

The church must beware of the concept of "pluralism" as it is advocated today. I am not saying that we should be opposed to the fact that cultures and races are different, and they should be respected for what they are. This was the old concept of pluralism. But the new form is different. It says that a Christian should not seek to force his or her religious beliefs on another. Unfortunately this has led to a consensus within society that anything is acceptable. Nothing is right or wrong; it is only a matter of preference.

To say this runs contrary to the mandates of the Bible. There is truth and untruth. There is good and evil. Christianity is truth. In the Great Commission Christ charged the church to conquer alien belief systems and to convert the individuals holding them. The pluralistic concept promulgated by modern society is a way of keeping the church from fulfilling the cultural mandate. The Christian is to "make disciples" of individuals, institutions, and cultures, not cower before alternative belief systems.

The church, it seems, has learned, as a successful Volkswagen commercial once put it, "to think small." This idea must be reversed or it stands to reason that we face perilous days ahead. To put it bluntly, as a man "thinketh in his heart, so is he." If the church really takes the Bible seriously, it can think like God. His plan ends in victory for the church, not defeat.

What Can We Do?

The first step is to recognize the problems within the Christian community itself. We must remove the beam from our own eye by putting God and the Bible first and recognize that Christ is Lord over all areas of life. Then we are ready for action. Politics, the legal profession, social commentary, the press, all the fields of communication and academia are open to the Christian.

By sheer number the individual Christian can effect great change. We must be aware of the need to be educated on the issues and, once educated, wary of compromise. Many fine books have been written that deal with aspects of these topics. Here is a representative sample:

- Schaeffer, Francis. *A Christian Manifesto*. Westchester, Illinois: Crossway Books, 1981.
- Schaeffer, Francis. *How Should We Then Live?* Old Tappan, New Jersey: Fleming H. Revell Co., 1976.

- Schaeffer, Francis, and Koop, C. Everett. *Whatever Happened to the Human Race?* Old Tappan, New Jersey: Fleming H. Revell Co., 1979.
- Rushdoony, R. J. *This Independent Republic.* Fairfax, Virginia: Thoburn Press, 1964.
- Brown, Harold O. J. *The Reconstruction of the Republic.* New Rochelle, New York: Arlington House, 1977.
- Schaeffer, Franky. *Addicted to Mediocrity.* Westchester, Illinois: Crossway Books, 1981.
- Peters, Charles. *How Washington Really Works.* Reading, Massachusetts: Addison-Wesley Publishing Co., 1980.
- Jackson, Jeremy C. *No Other Foundation.* Westchester, Illinois: Crossway Books, 1980.

These books, plus those cited within the text, will give you a good start.

We live in a visual age, and the electronic media have great impact. It would be a good idea to purchase or rent the films *How Should We Then Live?* and *Whatever Happened to the Human Race?* and show them to community groups and individuals, as well as *The Second American Revolution,* the film counterpart to my book.

Once you have developed a knowledge of the issues, keep informed on current legislation. If you are involved in Christian broadcasting or publishing, begin a radio spot or a column that will feature issues that affect our religious liberty. If you are a lay person, suggest such a program to your Christian network or favorite magazine.

The most important contribution the individual can make is to become actively involved in local community affairs, politics, and legal battles. If America is going to be revitalized or reformed in a Christian sense, it will be done at the local level. America was meant to be primarily a system of local governments. The giant federal machine we have today in Washington, D.C., was never intended by the framers and must eventually be dismantled piece by piece.

Getting involved in local politics will eventually mean Christians running for office. This will include attending and eventually taking control of party conventions where grass-roots decisions are made. But you must begin right now by becoming involved in various political committees, thereby getting your name before party leaders as well as the electorate. We simply cannot expect a consistent Christian response to issues from non-Christian officials.

At the local level committed Christians, who understand the lordship of Christ over all of life, can have a tremendous impact. I have seen instances where one Christian sitting on a public board composed of seven members tipped the balance on the most crucial issues. Public school boards are probably one of the most important and influential organizations at the local level. They determine which books and educational materials go into the schools as well as the curriculum teachers teach. The potential for influencing the education of young minds is staggering.

Short of running for office, your contact with your local, state, and public officials is vital. In my involvement on the federal level with senators and congressmen, it has always amazed me how little input these men and women receive from the Christian community before voting on legislation. Many of the problems churches and Christian schools face with state intervention and interference today would never have arisen if the church and individual Christian had done their homework.

Letter writing is very important—not form letters, but handwritten letters voicing objection or approval concerning a piece of legislation. Christians within the various churches can form local political groups to coordinate letter writing. This means getting organized. These groups can also make sure that your representatives receive personal visits from people in the community. These are the tactics used by the proponents of legislation designed to destroy the Christian way of life. If done with honest and sincere motives, there is nothing wrong with telling your representative how you feel on an issue. In fact, your letter may tip the scale on how he votes.

The most powerful tool available to the individual, and individuals as organized in a group, is the ballot box. If your representative does not heed your advice on the central issues, then unseat him. This may involve running your own candidate.

Where possible seek out lawyers and judges who are sympathetic to your cause and push hard for their appointment to judgeships. Moreover, by placing pressure on your elected representatives, try to stop the appointment of anti-Christian judges. Something must be done to balance the courts. Forcing your representative to appoint judges who are sympathetic to the Judeo-Christian world view could very well impede the activism of the courts.

The Moral Majority has proven that grass-roots efforts can have a tremendous impact on the national level. No matter what else can be said about the Moral Majority, it has used the freedom we still have in the political arena to stand against the state. The ordinary citizen can affect the political process.

Humanistic Influences

We also need to be constantly questioning the influences that surround us. Much of the humanistic indoctrination of society is being carried on by agencies that appear to be independent private groups but, because of their funding by the federal government are, in reality, arms of the state. An example of such an organization is the Public Broadcasting Service (PBS), which, although providing some good program content, consistently airs programs that favor unbiblical choices. Besides the program "Choosing Suicide," PBS has aired other programs such as "Guess Who's Pregnant Now?" Forty-five minutes of this one-hour special was given to directors of Planned Parenthood and others who advocated liberal sex education in the public schools. In contrast a few minutes of a film clip from a Southern pastor's sermon represented the Christian stand. Throughout the program Christians were depicted as being against all sex education, as expecting their children to blindly follow the Seventh Commandment. Actually Christian groups are objecting to the promiscuity and amoral standards taught in some sex education programs, not sex education itself. The commentator's denouncing of the Christian stand as ignorant and irrelevant was veiled but insidious.

Public Broadcasting Service also aired a six-part program, "Hard Choices," which discussed without moral comment such issues as genetic screening and amniocentesis, the inserting of a hollow needle through the uterus to determine fetus sex, and the subsequent abortion of unborn children because they are not the sex parents desire.

An organization which is responsible directly or indirectly for much of the proabortion propaganda that has been infiltrated throughout the United States is Planned Parenthood Federation of America. Amazingly enough, Planned Parenthood and its over one hundred affiliates have received over $100 million by direct grants and reimbursements from the federal government to promote, in effect, genocide.

Through such groups the federal government has placed itself in the position of advocating a prodeath position. Moreover, the federal state is using taxpayers' money to do it. Your representatives in Congress should be encouraged to remove the government funding for these projects. It is certainly not a province of the government to urge such policies. If your representatives do not respond, then it is time to institute legal action to stop this abuse. Don't let the false political dictum of separation of church and state stop you from getting involved.

After all is said and done, the basic change in our country will come through the truly Christian family. In view of the fact that the present humanistic culture is tenaciously attacking the institution of the family, Christians must take a hard look at what they are doing in their own families.

The family should be the center of Christian life. No other institutions (including the church) or activities should get in the way of family life. Parents must develop relationships with their children, and this means spending time with them. There is nothing more spiritual than this.

Christian parents must counter the influence of the brainwashing of public schools, television (all media), and literature. Most television turns every home into a classroom where basically humanistic principles are taught. Allowing your children to watch very little television is an excellent idea. In fact, eliminating television entirely would bring more gain than loss. Television is a violent invasion of the privacy of the family. It not only consumes valuable time, but it is also stealing your children's minds.

As Christian parents, you must make sure that your children are being raised as complete Christians. This will involve instructing them in the realities of the culture we are living in as well as the Bible. For example, are you teaching your children that Christianity is a system of thought that applies to all of life? Are they being educated to be a generation that will vigorously resist humanistic values and infringement on their rights? Are you guiding your children to help them understand twentieth-century problems so the coming generation will know how to attack the desperate cries we face from a Christian perspective?

Finally, in the context of the family, it is important to note that the cultural mandate given in Genesis 1:26-28, "Let us make man . . . to be the master of all life upon the earth and in the skies and in the seas" (Living Bible), was bestowed upon Adam and Eve collectively as a potential family. Intimately connected to the cultural mandate is the command to have children in verse 28: "Be fruitful and multiply." God expects us to disciple the children he has entrusted to us.

The Law Student

Those planning to attend law school and those presently involved in law school can have a great impact on the systems of law and civil government. Much of what is taught in law school today is directly opposed to the teachings of the Bible. It is a humanistic system in need of a Christian orientation.

In my third and final year of law school, one of my law professors began his class by making this statement: "Always remember that you are never in the courtroom to get justice, but to win!" This is the legal mentality that is passed on to thousands of law students yearly. It is a survival-of-the-fittest mentality. When it is applied to the criminal justice system and legislation, we can see why we are facing a trauma in law today.

The apostle Paul in 1 Timothy 1 spoke about those who teach the law without biblical content:

> Now the end of the commandment is charity out of a pure heart, and of a good conscience, and of a faith unfeigned, From which some, having swerved, have turned aside unto vain jangling, Desiring to be teachers of the law, understanding neither what they say, nor whereof

they affirm. But we know that the law is good, if a man use it lawfully (vv. 5-8).

A number of those in legal education today teach a legality without the content of true law. The Christian student cannot sit in class and allow this to happen. A vocal Christian law student can be an effective witness of the truth. Christian students must challenge professors who urge an immoral, pagan base to law. Law professors need to be reminded that much of law is still based on the Bible.

Christian law students should propose a course on William Blackstone or the common law, if their school does not have one. This can be done through the various student-faculty committees. Most contemporary law schools attempt to cover all the historical bases of law in one three-hour course called jurisprudence. It is not sufficient.

If the school refuses to alter the curriculum to study the Christian foundation of law, then Christian law students and those concerned should start their own extracurricular study group. Make it an honor society with prestige. More could be learned in one of these groups than in many courses taken in the current legal education system.

Many Christians believe and accept the fact that they are second-class citizens. Too often it is true that they are. However, this should not be the case. The Christian law student should be an example to the rest of the students. He or she should excel, if possible. If you are a serious law student, you can do well. Be the best.

Eventually, I believe more Christian law schools will come into existence. There are several in operation at this time. As this occurs more Christians will go to these schools. Until this happens, however, the Christian must be prepared to enter the humanistic schools of law and thrust Christian ideas into the system. Moreover, as Christian law schools open, they must, if they are to serve any viable purpose beyond adding to the present pietistic jargon, teach law in a way that will lead to Christian activism by their graduates on all the frontiers of the justice system.

The lawyers who graduate from these schools should have a firm knowledge of Christian philosophy and of the true legal roots of American society. They should have studied the works of those writers cited in my book, *The Second American Revolution,* thoroughly and should leave with a sense that their practice of law is not as much a livelihood as a vocation to take society by the horns and turn it around.

We who are Christian lawyers have reason to be ashamed. We, who supposedly have a working knowledge of God, have often lagged behind in dedication to the truth. Christian attorneys have simply failed to use their profession effectively.

In Matthew 13 Christ says, "Therefore every scribe [or lawyer] which is instructed unto the kingdom of heaven is like unto a man that is an householder, which bringeth forth out of his treasure things new and old" (v. 52). The lawyer who is learned in biblical law and applies it in the external world will produce much good fruit.

The role of the lawyer in modern society cannot be exaggerated. The entire American system is structured upon law. If the lawyer who professes Christ so desires, he or she can have a major influence in the direction of the culture. However, many attorneys believe their professions are somehow separate from their Christian calling. They compartmentalize their faith and practice.

The person who becomes a lawyer must see that he has taken on a high calling and, as such, must be a steward of what God has given him. One cannot be a lawyer from the hours of nine to five during the working week and thereafter act as a Christian. His Christian faith and his legal practice must be integrated.

The attorney who is a Christian must see the practice of his profession as a vocation, not a business. This may, and often does, mean that not all he does will be profitable financially. However, Christians have not been placed on this planet solely to make money but to communicate the consistent Christian message to the whole culture and change history.

At one time in the profession, attorneys were routinely called "counselors at law." That is an important term, which indicated that attorneys were advisers not only in legal and technical matters but consolers and counselors in the biblical sense. Proverbs

11 instructs: "Where no counsel is, the people fall; but in the multitude of counselors there is safety" (v. 14).

We need fewer legal technicians and more attorneys who can counsel their clients on matters of divorce, abortion, child abuse, and other areas of moral concern. The Christian attorney's first prerogative should be to help people solve their problems.

Christian attorneys need to become aggressively and actively involved in local community affairs and politics. Most people will listen when an attorney speaks. The problem has always been in getting the Christian attorney to become involved in something other than church activities. The world needs the counsel of the godly lawyer.

Christian lawyers need to organize in local attorney groups not only to fellowship but to strategize on how they can influence their community. Imagine a strong local Christian lawyers' group threatening legal action against abortion clinics or upholding the right of a Christian teacher to talk about Christ in the public school classroom.

An involvement in local, statewide, and national bar association functions is important. Most of these groups have degenerated into social outlets. With proper guidance, they could become vocal on the issues and an excellent educational tool for both lawyers and society at large. Attorneys, however, must realize that their first loyalty is not to a bar association (or to keeping peace with their colleagues) but to Christ himself. In that spirit these lawyers should be willing to shoulder the burden of creating controversy locally and nationally in the cause of Christian absolutes.

We are all aware of the downward plight of the legal profession—that in and of itself should be the motivation for change. However, change in the Christian sense will not come unless those attorneys who profess Christ become visible in their profession. The legal system should be flooded with Christian lawyers dedicated to bringing change and fighting the evil that now pervades the courts and the whole enterprise of law. In this way, there is hope for a troubled profession. The challenge to the Christian attorney is to be a vocal, dynamic spokesman for the true legal profession—the one with Christ at its center—and to stop at nothing less than reclaiming the whole system.

The Church

Most of the books of the New Testament, as well as Christ's references in the Book of Revelation, are letters written to local churches. I believe this is because God first desires action to be taken there. Failing this, God works through organizations and individuals outside the local church. Those pastors who have voiced their dismay at the numerous evangelical groups who have organized outside the local church have only themselves to blame. Those groups are in essence a judgment on local churches and on the institutional church as a whole, a church that has not fulfilled the requirements God has set forth for it. These words are not written merely to be critical but in the hope that they will be heard. Tragically, the church has been apathetic to much of what has been going on outside its four walls.

Sermons, seminars, lectures, and books are all geared by the church for the individual Christian within the congregation. The same ideas are always being presented to the same people. Christ broke with the Pharisees on a similar issue. Jesus ate with sinners because he came to give a Christian message to them. Christ thus taught that the Christian message is an external thing. It has to flow out into the world, not be entombed within the church building.

The grave problems in the courts, in the law, and in civil government are the consequence of a century of church teaching that involvement in church activities is more important than involvement in the affairs and institutions of the world. Christian pastors must define church activities in such a way to recapture the biblical emphasis that involvement in all areas of the culture is a necessary part of true spirituality. In this way the church will thrive, instead of having to fight for its very existence as it is today.

The true church, by its very nature, is a political institution—political from the standpoint that, as Christ's exclusive preserve, the state has no legitimate authority over it. The true church says "hands off" to Caesar. This is a political statement—a delineation of the authority of the state. When this principle is aggressively upheld by the church, a balance is maintained between church and state.

An excellent program for churches to sponsor would be a free legal aid clinic to the poor and the helpless, which is now sadly lacking. As James states: "Pure religion and undefiled before God and the Father is this: to visit the fatherless and widows in their affliction, and to keep oneself unspotted from the world" (James 1:27).

Local churches, as missions, could sponsor young people who want to go to law school. Churches should encourage their young people to study law and encourage Christian lawyers to reexamine ways to apply their faith to their profession. The church, if it took its task seriously, could flood the law schools with Christian law students who would eventually influence the legal and governmental systems. If any institutions need missionaries, it is the law schools. It is a mission field ripe for harvest.

Most important, the local church, as the pillar and the ground for truth, should instruct all its people in the laws and mandates of God. Instead of the numerous conferences on how to feel good spiritually, seminars on biblical law and the political system would be profitable. The people could be educated and given the tools to exercise the cultural mandate. The local church should be a teaching institution, not just a fellowship group. Through the teaching church a generation of Christians who know the issues and dare to speak out will be born. It was with twelve men like this that Jesus changed the world.

Summary of Action

I would like to summarize the immediate objectives of Christian action for everyone—the individual, the law student, the lawyer, and the church.

First, the power of the federal government must eventually be broken down to its constitutional limit, returning much of the power of the federal bureaucracy to the state and local governments. This is the federalistic principle upon which the American government was originally founded. This would entail curbing and, if necessary, eliminating the massive federal bureaucratic agencies such as the Internal Revenue Service. It will also mean a severe delimiting of the authority of the federal courts.

These objectives can be attained in several ways. An initial effort must be made to influence Congress to act against these agencies and their programs. Congress can effectively curtail the power of the federal government and its agencies by withdrawing funds to them or by eliminating certain agencies in their entirety.

As for the courts, Article III of the Constitution of the United States affords Congress the authority to restrict the Supreme Court's and the lower federal courts' power to hear most cases. Although it has been seldom used, under this constitutional provision Congress could virtually eliminate the federal courts. Certainly Congress could use this provision to limit the number of federal courts that are established, which would curtail the awesome power now claimed by the courts.

If Congress fails or refuses to respond to efforts to curtail the federal bureaucracy, then possibly legal actions could be instituted to attack various acts and programs carried on by the federal agencies. There is a problem, however, in petitioning the courts to limit a federal bureaucracy of which they themselves are an integral part.

Ultimately, the people themselves will have to take control of their own affairs and refuse assistance from and control by the federal government. States, towns, and communities are often taken over by the federal government, in effect, if not in fact, because they accept funds from federal agencies. Many local governmental entities have become more or less addicted to the federal purse. When and if they decide to disobey some agency, the federal government threatens to withdraw its funds. It's like getting hooked on heroin. The pusher knows he can control the addict by threatening to hold back on selling the drug.

The pusher also pushes the price higher and higher. Writing in *U.S. News & World Report,* Gerald Thompson, who was serving as the secretary of the Washington State Department of Social and Health Services at the time, said: "And the addition is progressive. As we rely more on government agencies to handle our problems, we become less effective in dealing with them ourselves, as individuals, in families, in communities. We lose skills. We forget how to do certain things, and if the process goes on long enough, we may even forget that there was ever another way." Moreover, whatever the federal government funds, it usually controls. Loss of freedom is a heavy price to pay. (This is true not only of local governmental entities but of Christian institutions as well.)

Second, situations will arise when the Christian community, either through groups or individuals, will be forced to pursue legal action. At some point all avenues to alternative action may be closed. If legal action becomes feasible, it should be pursued aggressively. Humanist groups such as the American Civil Liberties Union (ACLU) have taken the offensive in pushing their version of social change onto society through the courts and with great success.

It is emphasized that court battles cannot be won, as a whole, from a defensive posture. The Supreme Court cases removing Judeo-Christian practices from the public schools serve as a good example of this principle. In every one of those cases, the local school boards or governmental entities were the defendants. They had been sued for establishing Bible reading, prayer, or what have you in the schools. Moreover, no Christian groups intervened or attempted in any way to join in the lawsuits and in no way supported the school boards in those cases. The defensive posture is clearly a losing situation.

There is an advantage to suing before being sued. The principal advantage is that the entity suing chooses the court in which the case will be heard, and, by suing, frames the issues and arguments from his point of view. There are other advantages, but they can be summed up by saying that the first man out of the chute has the jump on the others involved in the race. It is a matter of strategy and planning.

An example of aggressiveness in handling a court action was epitomized in the case of *Walker* v. *First Orthodox Presbyterian Church of San Francisco*. I acted as lead attorney for the church, and was assisted by two other attorneys (Tom Neuberger of Wilmington, Delaware, and Susan Paulus of San Francisco). In that case the church was sued by a practicing homosexual who had been dismissed from his position of church organist after his homosexuality had been discovered and the pastor of the church had talked with him without result. The man alleged employment discrimination based upon a San Francisco gay rights law.

Note that the church was sued. However, due to careful planning and strategy, we filed a motion for summary judgment several months later, asking the court to decide the case on the Constitution (because there was no dispute among the parties on the facts). By doing this, a lengthy trial analyzing the discrimination charge was avoided. Instead of staying on the defensive, we put the church on the offensive; the homosexual (and the homosexual legal organization backing him) were placed in the position of having to defend their position. In April 1980, the court ruled that the gay rights ordinance was unconstitutional as applied to the church. An entirely different outcome could have resulted if we had gone on the defensive.

Third, the public education system, which includes the entire educational structure up through the university level, must be reinstilled with Judeo-Christian theism. The education system is of primary importance because it trains the citizens of tomorrow. At present, the system is producing wave after wave of graduates who have little or no knowledge of Christianity and who, in most instances, are actively anti-Christian. The secularizing of the public schools has effectively been carried out through decisions removing the Judeo-Christian base from education. Humanist Paul Blanshard writing in *The Humanist* in an article entitled "Three Cheers for Our Secular State" said:

> I think that the most important factor moving us toward a secular society has been the educational factor. Our schools may not teach Johnny to read properly, but the fact that Johnny is in school until he is sixteen tends to lead toward the elimination of religious superstition. The average American child now acquires a high school education, and this militates against Adam and Eve and all other myths of alleged history. . . . When I was one of the editors of *The Nation* in the twenties, I wrote an editorial explaining that golf and intelligence were the two primary reasons that men did not attend church. Perhaps I would now say golf and a high-school diploma.

If there is little hope of revamping public education—and this is more than a probability—then Christians must remove their financial support from the system. In most states, the highly suspect real estate tax is used to support the public educational system. Legislation should be passed exempting those opposed to the materialistic world view taught in these schools from having to support them. If the legislature fails to act, then the people can, by referendum, place such a measure on the ballot and, in effect, pass their own law.

Christians should establish their own institutions while fighting the decay of the public education system. Already Christian schools are flourishing and growing at a rapid rate. We must take care, however, that these institutions produce children who know how to affect the world they live in for Jesus Christ. If not, Christian schools will simply be the "religious" counterparts of the secular school system.

Fourth, the massive federal government we have today is by and large the result of a church that has not taken its duty seriously and provided for the education and welfare needs of the people. It is a function of Christ's church to care for the sick and needy. The reason many non-Christians see no value in the church today is because the church does little to meet the physical needs of the people. The church should be a servant church, one designed to provide health, education, and welfare. If the people could be served in this way, the need for welfare would be nonexistent. All it takes is the church serving its proper function: externalizing the faith.

Taking a Stand

The church cannot be timid in the face of crises. One strong local church can demand respect from the entire community. The world is looking for someone or something that will take a stand. Moreover, the bolder the church becomes, the stronger Christians in general become. The church is not to have a spirit of timidity but of power: the power of God, which is at the church's disposal.

As we face the massive machine of government, we are at a very similar position to that of the colonists who congregated to declare their independence from Great Britain in 1776. They brought about a revolution. It is now time for another revolution, a revolution in the reformative sense. It should not be a revolution designed to kill people or to tear down and physically destroy society, but a revolution in the minds and the souls of human beings—a revolution promulgated to be a total assault on the humanistic culture. A Second American Revolution founded upon the Bible in its totality. In this, and only this, is there hope for the future.

12. Public Justice and True Tolerance

James W. Skillen

Politics in our day usually begins and ends with "The People," perhaps in the form of "We the people of the United States . . ." or "The People's Republic of China" or "the will of the people . . ." or "return power to the people."

Christian politics begins and ends with "The King of kings and the Lord of lords."

> Great and wonderful are thy deeds, O Lord God the Almighty! Just and true are thy ways, O King of the ages! Who shall not fear and glorify thy name, O Lord? For thou alone art holy. All nations shall come and worship thee, for thy judgments have been revealed (Revelation 15:3-4, RSV).

Jesus acknowledged, as we know, that *people* do have political responsibilities and that *people* do indeed belong in certain political offices (cf. Matthew 22:15-22; Mark 12:13-17; Luke 20:19-26; John 19:11). But in the biblical view of life, human responsibility in earthly politics is never a self-contained and self-sufficient affair of "The People." Human politics is always God's business.

The biblical perspective always places human political responsibility in the context of God's sovereignty and Christ's lordship. The Old Testament revelation placed human politics in the context of the anticipation of One who would come as the Prince of Peace, the Just King, the Righteous Lord, the Perfect Judge, the Mighty God (Isaiah 9:6-7; 40:9-11; Jeremiah 23:6; Psalm 82:8; 98:4-9). And when Christ did appear for the first time, he announced boldly that "All things have been delivered to me by my Father" (Matthew 11:27, RSV). All authority in heaven and on earth, he said, has been given to me (Matthew 28:18). Christ has come to establish the rule of his Father over the whole earth (Luke 4:1-21; 1 Corinthians 15:20-28; Philippians 2:5-11; Colossians 1:15-20; Revelation 10:1-16).

The Politics of Grace

The biblical revelation also shows us that the time between Christ's first appearance and his second coming is a time of great patience, long-suffering, and grace on God's part. He is not willing that anyone should perish, and so the call goes out for people to repent and to believe the gospel of his kingdom (Mark 1:15; 2 Peter 3:9). God's gracious patience has considerable significance for politics because Christ does not ask his people to administer any kind of forceful, political separation of non-Christians from Christians. In fact Christ gives the opposite responsibility to Christians. We are to love our enemies (Matthew 5:43-48). We are to look after the welfare of those who might do evil to us (Matthew 5:38-42; Romans 12:20). We are to pray for God's will to be done on earth as it is done in heaven (Matthew 6:10). In all of this we are to leave the responsibility for separating the wheat from the chaff in the hands of the King himself (Matthew 26:51-54; Luke 3:15-17; Revelation 5:1-14).

A biblical parable which brings to focus the gracious character of this age is the one in Matthew 13:24-30. Jesus told the parable this way:

> The kingdom of heaven may be compared to a man who sowed good seed in his field; but while men were sleeping, his enemy came and sowed weeds among the wheat, and went away. So when the plants came up and bore grain, then the weeds appeared also. And the servants of the householder came and said to him, "Sir, did you not sow good seed in your field? How then has it weeds?" He said to them, "An enemy has done this." The servants said to him, "Then do you want us to go and gather them?" But he said, "No; lest in gathering the weeds you root up the wheat along with them. Let both grow together until the harvest; and at harvest time I will tell the reapers, Gather the weeds first and bind them in bundles to be burned, but gather the wheat into my barn" (RSV).

In the entire context of the New Testament, this parable seems to suggest that Christians must not try to establish an earthly state or political community that would be for Christians only or that would be fully open only to those who confess Christian faith. It is not *Christian* justice for Christians to enjoy any political privilege at the expense of non-Christians. Non-Christians must be given every blessing in the political arena that Christians themselves enjoy. Just as the wheat and the tares enjoy the same sun, rain, and cultivation, so Christians and non-Christians should enjoy equally the benefits of God's grace given to the field of this world in the present age.

The Christian view of political justice should be built directly on this understanding of God's gracious patience and love. If this is done, then Christian politics will manifest itself not as the Church's selfish attempt to control the state, nor as an interest-group effort to "get" benefits primarily for Christians, nor as a campaign to flood political offices with Christians so that Christians can control the government for the enforcement of Christian doctrine on the populace.

The biblical view of justice for every earthly creature will mean instead that Christians will work politically for the achievement of governmental policies that will protect, encourage, and open up life for every person and community of people, whatever their religious confession and view of life. Justice in political life cannot be based on the biblical teaching about church discipline since earthly states are not churches. The state is not a community of Christian faith; it is a community of public legal care for all people which must not favor or persecute any particular group or society.

Our difficulty in grasping this biblical perspective is quite understandable considering the history of politics in the West since the time of Christ's first stay among us. The Roman empire did not promote an evenhanded justice which came from God's grace, but frequently persecuted Christians and Jews. Later when Christianity was accepted by the Roman emperors as the established religion of the empire, these emperors frequently persecuted or discriminated against non-Christians instead of Christians. This was no more just in a biblical sense than the former Roman injustice. The Roman empire in both instances falsely identified itself with *God's* empire, and the emperors wrongly assumed responsibility for getting rid of heretics (rooting up the tares)—a responsibility which Christ gave to no human being.

Still later in history the church gained such strength and prominence that it became the chief power behind most of Europe's politics. "Christian politics" then came to mean "church-controlled politics," and the Roman church leaders assumed some of the same power and held on to some of the same ideas that the Roman emperors once had. Political justice reflecting biblical patience and grace was still not operative for the most part.

So much political debate, warfare, persecution, and turmoil occurred during and after the Reformation when most Christians were still confusing the church's and the state's responsibilities that many people came to believe that political life ought to be organized without reference to religion. Our American political roots go back to this period when people were trying to organize government and politics according to so-called "neutral," non-religious principles. They believed that if they could only keep religion in their private lives and in the churches, away from the political arena where all people participate in common, then religious conflict would not interrupt political life and everyone would enjoy peace and prosperity.

But this was no more "just" than the earlier systems of political organization because not everyone agreed that politics was "neutral" or that religion belonged only to private life. In the political arena, therefore, people were still discriminated against and frequently persecuted if they did not go along with this new idea of a common "religionless" politics.

New Political Religions

What we have seen in the last two centuries is that our supposedly "neutral," "secular" political communities have given birth to the most passionate and unjust *religions* that now control most of these political communities. Nationalism, a religious faith in the nation itself, has become the dominant power in modern political life around the world. Various forms of Marxism, a religion of materialistic humanism, dominate many states, persecuting and discriminating against those who do not confess the party line.

Many western democracies, including the United States, allow little or no room for minority participation in politics unless the minorities agree to play by the rules that supposedly keep religion out of politics (and out of the schools) and that keep the majority in charge of directing society. This means unjust discrimination against many people.

In reality what has actually happened is that American democratic nationalism has developed into one of the most powerful "civil religions" in the modern world. It is not Marxist; it is not Roman Catholic; it is not Protestant; it is not styled after the old Roman empire's elevation of the emperor to the position of God. It is rather a religion of secularized Christianity where the American nation has come to be seen as God's specially chosen kingdom—the political community through which the world will be saved politically. God's will is supposedly revealed through the will of a political majority, and all private religions have their primary place of honor as supporters of the nation's common, unified progress through history as God's nation.

The American civil religion not only leads to political injustice at home, but it promotes injustice abroad in so far as "American interests" dominate world politics and economics. "What is best for America is best for the world," is a slogan in the minds of many American citizens and U.S. officials. On the world scene this attitude operates in much the same way that the dominance of one group operates in the internal life of a nation. It means injustice and discrimination against the poor in favor of the rich, against one class in favor of another class, against one religious group in favor of another religious group.

We can see, then, that politics does not exist as a neutral enterprise. Religion cannot be kept out of the life of states. If a Christian approach of patient, gracious justice does not rule human political life, then some other religious dynamic will control it. If all people are not cared for in an evenhanded way in the public legal domain, then another religious impulse will lead to injustice and discrimination. Christians must wake up to this fact today and recognize that if they are not serving Christ in politics according to the norm of biblical justice, then they are serving some false god that will lead to injustice. In America today we believe that we are doing justice to all people by keeping religion out of politics and letting the majority rule. But actually we are keeping a truly Christian work of justice out of politics only to have a democratistic religion of the people dominate majorities and minorities in a way that oppresses and discriminates against certain people and communities of people. The only answer to the present difficulties facing democratic political systems (as well as non-democratic systems) is to recognize that people are basically religious creatures and that religion can, therefore, in no way be kept out of politics. Political life must be opened up to the full diversity of human religious impulses, and evenhanded justice must be the norm by which this diversity is allowed to live publicly.

A Christian Political Response

In the contemporary world of injustice, both domestic and international, Christian politics will begin with the repentance of Christians who come to see that they have not always been ministers of God's gracious, patient justice to others. Christian politics will grow when Christians begin to take seriously Christ's command for us to love our neighbors. The love command will lead us to be dissatisfied with the unloving injustice of the American civil religion, of Marxism, of church-controlled politics, of nationalism, and of every type of organization of political life which discriminates against some to the advantage of others.

Christian politics will mature in America when Christians recover the biblical vision of the *communal* responsibility they have for others. When we begin to see that the body of Christ is not a "part-time" or "private" organism unrelated to the political realities of human life on earth, then we will be able to break away from the *individualistic* conception of political responsibility which dominates our democratic political system. We will then no longer be willing to have the majority political parties do all of our politics for us on their own terms—terms which presuppose the individualistic character of political responsibility, the rule of the majority for determining what justice is all about, and the neutral secularity of the political dimension of life. Instead we will be driven by the Spirit of Christ to begin working together as a *political community* and not just as an ecclesiastical community or as an educational community. We will see that politics is our business as a community with a distinct view of life unlike the views that other communities of people have. We will begin to do politics as unto the Lord.

Once we begin, as Christians, to take our political responsibilities seriously, we will be able to take up the complex issues of inflation, poverty, taxation, education, foreign policy, racism, and so forth, in order to examine present government policies and political processes in the light of the Christian norm of patient, gracious, loving justice. Then, as the Lord guides us into a deeper understanding of modern political realities from the standpoint of his merciful justice, we will be able to make the necessary tactical decisions about how we should organize our talents and energies for the service of justice. We may find that the present political system will allow us little room for unique Christian service besides writing and speaking about alternative policies. Or we may find that after considerable labor some significant avenues will open up for our organized efforts to restructure the system and to enact policies and laws of greater justice.

To develop a Christian political option, therefore, we must begin by studying the Word of God together in order to see what it teaches about the kingdom of God in Christ. We must pray and talk together in order to grasp the principles of that kingdom as they hold for earthly politics. We must grow up into Christ so that we can gain a *common Christian political mind*. It is not enough for us to say that we have Christ in common if our lives manifest a confusion of divergent approaches to politics. It is not enough for us to say that we all believe that Christ's kingdom is coming if we live in a way that shows no communal unity in our service of the King. If we are children of the light, then our lives should manifest the communal bond that the light gives to us. Politics is a major part of the life we now live by faith. We need the mind of Christ in us. We need to be renewed in all our thought and life by Christ, including our thinking and living in politics.

Right along with our communal growth as the body of Christ, we must also encourage particular ones among us to give leadership in working out the details of our Christian political option. What are the problems facing modern nations today? What can be done to reform our present systems and policies so that greater justice can be done? What is an equitable tax policy? What is justice in education, or in broadcasting? If we are to get answers to these and thousands of other questions, we will have to have economic, legal, historical, and political experts to guide us. They will need to work full time as part of a Christian team, developing the implications of the biblical view of God's rule in Christ over the whole earth. We must work and pray together for the Lord's guidance in our lives as we seek communally to fulfill our political responsibilities before His face. But to do this we must be sure to recognize the talents and gifts that God has already given to certain ones among us in the area of political understanding. If we do not seek to discover and encourage such men and women to do this special service, and if we do not organize for the support of them, then it will not be enough for us to pray and ask God to help us in our political service. God is already richly blessing us with men and women able to give political leadership. Let us consider how we can be good stewards politically of what God has already given.

Christ is King! Will we now serve him in our political offices or will we continue to limp between the part-time service of Christ and the part-time service of other gods? Christ calls us to his service with all our heart, soul, strength, and mind.

> And I heard every creature in heaven and on earth and under the earth and in the sea, and all therein, saying, "To him who sits upon the throne and to the Lamb be blessing and honor and glory and might for ever and ever!" (Revelation 5:13, RSV).

Study Questions

Is There a Response That Is Christian?

1. How does Whitehead define pluralism? How is it different from the way McCarthy defined pluralism in chapter 10?

2. In what ways is Whitehead's understanding of the power of law in American society parallel to Hammond's argument that law is the defining and enforcing power of American civil religion?

3. How do you read Whitehead's statement that since the church is "Christ's exclusive preserve," the state has no authority over it? Do you agree with him, or do you see problems with his statement?

4. Do you agree with Skillen that it is just as unbiblical to use public legal institutions to support Christian beliefs as non-Christian beliefs? Or do you agree with Whitehead that using public legal institutions to support Christian beliefs is just what biblical public action is all about?

5. What do you think of Skillen's argument that Christian politics means following a pattern after God's grace?

Afterword: A Personal Comment

Reflecting upon the readings presented here, and the larger Christian America debate they represent, I am struck by the strength of a common commitment shared on all sides. *Evangelicals are convinced that Christian political activity must resist the secularizing tendencies of modern America.* Despite the real differences over America's founding that divide them, it seems to me there is an overwhelming agreement among evangelicals that true biblical witness requires a public stance that clearly opposes the cultural pressures driving our society into modern secularism. In fact, I am beginning to think the way evangelicals resist these pressures is linked directly to their stance on Christian America.

In an important new book on American Evangelicalism, James Davidson Hunter (an evangelical himself) explores the uneasy relationship between the convictions of evangelicals and the social forces of modern society.[1] He summarizes how the pressures and practices of modern society (what he calls modernity) erode the very plausibility of transcendent religious beliefs. Describing some of the same social forces touched upon by our authors, Hunter shows how modernity (through rationalism, cultural pluralism, and the privatization of religion) has worked to undermine the public authority and credibility of traditional religion.

Hunter's thesis is that evangelicalism for the most part is resilient to modernity, resisting the pressures of modern society rather than withdrawing from or simply accommodating them.[2] This resonates with my own conclusion above about the shared commitment of evangelicals in the Christian America debate. But what I find interesting in the light of our readings are Hunter's comments on civil religion and his analysis of the type of accommodation to modernity found even within evangelicalism.

In his discussion of civil religion, Hunter explains how evangelicals often identify their public religious activism as an essential expression of what they believe. He argues that civil religious activism frequently is an expression of protest against modernity. It is a reaction to the secularized public sphere. Despite their protests against secularism, however, he shows how evangelicals exhibit a kind of marginal accommodation with modernity. Such accommodation may include a rise in apologetic activity to demonstrate the rational credibility of belief, or a rise in toleration of other beliefs even while maintaining commitment to one's own belief as the one and only truth.[3]

While reading our authors' discussion, we have learned that those favoring the Christian America idea protest the secularization of the public sphere and work eagerly to reassert the generalized Judeo-Christian consensus of early America. They argue that working to reassert that early consensus is an essential expression of Christian faith. Opponents of the Christian America idea also protest the secularized public sphere. But they do so by calling into question the credibility of assuming that rationalism is purely secular. They argue that rationalism is as much a faith as Christianity.

We also have discovered that evangelicals sympathetic to the Christian America thesis, while stressing the absolute truth of biblical faith, tend to tolerate (minimize) differences between evangelical Christianity and the unchristian aspects of the generalized public consensus (civil religion) of early America. Those critical of the Christian America thesis, on the other hand, emphasize how different evangelical faith is from civil religion.

What this suggests to me is that in the Christian America debate we see at least two different ways by which evangelicals resist modernity. The style of resistance seems closely tied to the kind of accommodation each side is willing to make. Advocates of Christian America fear the relativizing influence of modernity's cultural pluralism. Thus they seek to use public and legal institutions to enhance more traditional (Christian) modes of thought and behavior as well as a more homogeneous world view. But their refusal to accommodate cultural pluralism is accompanied by a measure of accommodation with the other-than-Christian influences found within our nation's civil religion.

Critics of Christian America are willing to accommodate modernity's cultural pluralism to the extent of raising a Christian apologetic (to use Hunter's term) which exposes the "religious" character of rationalism. Thereby, they can credibly reject modern society's notion of "neutral" public institutions and provide a rationale for the equal public footing of Christianity alongside secular humanism, as well as other "religious" world views. But their accepting a measure of accommodation with cultural pluralism is accompanied by a refusal to accommodate rationalism, or any other non-Christian influence, found within America's civil religion.

What Hunter's helpful analysis has led me to consider is the connection between one's opinion about Christian America and one's attitude toward the social forces of modern society. What is important is the way in which one is inclined to resist the forces of modernity. The data marshalled by most studies which deal with the issue of America's Christian founding are frequently ambiguous and sometimes plainly biased. Such data may be compelling, then, only to the extent that they confirm a previous predilection about modern society. Where evangelical Christians come down in this debate over whether America ever was, or ought to be, Christian may well be shaped more by how they resist modernity than by the arguments of historical, sociological, or theological analysis.

Afterword: A Personal Comment, Notes

1. James Davison Hunter, *American Evangelicalism: Conservative Religion and the Quandary of Modernity* (New Brunswick, N.J.: Rutgers University Press, 1983).

2. Hunter, *American Evangelicalism,* see esp. ch. 7: "Resistances: Public Piety and Politization," pp. 102-119.

3. Hunter, *American Evangelicalism,* pp. 15-18.

Selected Readings

This is not an exhaustive bibliography. It is simply designed to help the reader with a beginning interest in the issues of civil religion and American Christian history. An attempt has been made to provide a balanced selection of readings from a variety of viewpoints.

Ahlstrom, Sidney, *A Religious History of the American People*. New Haven, Conn.: Yale University Press, 1972.

   From the founding of the "Protestant Empire" to "Post-Puritan America," the author provides a superb, comprehensive history of the religious dimension of American life.

Anderson, John B. *Vision and Betrayal in America*. Waco, Tex.: Word Books, Publisher, 1975, ch. 2, "The Crisis of American Ideals."

   A Christian layman and well-known statesman calls for a recommitment to the moral ideals, values, and national ideology and traditions of our civil religion.

Brown, Harold O. J. *The Reconstruction of the Republic*. Milford, Mich.: Mott Media, 1981.

   An evangelical scholar, showing how Christian withdrawal from public life creates a moral and spiritual vacuum, calls for a return to the biblical heritage of America while allowing for pluralism; hence avoiding the "Christian America" model.

Clebsch, William A. *From Sacred to Profane America: The Role of Religion in American History*. New York: Harper & Row, 1968.

   Although acknowledging that current religious trends accommodate the "profane," the author rejects the idea that modern secularism is contrary to our religious heritage, arguing instead that American religion cultivated pluralism outside and within itself.

Cotham, Perry C. *Politics, Americanism, and Christianity*. Grand Rapids: Baker Book House, 1976.

By distinguishing "good" civil religion from secular cultural religion, an evangelical political scientist explains how America is a Christian nation and how Christian realism can shape our politics to allow biblical service to both God and Caesar.

DeMar, Gary. *God and Government: A Biblical and Historical Study*. Atlanta: American Vision Press, 1982.

Analyzing the Bible's teaching on God and government, a concerned Christian studies America's civil government, showing how America started as a Christian nation and urging a return to her biblical foundations.

Falwell, Jerry. *Listen, America*. New York: Bantam Books, 1981.

A famous fundamentalist issues a call to political action for restoring America's moral and spiritual heritage to its traditional Judeo-Christian foundation.

Fackre, Gabriel J. *The Religious Right and Christian Faith*. Grand Rapids: William B. Eerdmans Publishing Co., 1982.

An evangelical scholar shows how Christian orthodoxy has been adulterated by right-wing secular humanism in a confusion of biblical faith and American nationalism.

Foster, Marshall and Swanson, Mary-Elaine. *The American Covenant: The Untold Story*. Thousand Oaks, Calif.: The Foundation for Christian Self-Government, 1981.

A historical guide detailing America's unique Christian history that allowed the full flower of Christian civilization and government to be expressed in the United States as in no other nation.

Hall, Verna M., ed. *The Christian History of the Constitution of the United States of America: Christian Self-Government with Union*. San Francisco: Foundation for American Christian Education, 1979.

A compilation of historical documents tracing the Christian foundations of the nation and showing how biblical principles of government were used to construct the American Christian republic.

Handy, Robert T. *A Christian America: Protestant Hopes and Historical Realities*. New York: Oxford University Press, 1971.

Focusing on the evangelical Protestant hope that someday America would be fully Christian, the author traces how Protestants envisioned a Christian civilization and how they worked toward it in the nineteenth and early twentieth centuries.

Hatfield, Mark O. *Between a Rock and a Hard Place*. Waco, Tex.: Word Books, Publisher, 1976, ch. 7, "Civil Religion and Biblical Faith."

A prominent evangelical statesman decries the shallow public expressions of religious values that mask civil religion as "Christian" while distorting the true biblical relationship between the state and Christian faith.

Herberg, Will. *Protestant, Catholic, Jew: An Essay in American Religious Sociology*. Chicago, Ill.: University of Chicago Press, 1983.

Originally published in 1955, this landmark study of religion in American life critically analyzes the way America's three major faith communities express in slightly different ways a common spiritual reality identified as "The American Way of Life."

Linder, Robert D. and Pierard, Richard V. *Twilight of the Saints: Biblical Christianity and Civil Religion in America*. Downers Grove, Ill.: InterVarsity Press, 1978.

Two evangelical historians critique the development of civil religion and call for a Christian political witness that avoids civil religion's pitfalls and remains true to biblical faith.

Marsden, George M. "America's 'Christian' Origin: Puritan New England as a Case Study," *John Calvin: His Influence in the Western World,* ed. W. Stanford Reid. Grand Rapids: Zondervan Publishing House, 1982.

In the light of the ambiguous character of much of the Puritan cultural achievement, the author argues that the case for a Christian America rests on rather nebulous foundations.

Marshall, Peter J., Jr., and Manuel, David B., Jr. *The Light and the Glory*. Old Tappan, N.J.: Fleming H. Revell Co., 1977.

    An evangelical minister and a journalist join to trace the early Christian history of the United States' founding, concluding that America's rich Christian heritage is due to a plan of God which both shapes and judges American history and destiny.

McCarthy, Rockne M.; Oppewal, Donald; Petersen, Walfred; and Spykman, Gordon. *Society, State, & Schools: A Case for Structural and Confessional Pluralism*. Grand Rapids: William B. Eerdmans Publishing Co., 1981.

    The Fellows of the Calvin Center for Christian Scholarship at Calvin College critique America's political and legal heritage, and then offer a biblical alternative for American public life.

McCarthy, Rockne M.; Skillen, James W.; and Harper, William A. *Disestablishment a Second Time: Genuine Pluralism for American Schools*. Grand Rapids: Christian University Press, 1982.

    Research Associates of the Association for Public Justice show how secular humanism is the established religion in the public schools because America's law and politics are based not on Christian but Enlightenment thought.

Mead, Sidney E. *The Old Religion in the Brave New World: Reflections on the Relation Between Christendom and the Republic*. Berkeley, Calif.: University of California Press, 1977.

    Showing that orthodoxy in Christendom is at intellectual war with the basic premises of the Republic, the author argues that insofar as America rests on belief in reason and persuasion, it is more "Christian" than the orthodox defenders of Christendom who try to make religiosity part of the common law of the land.

Montgomery, John Warwick. *The Shaping of America*. Minneapolis: Bethany Fellowship, 1976.

    Believing America's current malaise results from a fundamental tension within her spiritual heritage of Christian and Enlightenment belief, a noted evangelical theologian and legal philosopher calls for a national restoration by rejecting "secular" civil religion for the Reformation principle of Law and Gospel.

Noll, Mark A. "The Bible in Revolutionary America," *The Bible in American Law, Politics, and Rhetoric,* ed. James T. Johnson. Philadelphia: Fortress and Scholars Press, 1983.

An evangelical historian finds biblical influence inconclusive in Revolutionary political theory and virtually nonexistent in the political theory of the early national period.

_____. *Christians in the American Revolution.* Grand Rapids: Christian University Press, 1977.

A historical study which shows how Christians had a profound impact in revolutionary America, as well as how the Revolution shaped the basic outlook on life of Christians.

Noll, Mark A; Hatch, Nathan O.; and Marsden, George M. *The Search for Christian America.* Westchester, Ill.: Crossway Books, 1983.

Evangelical historians present historical studies of the biblical, classical, and Enlightenment influences shaping the American heritage, thus arguing that a "Christian America" never existed.

Richey, Russell E. and Jones, Donald G. *American Civil Religion.* New York: Harper & Row, 1974.

A collection of articles which brings together ten distinguished scholars from a variety of disciplines to examine and discuss the concept, complexity, and implications of civil religion.

Rushdoony, Rousas J. *The Nature of the American System.* Nutley, N.J.: Craig Press, 1965.

The founder of Chalcedon Foundation examines America's Christian political heritage, arguing that limited government is based on biblical principles but modern liberalism is attempting to replace it with an idolatrous, unlimited, monolithic state.

Schaeffer, Francis A. *A Christian Manifesto.* Rev. ed. Westchester, Ill.: Crossway Books, 1982.

An appeal by a renowned evangelical for Christians to work to return America to her Christian social and political base to thwart the threat of secular humanism.

_____ . *How Should We Then Live? The Rise and Decline of Western Thought and Culture*. Old Tappan, N.J.: Fleming H. Revell, 1976.

An introductory survey of the problems of ancient, medieval, and modern humanistic thought, showing the roots and failures of humanism and offering biblical Christianity as the only basis for a society of order and freedom.

Singer, C. Gregg. *A Theological Interpretation of American History*. Rev. ed. Nutley, N.J.: Presbyterian and Reformed, 1981.

A Christian educator analyzes the intellectual mainsprings of American thought and history, tracing the impact of Puritanism, Transcendentalism, Deism, and later systems of theologies in shaping American public life and institutions.

Skillen, James W., ed. *Confessing Christ and Doing Politics*. Washington, D.C.: APJ Education Fund, 1982.

The executive director of a national Christian citizens' association compiles a series of articles by evangelical leaders and scholars which argues for political service that is thoroughly biblical and avoids the pitfalls of civil religion.

Stringfellow, William. *An Ethic for Christians and Other Aliens in a Strange Land*. Waco, Tex.: Word Books, 1973.

A critical look at America that identifies its way of life with Babylon, summing up the social purpose of American economic and political organization as a commitment to death.

Tuveson, Ernest L. *Redeemer Nation: The Idea of America's Millennial Role*. Chicago: University of Chicago Press, 1968.

Showing the religious origins of the belief that God is operating through America to build a civilization in which Christians and Christian principles would triumph in history, the author traces the persistence in American thought of this idea of a redeemer nation.

Wallis, Jim. *Call to Conversion: Recovering the Gospel for These Times*. New York: Harper & Row, 1981.

The editor of Sojourners magazine argues that true conversion involves the Christian in a rejection of the American way of life in favor of a more thoroughly biblical politics and lifestyle.

Walton, Rus. *One Nation Under God*. Washington, D.C.: Third Century Publishers, 1975.

    Shows how America traditionally operated on the basis of biblical principles for government, economics, education, and the family, and argues that socialism and humanism are undermining these principles today.

Whitehead, John W. *The Second American Revolution*. Elgin, Ill.: David C. Cook Publishing Co., 1982.

    A Christian lawyer decries America's drift into secular humanism and calls for a Christian-led "revolution" to restore America's moral and political strength on her traditional biblical base.

Wilson, John F. *Public Religion in American Culture*. Philadelphia: Temple University Press, 1979.

    A noted scholar of religion in American culture offers an important historical and theoretical clarification of the concept of civil religion.

Zwier, Robert. *Born-Again Politics*. Downers Grove, Ill.: Inter-Varsity Press, 1982.

    A Christian political scientist analyzes the Christian New Right and its immediate roots, asking "Is it right for any group to shape a nation after its own image?"

Subject Index

Adams, John
  and body politic, 237
  on civil religion, 80-81
  deism and, 139
  on founding of America, 125
  influence of religion on, 132
  on liberty, 122
  as a religious rationalist, 142
  on settlement of America, 238
Adams, John Quincy, 19
Adams, Samuel, 68, 123, 141
Ahlstrom, Sidney, 132, 135, 143
Allen, Ethan, 141
America
  Christian
    debate, 22-24
    defended, 18
    denied, 20-21
    essence, 196
    extent of, 195
    influences, 35-36
    Noll on, 22
    origins, 17
    predestined, 238
    as a republic, 68, 69, 70
    Schaeffer on, 22
  Christian Commonwealth,
    111-13
  destiny of, 238
  dream of paradise, 103-4
  early foundations, 186-92
  faith and foundation of,
    143-45
  messianic mission, 239
  newness of, 102-3
  origin time of, 100-102
  revolution, 238
  time of testing, 99
  as wilderness, 104-5
American Civil Liberties Union,
  172

Anabaptists, 186, 215
Anarchism, 126
Anglican churches, 133
Antinomianism, 126
Arendt, Hannah, 101
Arminianism, and freedom of
  will, 137
Atheism, 159
Augustine, 68, 111, 119
Authority
  in education, 60
  resisted, 60

Backus, Isaac, 114
Baptists, 134
Becker, Carl, 150, 152
Bible, influence of, 42
Bickel, Alexander, 222
Black, Justice, 62, 224
Blackstone, William, influence on
  American law, 44
Bolingbroke, 148
Boorstin, Daniel, 44
Brewer, Justice, 223
British Parliament, 47 n. 7
Brown, Harold O. J., 202-3
Burr, Aaron, influenced by
  Witherspoon, 43

Calvin, John, 70, 112, 135, 159,
  185
Calvinism
  and Congregational churches,
    133
  and freedom of will, 137
  influence on Puritanism, 185
  Jefferson on, 159
  and Puritanism, 135
Capitalism, 55
Carnegie, Andrew, 198
Catholic Church

America, Christian or Secular?

Readings in American Christian History and Civil Religion

MANY OF US HAVE BEEN TAUGHT that America was founded on Christian principles. Yet evangelicals today differ in their perceptions of the religious character of our nation's origin.

Just how Christian was the "Faith of our Fathers," and how does the foundation they laid relate to the way Christians ought to act in America's present public arena?

Most evangelicals agree that Christians ought to influence the life of our society, but they question how we ought to, and on what basis.

With these issues in mind, Jerry S. Herbert has compiled the views of several spokesmen representing a divergence of opinion. Their debate seeks to answer such questions as: Is America Christian? Were its founders Christian? Is American civil religion Christian? Is there a response that is Christian? These readings on that controversy are designed to provide a balanced overview of some of the debate's major arguments.

Designed for college students taking courses in American society, history, and politics, this volume should also prove helpful to those of the general reading public who are interested in the contemporary debate over our nation's Christian heritage, and in how Christians ought biblically to participate in American public life today.

JERRY S. HERBERT is Associate Director of Christian College Coalition's American Studies Program, Washington, D.C. He earned his Ph.D. in political science from Duke University and has taught and researched a variety of political topics.

ISBN 0-88070-067-1